"How many people do you know who grew up playing ice hockey, nearly reached the Olympics in team handball, mastered the sport of polo, built three of America's most successful minor league baseball teams, became one of the world's most renowned fishermen, excelled as a writer, and swam in a race around Key West? I can think of only one: Bob Rich. In *The Right Angle*, Bob, an admitted sports junkie, leads us through his incredible life's journey, both as an athlete and as a businessman responsible for building one of America's most successful companies. Filled with wit, humor, and an underlying theme of passion and competitiveness, Bob shares his most sacred secrets for success in sports, in business, and in life. *The Right Angle* is a must read for anyone who needs to be reminded that life can be both fun and successful."

—Gary W. Hall, MD,
three-time Olympic swimmer

"There are few sportsmen who can match the breadth of experience and variation of Bob Rich's life. *The Right Angle* is a wonderful collection of autobiographical tales. This truly passionate angler, sports fan, friend, and now English Lord can tell a super story all the way back to his French ancestors! '*La bonne vie est inspirée par l'amour et guidée par la connaissance.*' ('The good life is inspired by love and guided by knowledge.') Thanks Lord Bubba for this great read that had me laughing out loud on almost every page."

—Howard Taylor,
English chalk stream outfitter and guide

THE RIGHT ANGLE

Sometimes you win, sometimes you lose,
sometimes it rains.

Tim Robbins as Ebby Calvin "Nuke" LaLoosh
in **Bull Durham**

TABLE OF CONTENTS

PREFACE

I am an angler. The word dates back to sixteenth-century England, when fishing rods were made of bamboo and fishing lines of fine strands of woven silk. Tackle was fragile then, and its user's success often depended on maintaining the right angle between his or her rod and the line and the position of the fish.

My first two books, *Fish Fights* and *The Fishing Club*, explored the character of both fish and angler and how they came to be connected over the years in mini-battles of willpower.

The right angle has also come to play an important role in many other sports and professions ranging from architecture and journalism to politics and business.

Anyone who ever shot a ball or a puck at a net or a goal understands the importance of finding the right angle, just as anyone who has ever tried to protect a goal learns to succeed by cutting down that angle.

Entrepreneurs search for an angle to create successful products and services just as architects work to create angles that are both functional and pleasing to the eye. Politicians look for angles to get votes while journalists seek angles for a good story.

At a given time, all of us grasp for an angle to support our position, and who among us hasn't angled for praise or a compliment?

Angles can take on a pejorative connotation when they become schemes, and schemes can become scams that speak volumes about their perpetrators. All of us then, whether talking or listening, writing or reading, become charged with deciding for ourselves which angle is right.

From my vantage point, life is itself a game, sometimes more serious than others, and learning the rules is as important as finding the right angle.

INTRODUCTION

Like many others, I learned the rules of life while growing up. My hometown of Buffalo, New York, provided the wonderful and diverse backdrop of a city in transition from an industrial powerhouse to a back-office services provider. The old city is burdened by the vestiges of the past—like too much government and infrastructure—but enriched by iconic cultural institutions, big league sports, and outdoor venues. Buffalo is maligned for its severe winter weather and unappreciated for its beautiful springs, summers, and falls. I've always believed that if the weather is too harsh or the city is too far out of the mainstream for some then they shouldn't come. On the other hand, those who venture in are well rewarded. I have never heard of anyone who has arrived and then left because of any shortcomings of the region; on the contrary, most newcomers are delighted. Our region's largest problem continues to be job creation.

As for the people themselves, I believe that Buffalonians are defined by seven and a half virtues.

1. Indomitable Spirit

We are incredible fighters; we may get knocked to the canvas but we will always get up for the next round.

2. Strong Work Ethic

Attribute it, if you wish, to lack of year-round access to beaches and golf, but productivity numbers in Buffalo are always among the highest in the country.

3. Optimism

Buffalonians keep the faith and believe that tomorrow will be a better day.

4. Good Humor

We know how to laugh at a good joke, even if it is on us.

5. Passion for the Outdoors

With great skiing, hockey, hiking, boating, and fishing nearby, people in the community get off their couches and take advantage of their surroundings through all four seasons.

6. Caring for the Less Fortunate

Ask any charity from the United Way to the Jerry Lewis Telethon, Buffalo digs deep and shows its collective heart and generosity in spite of national or local economic conditions.

7. Ethnicity

We are proud of our diversity and celebrate it everyday with the friends we meet, the customs we adopt, and even the food we eat.

7½. Sustenance

We love to eat chicken wings that originated in our hometown and wash them down with our favorite beverage of choice: beer.

I am who I am, whoever that may be, because I was forged in Buffalo. I am proud of my roots and my hometown. In that spirit, I wish to dedicate this book of short stories to Buffalonians everywhere and to commit my proceeds from this endeavor to the Boys and Girls Clubs to help in their work of teaching sportsmanship and fair play.

BOOK 1
FROM BUFFALO WITH LOVE

A CHILDHOOD MEMORY

He was my first friend in life—at least, my first friend who I can remember now in adulthood. He lived with his family on the other side of the street in a quiet, middle class neighborhood in Buffalo, New York.

I saw him standing across the street from my parents' first purchased home, watching as the last of the empty moving vans pulled away from the curb after depositing all of our worldly possessions in the small, central-entrance, red brick house that would be my home for ten years until I went away to college. He was short for his age and wore thick glasses. His hair was light brown and slicked down in the back but up in front, as was the custom in the early fifties. He was wearing sneakers and jeans and a red jacket that matched exactly the color of the wagon he was

The house where I grew up; my father constantly reminded us that he bought it for $12,500. *Author's photo.*

pulling to help his older brother deliver Buffalo *Courier-Express* newspapers. We were both eight years old.

We played more at our house than at his. I think it was because my mother didn't let me cross the street by myself and his did, but maybe it was because my dad bought a television set before his dad. It was also easier to be at my house because his mother had certain room restrictions. Her living room, decorated in deep reds and browns and with all the furniture eternally covered in plastic, was totally off limits. In fact, the only time I was ever in that room was some thirty years later when I attended her funeral. She was laid out in her living room in an open coffin. As I bowed my head at the kneeling rail I snuck a peek at her, almost expecting her to sit up and chase us all out of her living room.

My friend and I became inseparable. We played together every waking hour. Cowboys and Indians, soldiers, tag, hide and go seek, pick on my younger brother (David) and cat toss (just what it sounds like) were some of our favorite pastimes at first. Later on came baseball, football, basketball, and street hockey. In sports I was a little stronger, but he could run a lot faster than I could.

He was like my sponsor to the neighborhood, known to the outside world as Saint Mark's parish. He introduced me to many of his classmates, all of whom seemed to be Irish or Italian and had many, many brothers and sisters at home. The only time we were apart was on Sunday mornings when we went to church—he to Saint Mark's and me to Central Presbyterian. We often asked our parents if we could visit the other's church, kind of an ecclesiastical home and away, but our requests were summarily turned down. In those days, interfaith church visitations were taboo. The only fight we got into was, in fact, about religion . . . kind of. It was a sunny Saturday afternoon in the fall, and we were re-creating a pro wrestling match we'd seen on black and white television the night before. He just got up and slugged me in the nose—for real. I asked him what he'd done that for as the taste of blood from my nose trickled over my lip. He said that I had pulled the chain he wore around his neck, which held his catechism. I said that I hadn't meant to as I punched him in the eye, making a note to myself to avoid chain grabbing in future matches. The fight, our first and last, thus ended in a draw. We repaired to his kitchen for some homemade buttered Italian bread that his mom had just baked.

He and I kind of drifted apart when we started high school. He went to a Catholic city high school and I went to a toney country day school; we kept busy and found new sets of friends. We both played football, and he starred as a sprinter in track while I played ice hockey. I heard reports from mutual friends at his school that he was considered to be a "brain," especially talented in science and math. I would see him occasionally in "the hood" and we'd chat, but things were different. Without our knowing or reflecting on it, we'd grown up and grown apart. Our good-byes reminded me of the words of Harry Chapin's hit song, "Taxi"; that "we must get together—but I knew it would never be arranged."

College really divided us. Then all of a sudden we had graduated, served in the army, gotten married, gone to work, and had kids. Then just like that we were divorced and living in apartments across the street from each other, just like the old days. After ten years of marriage, my wife decided that she no longer wanted to be married to me. His wife had apparently made the same decision about him, but their story was far more interesting.

Through track he had met and married a beautiful blonde girl with the palest blue eyes I've ever seen. They used to train together after they were married—until they discovered booze. Apparently, he has a very addictive personality. To shorten a long story, his bride used to pour martinis for him when he returned home from work nightly, which he consumed until he passed out.

One day my friend awoke from his stupor, reflected on how his life had been getting away from him, and got sober. Within a few months, his wife packed up and left him. It seems that she would pour him drinks until he passed out and then head out on the town for her other social life. With him back at home, sober and awake, she could no longer rendezvous with her "friends." Ironically, his sobriety cost him his marriage.

Unfortunately, his choice in women never seemed to improve. He went through a string of failed relationships, unable to find that one special woman he was looking for.

Eventually, he moved out of town a wizened, recycled bachelor with a healthy disrespect for the opposite sex and for the eternal dating game. He stopped sending me Christmas cards, which had become our only means of communication.

Fifty-two years after we met, I wrote a fishing book, and the first reader response I received after publication was an e-mail from my old pal. He told me that he'd retired, moved to Naples, Florida, and was now literally addicted to beach fishing for large snook.

I had a business meeting coming up in Naples, so we arranged to get together for lunch at one of those trendy beach bar–restaurants. My wife, Mindy, came along, and we met him and his live-in girlfriend at an umbrella-shaded seaside table for what I thought would be a pleasant reunion.

I was glad to see that he didn't order a drink and assumed that he was still off booze. From the get-go it seemed that something was a little off. My boyhood friend looked physically fit and well, but his demeanor had changed dramatically since I knew him as a child. It seemed almost as if the world had beaten up on him, and he bore a major chip on his shoulder. He smiled a lot, but it seemed that almost everything he said was either negative or confrontational.

Our luncheon ended none too soon. I insisted on picking up the tab and invited him to call me if he was ever planning a fishing trip to the Florida Keys. We said awkward good-byes and headed for our cars.

On the drive home, Mindy confirmed the obvious when she said, "That was uncomfortable. What's he so angry about?"

"Beats me," I said, "maybe he's just having a bad day." But I knew that wasn't the answer and wondered if it had been something that I'd done or said.

It turned out that I would hear from him only one more time. Apparently, he had made that trip to the Keys and called my home only to find out that I was out of town.

Getting word that he'd called, I returned his call a few weeks later only to have him curse and berate me; for what, I'm not even sure. I felt strangely like I had once again inadvertently pulled on his catechism chain. Apparently we had—by design or inadvertently—fired each other as friends. Using our own methods, we had decided to move on, leaving our childhoods in the past . . . probably where they belong.

For me, it was way too late to entertain any feelings of loss let alone sadness or remorse. We had been friends, and now we were strangers. No more, no less. It simply was what it was.

Over the years, I've thought about old friendships a lot and how we make allowances for friends from our past—maybe because we know how they got to where they are now.

I used to think that people did not change, that at most they modify or mask their comfortable behavior because of positive and/or negative reinforcement from those around them. Now I know that I was wrong. It seems to me now that life, like the forces of nature, can beat you down easier than it can build you up. Albert Schweitzer said, "The tragedy of life is what dies inside a man while he lives."

I've now come to place a high premium on people in my life who are optimistic as opposed to those whose "sky falling down" mentality seems to be a self-fulfilling prophecy. I've decided that I want my life to be a musical comedy and not a tragedy.

So, I wonder, should friendship be unconditional with no term, stretching out forever like a lifetime contract? I guess my answer is a categorical *no*. People do change and grow and move on. A friendship that precludes that process simply is no longer a friendship but more a past acquaintance.

I've learned something else along the way, too. As we get older, there seems to be a strong inclination to become grouchy if not downright angry. I've felt the urge myself and seen it in old friends who seem to be auditioning for *Grumpy Old Men*. I believe the major contributing factors are the stress of health and finances; a growing sense of one's own mortality; a self-realization that we are not going to hit all of our goals or reach all of our dreams; and a growing impatience with others.

My antidote is to keep or find a sense of humor. My dad used to say that "old age is no place for sissies," and I believe it. I don't want to spend my time with friends railing at the moon. That's not the way I want to "go gently into that good night."

THE BENCHWARMER

Benched. Riding the pines. Me. I couldn't believe it.

Winter of 1960, my sophomore year at Williams College, and I was starting out the hockey season as a second-string goalie, sitting on the bench with a towel around my neck, opening the door between shifts, and tossing water bottles to my teammates when they got thirsty. All of this coming off a great freshman team, undefeated, recording shutouts in half of our games. Meanwhile, the varsity won only five games and lost fifteen.

Our starting goalie, Allen Lapey (LAY-PEE), was a senior who was

Williams College varsity hockey team, '61–'62; notice the outdoor rink.
Williams College Sports Information Department;
Courtesy of Williams College Archives and Special Collections.

intermittently brilliant or invisible, long on quickness, short on technique, and off the ice a flake (probably like all of us goalies). He played the drums, whether real or imaginary, always tapping on things, probably hearing music in his head. He was nicknamed "Goog," and, to make matters worse, we had gone to the same high school in Buffalo, New York. My roommate, Tommy Roe from Minnesota, counseled patience. Easy for him to say; he had been installed as center on our second line and had taken over from where he left off the year before, scoring goals left and right. He, by the way, would go on to become an all-American and high scorer in the country.

But that would all unfold later. All I knew then was that I was a benchwarmer. "Coach is just being loyal to his last year's starter," Tommy would say. "Just keep on working hard in practice; you'll get your shot, sooner than later." Little did either of us know how accurate his prediction would be.

Our team was playing well; we were 5–1 after winning a Christmas tournament, and were already starting to get some attention from those who followed college ice hockey. Being a small school of about 1,200 male students, we were considered a cut below the major teams like Clarkson, Saint Lawrence, RPI, and Boston College. While some National Hockey League scouts were beginning to show up, I think most of them were en route to see another small college team that was setting a torrid pace with a team of recognized superstars: Middlebury College.

Middlebury was absolutely annihilating competition. Their first line center was a French Canadian named Phil Latreille (LA-TRAY) who was averaging four goals a game and was on his way to resetting all of Middlebury's scoring records. He had already been signed by an NHL team. (He scored ten goals in one college game!)

Their second line was also unique: three brothers named Fryberger—Jerry, Bob, and Dates, two seniors and a sophomore. Rumor had it that their father, a successful attorney from Duluth, Minnesota, had wanted his sons to go to Williams so badly that he had offered to build the college a new hockey rink, but they got turned down. So here we were, playing in an old outdoor rink in Williamstown, while the Frybergers were flashing around a beautiful rink in Middlebury, Vermont. If the rumors were true, they were no doubt harboring thoughts of revenge when they played against the school that rejected them and their new rink. They wouldn't have to wait long for revenge because we were scheduled to play them a few weeks later in their building and, to make it worse, on their Winter Carnival weekend.

A couple of weeks after we returned to school from Christmas break, Coach Bill McCormick called to tell me that Middlebury was playing RPI in nearby Troy, New York, and asked me if I wanted to join him on a scouting mission. I said sure, thinking that he was feeling sorry for me because I was still on the bench—or maybe he just didn't want Lapey tapping out tunes on his dashboard for an hour and a half.

Either way, I was happy to be invited and looked forward to spending some time with Coach McCormick. He was a great guy and had coached our freshman team as well as the varsity the year before. Only twelve years older than me, he had been recruited from Hagerstown, Ontario, to play hockey for the Michigan State Spartans. He loved the game as much as Tommy and me and would often scrimmage with us in practice. Watching him fly up and down the rink, I'm sure a passerby would have taken him for a college athlete and not a coach.

I loved spending time with Bill, his wife, Marty, and their five kids, and I often volunteered for babysitting. Little did I know then that we were forging a lifelong friendship that I continue to cherish.

The game day came. After our own practice, Bill and I jumped into his station wagon and started our drive down Route 7 and over the Berkshire Mountains to Troy, all the time talking about the National Hockey League and what we two "big league scouts" should be watching for. It was fun and instructive. Bill had been an officer of the American Hockey Association, where he was well respected. He also had many pals who went on to distinguish themselves in the pros like Lou Lamoriello, boss of the New Jersey Devils.

Having skipped dinner, we were both pretty hungry when we arrived just before game time. After we found our seats, I took off to bring us back some concession stand food; coffee and a hamburger for Bill, pizza and a coke for me. I really didn't mind missing the national anthems—

"Star Spangled Banner" for Middlebury and "O Canada" for Latreille and most every player from RPI.

From the concession stand, I watched both teams standing at their respective blue lines and thought how repetitive that ceremony was, everybody standing there listening to the same songs over and over when all you want to do is drop the puck and hit some guy. The pizza looked delicious—big, cheesy, and gooey—so I ordered myself an extra slice, not caring that we had a road game coming up the next weekend against our arch rival Amherst College. *What's the difference*, I thought to myself, *I'll only be sitting on the bench watching Goog get shelled.*

Our seats were great: five rows up, at center ice, with a clear view of the players, and sitting right next to the section reserved for the RPI players' girlfriends. I was in hockey heaven. The game, or what I remember of it, went pretty much as predicted. RPI was too strong for the visitors and won by a couple. Every time Latreille came on the ice, the crowd stiffened. In spite of having one skater assigned to him and being double-teamed all night, he managed to keep his incredible record alive of scoring at least one goal in every college game he ever played in.

I learned something else that night. Dates Fryberger, "Datesy," was in fact the real deal. Though he was a sophomore, I thought he was the fastest skater on the ice. While he may not have had the big, barreling slap shot of his teammate Phil Latreille, he combined speed with finesse and some of the greatest moves I've ever seen. What a prize catch he'd been for Middlebury. A wisp of a guy, like Gretzky, he did it all—everything but drive the team bus. As a bit of a signature, he wore a Kent School hockey sock around his neck honoring the prep school where he'd played. He would go on to become a two-time all-American, one of the best hockey players in Middlebury's history, and he would play on the 1964 US Olympic team.

Speaking of moves, halfway through the game I managed to strike up a nice conversation with this incredible blonde coed who was wearing the fraternity pin of one of the RPI players. She asked me what I did. Fearing reprisals from the boyfriend, I told her I was an NHL scout.

"For what team?" she asked.

"We're not allowed to say," I said, keeping the lie going.

"Where's your clipboard?" she persisted.

"Um, my assistant here has it," I said, pointing to Coach McCormick. If Bill heard that conversation, he never let on, but I think he got a little cross with me when I missed the final buzzer. My new friend and I were at the concession stand, sensually sharing cotton candy.

Anyway, I slept most of the way home, thinking about how pretty the blonde was and how my career as a scout was probably the shortest in history.

The next weekend, we breezed through a rather hapless team from Amherst, no doubt looking forward to our Winter Carnival Weekend visit to Middlebury.

Our bus ride was uneventful, and we arrived for a 10:30 a.m. training meal of steak and ice cream. It was freaky winter weather in Vermont, grey and rainy with a temperature in the mid-forties. Our game wasn't until 2:00 p.m., but we saw a crowd with umbrellas already lined up at the rink as we drove to the main dining hall. Middlebury enjoys a great reputation for their mountains and ski teams. We should have figured out that all of those outdoor events had been rained out, leaving hockey as the only game in town—literally. The stage was being set.

After our meal, we made our way to our locker room in the arena to retape our sticks, get our skates sharpened, and get dressed for the game. Pregame stuff is always fun. Being with the team helps get rid of the butterflies. Some guys always played cards, while a few even napped.

But there would be no napping this day. Like many college arenas, the visitors' locker room was located under the bleachers. In the case of Middlebury, the bleachers were all made of metal. An hour and a half until game time and a standing room only crowd had already shoehorned themselves into the arena. Speaking of shoes, the crowd were wildly stamping their feet, either to keep warm or harass the visitors. It was so loud you couldn't even hear yourself think.

We strapped on the blades and got ready. Game time came, and I'm sure that none of us had ever been happier to get out from under the bleachers and onto the ice in spite of knowing that we had our work cut out for us. Pregame warm-up was a blur of noise and colors. The crowd was on its feet, and Middlebury, in their white shirts with dark blue trim, was zooming around the rink, energized by the ear-shattering noise of its hometown crowd, which it had missed the week before at RPI.

As starter, Lapey went right for our goal and began stretching and taking shots. He looked a little tight, but I figured it was pregame jitters. I chose a spot by our bench and stretched lazily, feeling the extra training meal ice cream in my stomach and wondering how badly Lapey would have to get shelled before I'd get a chance to play. I wasn't wishing him ill, mind you, but I hadn't resigned myself to being a "bench jockey" forever, either.

After a bit, I put on my gloves, grabbed my stick, and started skating slowly toward our net to spell the starter,[1] as is a time-honored tradition in hockey warm-ups. I got halfway there and Goog waved me off. *What's up with that?* I thought, retreating to the relative safety of my stretching place by the net. As we approached the opening face-off, the noise became deafening. I wondered if the Romans had cheered as loudly before they fed Christians to the lions.

I laughed in spite of myself and decided to surreptitiously take a panoramic look at the crowd. I'd seen enough of Latreille and the brothers Fryberger, so I started scanning the crowd looking for a friendly or even familiar face. Besides its winter sports, Middlebury is also famous for its coed population, all beautiful and bright. (Don't forget, I was being held hostage at an all-male school.) The girls had, in fact, turned out. Even bundled up in well-fitted ski jackets, the beautiful souls in attendance were easy to pick out.

Not everyone in the crowd was "bundled up." My eye was drawn to ten guys almost directly behind our bench. They were shirtless and each wore a big, blue, block letter painted on his chest spelling out M-I-D-D-L-E-B-U-R-Y. I'd never seen anything like this before. It was cold in that arena; those guys had to be nuts. Just as I thought that, some of them caught me looking at them. The first "D" yelled something at me and gave me the finger, followed by the second "D," who yelled something else and grabbed his crotch. *Man*, I thought, *this is really hostile.*

For the first time ever as a hockey player, I was happy when the announcer asked everyone to rise for the US and Canadian national anthems. Of course, everyone was already standing, but I thought we'd at least lower the decibel level for a recorded version of the songs.

I skated over to join my teammates on the blue line, and the music began. Somewhere between "the rockets' red glare" and "the bombs bursting in air," I heard someone standing right behind me, going, "Psst, psst, Bobby, Bobby." I glanced over my shoulder, and it was Lapey.

"Not now, Goog, I'm listening to the song."

"I can't play," he said.

"This is no time to joke," I said. "And that's not funny!"

"I'm not joking," he said, now bending over, apparently in pain. "I think I've broken my hand, and I can't play."

"Are you sure, Allen?" I gulped.

"Yeah, I'm pretty sure, and I think I'm going to be sick."

"You and me both," I said, drowned out by the crowd noise that was building as the anthem ended.

The next thing I knew, I was standing in the crease in front of our net. No doubt in shock, I have no idea to this day how I got there, whether I skated or was dragged or carried kicking and screaming by my teammates. NCAA rules prevent warm-up shots after the anthem, so I hadn't even touched a puck.

Incredibly, Tommy Roe, perhaps putting in extra effort for his roomie, scored a goal on a great shot to put Williams ahead 1–0 two minutes into the game. Unfortunately for us, that was to be our only shot that period.

Middlebury threw everything at us but the kitchen sink. Our wings were back checking, and our defensemen were blocking shots left and right. As for our goalie, I got in a groove. Don't ask me where I found it; maybe it was all that pent-up desire to play. Three-on-one rushes, man down on power plays, breakaways; everything but penalty shots, and we kept the net clean. The crowd's collective groan after every save I made was energizing. I don't think I've played like that, before or since.

The buzzer sounded to end the first period, and I looked at the scoreboard to verify: Williams 1, Middlebury 0. A secondary scoreboard showed shots on goal: Williams 1, Middlebury 25.

While I don't remember how I got to the net, I do remember how I got to the exit door—very slowly. I was exhausted. Every muscle hurt. I had contradicting thoughts going through my mind. On one hand I needed a rest, on the other I was afraid to sit down for fear I wouldn't be able to get up again. I also knew that if I started to think about what was going on, we were all dead.

The foot stomping in the stands above our heads had slowed. Maybe we'd thrown a scare into 'em. The ref came to the door and said, "Five minutes, Williams!" Our locker room was subdued.

Then Tony Stout, one of our senior defensemen, jumped to his feet and yelled, "Let's go, you guys. These guys aren't that good; we can beat them. Let's go!" Twenty-three Williams hockey players jumped up and screamed, "Yeah, let's go, we can beat these guys!" The twenty-fourth, yours truly, the goalie, thought, *Beat 'em? Yeah right, we're being out-shot 25–1*. Was Tony serious? I didn't know whether to stand up or throw up. As is hockey custom, I, as starting goalie, led the team out of the locker room and onto the ice.

Back in the cage and five minutes into the second period, the barrage continued till an offside brought a whistle and play stoppage. Then came a line change, and the boys from Duluth skated onto the ice for a face-off in their own zone. Middlebury was still being shut out 1–0. All the way from where I stood, I could see a change come over Datesy's face. It was like he was thinking *That's enough of this BS. Let's get it started.*

Face-off to Bob, to Jerry, to Datesy at center ice, skating in all alone against Tony Stout and John Whitney. *No problem*, I thought as he picked up speed and headed for the middle of the ice and our blue line. He faked one way then the other, then slid the puck between our two super star defensemen. As they came together to put the crunch on him, Datesy jumped in the air over both of them, and they crashed into each other and slammed to the ice. All of a sudden it was me against Datesy, one on one, *mano a mano*; a defining opportunity. I slid forward slowly to cut down his angle and braced for the attack. Datesy closed fast, drew the puck to his left, and then swept it to his right and stuck it in the upper right corner. As for me, I might as well have been at the concession stands. "Faked out of my jock" is the only expression I can think of.

The crowd erupted and the score was tied 1–1. I knew the worst was yet to come, and I was right.

The shelling continued and the flood gates were open for the rest of the second period, and the third as well. The foot pounding exploded as the score mounted. Datesy got two more goals for his three-goal hat trick and won forever the hearts of the Middlebury crowd. The goal light behind our goal kept flashing red. Some guy in the crowd yelled at me, "Hey sieve, the back of your neck is getting sunburned."

With a minute left in the game, it was Middlebury 7, Williams 1. A gray day indeed—but wait! The great one, Phil Latreille, hadn't scored a goal yet. This would have been the first game in his career that he hadn't scored at least one goal, and the clock was ticking down to the end of this (mis-) match.

I had new life, new purpose, a new goal: to keep this guy off the scoreboard.

Thirty seconds left and counting, and this big guy had been on the ice for almost five minutes straight with no success. The crowd knew the deal and were on their feet screaming.

They got the puck to Phil behind the Middlebury cage with twenty seconds to go. He looked up ice. Both of his wings were covered, so he swung around up ice and headed toward our net.

Now it was all about him. The crowd was going crazy. He hit his own blue line with fifteen seconds left, skating toward the center red line as the clock ticked off the remaining seconds of the game. All of the crowd—coeds and the scouts included, I'm sure—were on their feet, cheering together for the great one.

The clock ticked on: 10, 9, 8, 7, 6; he hit the center line. Frustrated and desperate, almost out of time, Phil let go one of his patented slap shots.

Oh somewhere in this favored land the sun is shining bright
The band is playing somewhere, and somewhere hearts are light
And somewhere men are laughing and little children shout,
But there's no joy in Mudville—mighty Casey has struck out.[2]

But Mudville was not Middlebury, Phil Latreille was not Casey, and Phil didn't strike out. On the contrary: with time running out on the clock, the puck propelled by his blistering slap shot dented the twine in the upper right-hand corner of our net.

I'll be candid with you, I never even saw it. What a blast! The place erupted as the clock took the final tick and ended the game. The crowd went crazy and then headed for parts unknown to party.

The scoreboard told the story: Middlebury 8, Williams 1. Shots on goal: Williams 7, Middlebury 73.

I was feeling pretty low. Some guy on his way out shouted, "Hey goalie, thank God you had that big basket behind you or you wouldn't have stopped anything!"

My teammates filed over one by one to lightly slap my pads with their sticks—a nice tradition that is hockey talk for "good game" and/or "sorry we lost." I looked up to see Datesy skating toward me, too. He had left the celebration at the other end of the rink, and, without saying anything, he skated up, touched my pads with his stick, and skated away. It was a class move that I'll never forget.

We would see Datesy again a year later when Middlebury came to Williamstown for our equivalent of their Winter Carnival, our House Party Weekend.

We had a strong team, mostly made up of juniors and seniors, and were well on our way to a 16–3–1 record; to this day, the best in Williams College history. Middlebury was going the other way. Having lost Bob and Jerry and Phil Latreille to graduation, Datesy had to carry the team. With a minute left, we were up 12–5. Datesy, as if trying to re-create the moment that turned their game around the year before, jumped on a loose puck in their end and started up ice. Tommy was on the ice for us and took off after him. Everyone on the ice literally stopped skating to watch what was going to happen. As the clock ticked down, it was like these two superstars were the only ones on the rink. All of a sudden, the scene seemed to become a frozen pond somewhere in Minnesota, and Tommy and Datesy became two boyhood friends out for a winter skate with no one else on the ice, re-creating an age-old hockey rite of passage: the

game of one-on-one keep away. Datesy "ragged the puck," closely shad-
owed by Tommy, who was trying to take the puck away. Then, with ten
seconds left, Datesy came to a full stop on the center red line and gently
pushed the puck away. Tommy, skating by his side, stopped too. The
Minnesotans looked at one another, smiled, and gave each other a big
hug. The sellout crowd in Williamstown went crazy. Both teams started
banging their sticks on the boards in another old tradition of honoring
great play. It was a sports moment that I'll never forget.

Tommy and Datesy would be on the ice together many more times,
playing on the same line for a USA team that went on a world tour. Tom
would go on to become a lawyer in Minneapolis and Datesy an architect
and amateur ski racer in Ketchum, Idaho.

I never saw Phil Latreille again after that game, although I knew he
went on to play hockey for the New York Rangers after graduation.

Come to think of it, I never saw Allen Lapey after that game either. I
don't know if he had his "broken hand" casted or if his hand was ever
really broken. He just hung up his skates, just like that, and never even
showed up again at the rink. I guess he was just done. Did I tell you all
of us goalies are a little flakey?

Years later, I heard that he had gone to medical school and then
became an immunologist of some renown in Boston. He probably taps his
instruments on his desk like drumsticks as he interviews his patients).

As for me, after graduation I turned down an offer to play for Los
Angeles in the Western League in order to play backup goalie for the Buffalo Bisons of the American Hockey League and train for a tryout with
the '64 Olympic team. Sadly for me, I got cut before the team—which
included Datesy Fryberger—headed for Innsbruck, Austria. Then I got
drafted, not by the Bruins or Blackhawks, but by Uncle Sam. After an
undistinguished military career, I finished my hockey career with equal
lack of distinction by playing left wing for the Town Edge Lounge in a
beer league in Buffalo. I never quite developed the moves of Tommy or
Datesy.

THE BUFFALO SABRES

A National Hockey League team was coming to Buffalo, and I had been invited to be part of the ownership—life doesn't get any better than that!

The team to be known as the Buffalo Sabres was actually the dream of another Buffalonian, Seymour Knox, and his younger brother, Northrup "Norty" Knox, who had been lifetime friends and mentors of mine. Both Knoxes were from a most prominent family in western New York. Their dad had been the primary shareholder in the Woolworth Company and Marine Midland Bank, which was later to become part of Hong Kong Shanghai Bank (HSBC).

Both superb athletes, Seymour was an investment banker with Kidder Peabody, and Norty ran the family farms in nearby East Aurora and in

Rookie NHL owners Seymour Knox, center, and his brother, Norty, right, meet the press. *Courtesy of the Buffalo Sabres.*

Aiken, South Carolina, before becoming chairman of Marine Midland and, later, HSBC.

The Knoxes had put together a local team of investors that had tried to purchase an NHL franchise in 1967 when the league added six new teams. My dad had been part of that group, which came home empty-handed in spite of a great presentation.

Then my father stepped down, and I was included in the new group that tried again when the NHL added two new teams in 1969.

On December 2, 1969, franchises were awarded to two cities: Vancouver, British Columbia, and Buffalo, New York, for the then-lofty price of $6 million apiece. Representing a smaller city, the Knoxes' quest was heroic and full of drama up to the last minute.

At the expansion meetings, National Hockey League President Clarence Campbell thanked the Knoxes for their determination and was in the process of dismissing them. Seymour, ever the gentleman, thanked the committee for their consideration and was preparing to leave when Norty, the firebrand, jumped in and said words to this effect: "Listen, we've supplied you with everything you asked for, we've met your criteria, and we have a right to a team. If you turn Buffalo down again, we're going to sue you and demand treble damages— and if you don't know what that means, ask your lawyers. We'll be in our room, waiting for your call. C'mon, Seymour," and then he walked out of the room.

Within an hour the call came. It was for the polite gentleman, Seymour, of course, telling him that Buffalo had been approved for an expansion franchise in the National Hockey League.

That story, and many more like it over the course of his lifetime, is one of the reasons why Norty Knox was a hero of mine. He had a unique ability to identify important issues and cut to the chase. He was an up-front, no-nonsense kind of guy, confident enough to act on his convictions. That's why Norty's telephone call asking me to be an investor and to become a director before the franchise was awarded meant so much to me personally. Little did I know then what my role with the team would evolve into years later when I became a vice chairman or what decisions we would face after Seymour and Norty's untimely deaths, both ironically at seventy years of age.

Growing up in Buffalo, hockey had been my life. First it was street hockey, then pond hockey and trips over the Peace Bridge to play in nearby Fort Erie, Ontario, then city leagues and high school hockey.

We could barely get Canadian Television (CTV), so when we would watch the six original NHL teams play in black and white on *Hockey Night in Canada*, it was like watching a game in a blizzard. Fearing loss of vision, my father would always insist I turn off the set, which made watching the games all the more appealing, like stealing cookies.

I was literally raised on the old Buffalo Bisons of the American Hockey League. The minor league team played in the 7,500-seat Memorial Auditorium, also known as "the Aud." From the time I was a child, my favorite seats were those closest to the rink, front row, center ice browns, where you felt you were part of the action. Sunday evenings meant hockey at the Aud. Eventually, my closest friend and I were allowed to take the bus to games alone. We would wonder at the moves of scoring leaders like Zellio Toppazzini of the Providence Reds, Bronco Horvath of the Rochester Amerks, and Bill Sweeney of Eddie Shore's Springfield Indians. Together we would boo the "bad guys"—like a young high school draftee defenseman, the inimitable Don Cherry of the Hershey Bears or the rogue villain Freddy Glover of the Cleveland Barons.

We cheered loudly for our hometown heroes, the Buffalo Bisons. As a goaltender, my all-time favorite was Buffalo goalie Jacques Plante, who later went on to star for the Montreal Canadiens. Playing without a mask, as all us goalies did then, Plante, a good skater, not only cut down shooters' angles but became famous for ranging all over the ice to handle the puck and make plays. I copied his every move. Off the ice he was also famous for his knitting—you know, scarves, sweaters, toques. I didn't copy his off-ice hobby.

It was ironic that this same team that I'd watched and loved as a child would later sign me to a contract.

Norty's call came at a great time for me. I was twenty-eight years old, married with three young children, and I was just finishing the start-up of a family company in Canada and a master's degree in business at the University of Rochester. On my way back to Buffalo to oversee sales and marketing for our US company, I hoped I'd have some time to help the Knoxes in any way they wanted.

Ownership in the team was divided into four basic pieces: one owned by the Knox family; one by me and my family; one by several small local shareholders hoping to increase local interest (and ticket sales as well); and one by a chap named George Strawbridge from Philadelphia. George, a member of the Dorrance family that owned the Campbell Soup Company, was a handsome Pierce Brosnan look-alike and accomplished equestrian. We would become good friends. He and I were more than happy to be silent partners while Seymour served as the general partner and chairman. It was his team, and he was ready to make it his profession as well.

There was a lot to do before the team opened in the fall of 1970. To be granted the franchise, we'd had to buy the American Hockey League Bisons, which now had to be relocated. There was also a lot of planning and marketing required to facilitate the sale of tickets. Radio and TV contracts had to be negotiated, and most importantly, we needed players. Norty and Seymour wisely hired a wily old veteran, Punch Imlach, to be the team's GM and oversee the draft that spring that would determine our first year's players.

The highlight of the draft in Montreal came with the selection of the first player in the amateur draft by either the Buffalo Sabres or Vancouver Canucks. Building the excitement, NHL President Campbell, not a natural showman, had had a giant roulette wheel set up. The board showed numbers from one to twenty. It was predetermined that if any number between one and ten came up, Vancouver got to choose first. If a number between eleven and twenty came up, the first choice belonged to Buffalo.

The prize awaiting the winner was an exciting young French Canadian junior named Gilbert Perreault, available only because this was the first year that the Montreal Canadiens did not have preference on all Quebec-born players. Gilbert was one of those "do it all" players in the image of Montreal's Jean Beliveau, who you could build a team around.

The spin came and the wheel apparently stopped on number 1. Clarence Campbell announced that first choice belonged to Vancouver and their table erupted. Punch Imlach quickly pointed out that the number was actually a one on top of a one, or eleven. Campbell corrected himself and announced that the first pick belonged to Buffalo, and it was our table's turn to go crazy.

Punch stood up and said, "The Buffalo Sabres choose, from the Montreal Junior Canadiens, Gilbert Perreault."

Ironically, eleven would be the magic number that day, June 11. It was Punch's favorite number and the number that Gilbert Perreault had always worn as a junior. What was the number that Gilbert wore for the rest of his seventeen-year career exclusively with the Buffalo Sabres? Eleven, of course.

As for the team name, the "Sabres" was ostensibly chosen through a citywide name-the-team contest, although I suspect that it was always a name that Seymour had in mind. It had great symbolic power: a flashing blade, striking with speed, force, and rapidity, as well as a strong, sturdy weapon for defense. What about the team colors, blue and gold? Easy! Those were the Knoxes' polo colors.

That first season, the team would play in a smallish Memorial Auditorium, and plans were completed to raise the roof in the offseason to expand seating to 19,500.

Time went by quickly, and all of a sudden the team was opening training camp in nearby St. Catharines, Ontario. On the ice, they were a ragtag lot made up of a lot of guys who, by reason of age or lack of talent or something more obscure, were not in the long-term plans of the teams that had left them unprotected in the expansion draft. Punch knew that the first few years would be tough, so in the expansion draft he drafted some guys who loved to hit and/or were extremely entertaining to watch. Opening with guys like "the Enforcer" Reggie Fleming and Eddie "the Entertainer" Schack, Punch guaranteed that the fans would be amused and the opposition would keep their heads up when on the ice.

As for me, I was like a kid in a candy store, still focused on the excitement of the game on the ice. All of that began to change when the team broke camp. We got a call from US Immigration that when the team bus crossed the Peace Bridge, one of the players would be arrested as a fugitive. It seems he was a few years in arrears in his court-ordered child support payments. For me, this was kind of a loss of innocence; these guys weren't superstars, they were human like everybody else.

This incident also focused us on the need for lawyering, and Buffalo had a good one. Bob Swados, a friend of Seymour's, was the senior attorney in one of the city's law firms when Seymour asked him to be an officer of the corporation.

Bob Swados was tough and dogmatic and would go on to be elected secretary of the NHL. While he'd never win any popularity contests, he usually got the job done one way or the other. In his later years, he went on to write his memoirs, called *Counsel in the Crease*. I read the rather long opus and took exception with many of his "facts" and conclusions, especially around the subject of how the team came to be sold. Perhaps my umbrage stems from the fact that we goalies just don't like people in our crease, but that's a story for later.

We opened on the road against the Pittsburgh Penguins and won 2–1.

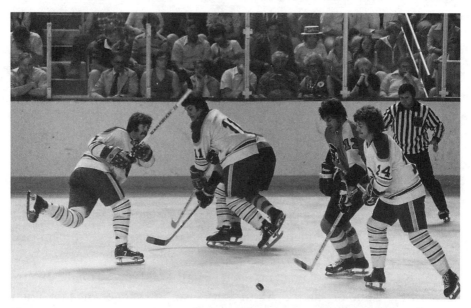

The French Connection in action. *Courtesy of the Buffalo Sabres.*

It was one of the most memorable games I've ever watched. Then we returned to the Aud for our first home game against my longtime favorite, the Montreal Canadiens! Who would I cheer for? Remember, I'd been watching those guys since I was a single digit old. I had to cheer for the Sabres, but how? I figured it out; I'd just think about how Montreal summarily traded Jacques Plante to the Rangers after eleven great seasons.

An opening home game loss to the Habs mattered little; our team was launched and on its way to great accomplishments on and off the ice. Off-season construction went even better than planned, and fans were thrilled to return to a totally refurbished Aud with 19,500 seats.

Punch Imlach proved to be a master; the next year, he drafted another young French Canadian, Rick Martin, who he teamed with Gilbert Perreault and René Robert, a winger he picked up in a trade from Pittsburgh. Together they formed a line nicknamed "The French Connection" that was as exciting to watch as any line in the National Hockey League.

Things were happy in Sabre Land as the team thrived and built a reputation as one of the best-run sports franchises in the country. We were selling out and retiring debt. Everyone seemed content.

Then in 1972 came a threat in the form of a rival league, the World Hockey Association (WHA), with ten new teams. The franchise fee per team was only $25,000, which ironically was the same amount that the average NHL player was making at that time. Our resident "hockey expert" and lawyer, Swados, counseled our board to "stay calm." The new league could only mean "modest" average payroll increases of "well under 30 percent." Then NHL superstar Bobby Hull led a mass defection of players to the new league by signing a contract with the Winnipeg Jets for just under $4 million. Disregarding informal drafting rules, the Houston Aeros of the WHA drafted Gordie Howe's two sons, Mark and Marty, who were considered underage juniors. They even brought their legendary father, Gordie, out of retirement at age fifty-one so that the three Howes could play together on a line for mega bucks. So much for modest payroll increases.

While the WHA folded after seven years, it helped change the economics of the game. All of a sudden there were large NHL markets and small markets, basically defined by the size of their television contracts. We went from retiring debt to adding on debt. The economics soon dictated that the Sabres had to get through first one, then two, rounds of the play-offs each year just to break even. In the meantime, player salaries were spiraling uncontained through the roof with the owners unable or unwilling to demonstrate even a modicum of restraint.

The years went by; the Sabres diversified as a way to increase revenue by expanding into several other ventures: television, a new training/ skating complex, an indoor soccer team, the Blizzard, and an indoor lacrosse team, the Bandits.

As happened in other cities, it also became imperative to move into a new building equipped with revenue enhancers like corporate boxes, more high-priced seats, and club lounges. The problem was financing. Most of the owners were in at small levels, growing older, with no interest in investing more money. Let me talk for a moment about "cash calls." Once invested, most sports owners receive all the psychic reward that they sought by being identified as "one of the owners." For most, answering a cash call does absolutely nothing positive for them—especially when the enterprise is losing money and building debt.

Only a few of us, like George Strawbridge and me, constantly responded to the cash calls, thereby avoiding dilution and increasing our percentage of ownership in the Sabres. Faced with his team's cash problem, Seymour sent Bob Swados out in 1994 in search of new capital. Based on the club's income statement and balance sheet, this seemed to be like mission impossible.

Then Swados made the dubious discovery of the Rigas family. Son of Greek immigrants, John Rigas, the family patriarch, had made his first acquisition when he bought a small movie theater in his hometown of nearby Coudersport, Pennsylvania. From there, he ventured into the burgeoning new field of cable television, first purchasing one then several cable networks. He was aided by his three sons, John, Michael, and Tim. Soon they had built their Adelphia Cable Company into one of the five largest systems in the country. Rigas continued to headquarter in Coudersport and literally turned the town once known as "Potato City" into Rigasville.

John Rigas seemed to be a natural investor in the Sabres, bringing with him a wealth of knowledge in cable television that would be needed for the team to survive. The Rigases invested $16 million into the franchise in what had to be one of the most one-sided, onerous agreements ever signed. First, their money went in not as equity but rather as debt, bearing a usurious interest fee of over 18 percent. Second, they could convert the debt to equity at any time they wished, and third, they demanded the right to approve any new investors. In short, they could watch the Sabres struggle while existing investors passed on cash calls and eventually take over the team by default.

In the meantime, Seymour and then Norty Knox became ill, unbeknownst to the rest of us. Construction funding was secured, and we were on our way to a new building while an internal battle royal began to determine who would become the new president of the Sabres. In one corner we had the incumbent, Larry Quinn; in the other, the challenger, newcomer Doug Moss. Larry was a longtime Buffalo guy who had been tapped by Mayor Griffin to head up development for the city when he was just out of Notre Dame. Larry was a young superstar who had then gone to New York as a developer, later to be wooed back to Buffalo to oversee the construction of our new home, Marine Midland Arena. Doug Moss had been brought in to manage the day-to-day operations. He had previously run MSGN—basically, a cable television network.

I knew there was trouble brewing when, before Doug's introductory press conference, Seymour proudly presented him with a Sabres logo necktie to wear.

Noticing he hadn't put it on, I asked him about it. He said, "Doug Moss does *not* wear polyester!" *This is going to be good*, I thought.

In the meantime, I received a somewhat ominous call to meet Seymour and Norty at the Knox family offices. This was a first, and I was curious to find out what was on their minds.

When I arrived, they were both courteous as always and very complimentary about the help I had been giving the Sabres, specifically on dealing with the city and the construction of the new arena. It was then that they asked me if I would step in as chairman and succeed them in running the team.

I was flattered. They had been my mentors, and I looked up to them both but I felt they deserved a prompt answer. I said, "No, I can't. I have major commitments to running our family business, which will always be my priority." Jumping in further, I thanked them and pledged that short of running the team, I would do anything I could to help them. Then, all but unable to bite my lip, I added, "From what I've seen in the last few financial reviews, if I were to run the team, the first thing I would do would be to sell it—to buyers who would keep it in Buffalo, of course."

Neither Seymour nor Norty liked what they heard from me, but after reviewing my rationale—small market, low mean income, marginal TV revenues, escalating player salaries—I know they understood. We shook hands, and I left with a sinking feeling inside, though I was hopeful that my candor would not cost me their friendship.

Seymour died on May 22, 1996, only a few months before the first puck was dropped at his beautiful new arena. He called a week before he

Under Larry Quinn's direction, HSBC Arena, the Buffalo Sabres' beautiful new home, was brought in on time and under budget. *Courtesy of the Buffalo Sabres.*

died, asking me to reconsider, but I had to turn him down. Two of his sons confided in me that his last deathbed wish was that I would run the club. This has been a heavy burden for me to bear.

A few months before completion of the arena, the Sabres ran out of money and the banks wouldn't lend them any more. I met with George Strawbridge, and we agreed to provide them a bridge loan of $3.7 million to allow them to complete construction.

The arena was finished. Larry Quinn brought Marine Midland Arena in on time under budget. Later in November, as if part of some weird, ominous foreshadowing, the huge four-sided video board crashed to the center floor of the arena and had to be replaced. Luckily, no one was under it.

Once the arena project was complete, Larry Quinn returned to the Sabres office full time, and the battle for the Sabres presidency heated up. It didn't last long. Larry had proven his skills, and Doug Moss, the slick marketer, had lost the trust of those around him. Larry became president. Doug left.

The arena opened and was a grand and unmitigated success. Norty called for a meeting that I had anticipated but had been dreading. He told me that his own illness, which had been in remission, had returned. "I know you won't change your mind on succeeding me and running this team, so I want you to sell it. I would, but I just don't have the strength. I trust you," he added.

"What about Mr. Swados?" I had to ask.

"You have more invested financially and I know that you understand what has to be done. Use any resources that you need," he said.

It was clear that the deteriorating financial condition of the club was taking its toll on Norty, and I that his patience was running out.

"Please find a buyer who'll protect our investors and keep the club here," he said.

I reminded Norty that the Rigases had the right to approve a buyer, and he told me to do what I had to, but get started.

I met with Peat Marwick, accountants in New York City, and came up with three prospects after two months of work. To the best of my knowledge, the Rigases had only a half-hearted meeting with one of the prospective buyers and refused to talk to the other two. I reported back to Norty and told him it was my impression that the Rigases were just waiting to take the team over. We agreed that I should talk with them again, this time about purchasing the team.

Our timing was good; we were forced to make another cash call. Norty and I stepped up along with George Strawbridge, sending a message to Coudersport that we were not going to walk away and let them take the Sabres, and that now they would have to step up too or watch their shares become diluted.

I set up a meeting with the Rigases knowing that I wanted a second in the ring for this one. James Haddad served as our company's corporate controller. He was bright and quick, with a good mind for deal-making, and he was someone I could trust implicitly. He also had a curiosity for numbers and a great self-deprecating sense of humor that I knew would help me keep my temper when this negotiation got tough—which I knew it would.

We chose a meeting spot, in the ski town of Ellicottville, that was symbolically halfway between Buffalo and Coudersport. We arrived fifteen minutes early; Tim showed up with his financial people forty-five minutes late, offering no excuse. His father decided not to come. This would turn out to be a hallmark of their style that showed true disrespect and contempt.

We asked if they were interested in purchasing the Sabres, and one of Tim's minions, Jim Brown, their CFO, went to a blackboard and scribbled for an hour to show us how bad off the team was. "Functionally bankrupt" were his exact words.

I'd chosen well; James Haddad refuted his every point. It was clear that he had more than enough firepower to deal with these guys.

Our meetings went on and on for several months, some with intercession from the NHL commissioner's office. The Rigases were late for, or skipped, every single meeting I can remember, and they tried every trick in the book (and some not in the book) to delay a conclusion and/or sabotage a deal. It was a very frustrating process. They wanted us to take Adelphia stock and not cash, and I luckily refused repeatedly. Then, just before Christmas 1997, it appeared that we had the makings of a deal. I had added a second professional from our Rich Products team, a young lawyer named Bill Grieshober. Bill, a good athlete himself, was a quick study and would give us the legal expertise we needed to draft an agreement.

I went to Barbados with my family and literally broke two fax machines and got cauliflower ear from a telephone trying to keep up with the work produced by multiple lawyers, accountants, and bankers.

Finally we got back a signed memorandum of understanding (MOU) on New Year's Eve, December 31, 1997. By this time Norty was becoming very frail and had allowed John Rigas to replace him as chairman. This would turn out to add to the difficulty of getting a closing and disbursements of funds.

The MOU called for us to come up with a formal Funding and Purchase Agreement. This, too, dragged on, but the agreement was finally signed on March 20, 1998.

In the meantime, apparently wanting to consolidate power and bring cash to his office in Coudersport, John Rigas fired Larry Quinn and replaced him with his son, Tim. Then he fired the chief financial officer for the Sabres and brought in his own financial people to replace the Sabres staff. He did this, he said, "to use our financial reporting systems, you know."

Four months after the signing, on July 23, 1998, Norty Knox passed away. It was a very sad day for me. I felt like I'd lost an older brother. While happy that he'd seen us get a signed agreement, I was frustrated that we hadn't yet been able to complete the task and get a closing.

Throughout my business career, longer than I like to admit, I've never seen or dealt with anyone like John and Tim Rigas. I always felt that, on the occasions that you could get their attention, they'd look you right in the eye and lie.

My spirits throughout the process were bolstered by the other shareholders. While many of them couldn't invest more money, they knew what an uphill battle we were fighting and they stayed in lockstep with us all the way.

The Rigases had claimed that, due to the complexity of the deal and the number of bank consents required, they would not be able to commit to a closing date. Getting them to close would be a daunting task that would end up taking an unbelievable two years and four months. They even contested the bank's desire to change the name of the Arena from Marine Midland to HSBC.

Amid our chasing the Rigases for a closing, the *Buffalo News* published the results of a survey they'd conducted on Buffalo leadership. In a front page story, complete with a large color picture, they announced that John Rigas was a runaway winner as "the most powerful and effective business leader in Buffalo." The voters were no doubt swayed by his role in "saving the Sabres" and his promise to build a multistory building on our waterfront. What a joke! At best, I believe that Rigas should have been given the "Artful Dodger Award."

This was a game of which I was getting tired, so I came up with a plan. The Rigases were legally bound to hold a board of directors meeting. When they did, I was ready. John Rigas, as chairman, called the meeting to order, and I asked for the floor. I said that on behalf of the other investors who'd been waiting for a closing and to be paid out, I'd had enough of their antics. I told them that I had retained the New York law firm Weil Gotshal and the forensic accounting department of Ernst and Young and would like to propose a motion to hire them to do an in-depth review of the management's actions since John Rigas had become chairman. The Rigas crew turned ashen. My intent was clear; Weil Gotshal had a reputation as one of the toughest law firms in the country, and Ernst and Young's forensic people wouldn't be trifled with. Rigas hemmed and hawed but finally called the motion, which passed on party lines as you might expect.

Once again, we called in Commissioner Bettman to assist. He requested that Tim and John meet with us in his office to try and move things along.

The day came, and both Rigases were no-shows, sending two of Adelphia's employees instead. I was furious and made my feelings known in no uncertain terms. Commissioner Bettman told both sides that he believed we were entitled to an investigation. The Rigas camp grasped for straws; it was clear they felt the noose tightening. But it wasn't fast enough for me, so I came up with another idea.

It was clear that we needed to take the heat up if we wanted to close the deal and get paid. Hockey, like any other enterprise, has a well-tuned grapevine; it was time to use it. We put the word out that the talking was over and that we planned to start the investigation.

Within a few weeks, we had a closing and proceeds were distributed. Coincidence? You be the judge. In retrospect, it was obvious to me how and why this tactic worked. In spite of all of their cable wheeling and dealing, it was clear that they were cash poor. More importantly, John and Tim Rigas had a lot to hide, and the last thing they needed was these legal/accounting professionals getting into their operations. The grapevine had done its job. I wish I'd used it sooner. My first call was to Norty Knox's widow, Cetta, to share the news of the closing.

The Rigases had their team, but their joy didn't last long. In the spring of 2002, Tim Rigas admitted during a call with investment analysts that $2.3 billion of Adelphia's debt was loans to entities controlled by the Rigas family. The market went crazy, the value of their shares collapsed to almost nothing, trading was suspended, and Adelphia was eventually delisted. An immediate SEC investigation began. The $2.3 billion was later adjusted to over $3 billion.

In May, John, Tim, and Michael Rigas were indicted and arrested for, among other things, conspiracy, wire fraud, and securities fraud for embezzling $2 billion from Adelphia, the public company that John had founded and now managed. It wasn't a pretty sight. John and two of his sons, Tim and Michael, were arrested at their apartment in New York City, handcuffed, and given the "perp walk" to the curb. The arrogant Jim Brown, who'd taken it upon himself to be our finance professor in Elli-cottville five years earlier, was indicted as well.

For Larry Quinn and I, there was no shock whatsoever. I, in the boardroom, and Larry, in the office, had both seen firsthand how these guys operated. If anything, like everyone else, we were surprised by the enormity of their "heist."

Their dealings followed a pattern. John, the "generous old father figure," seemed to want to be everyone's friend. His son Tim comfortably played the role of the arrogant *L'enfant terrible*, a cold, dispassionate know-it-all driven to build an empire. To the end, some people argued that John was a caring community benefactor, totally unaware of his son's malfeasance.

Their trial took place and a jury wasn't fooled by either of them. Father John and son Tim were both found guilty and eventually sentenced. John got fifteen years; Tim twenty. Michael, later judged to be more of a witness to it all, got a one year suspended sentence. Showing unusual compassion, or maybe wanting to give them a break, the Judge allowed them to stay out of jail during their appeal process. Leave it to the Rigases to stall; nobody's better at it.

After losing their appeal, they were remanded to prison. Ironically, they were later joined in the same facility by master Ponzi artist Bernie Madoff. They must have some interesting conversations in the cafeteria.

I had only one discussion with my dad about this "father–son tragedy." He came back from Florida one day, and we were getting caught up. He said how unfair he thought it was that John Rigas, then over eighty, was given such a long sentence.

"Why, Dad?" I asked him.

"Because he's such an old man," he said.

"That's interesting," I said. "Just what is the age, then, that you can put yourself above the law?"

We never spoke on the subject again.

After their indictment, the Rigases turned the Buffalo Sabres franchise over to the National Hockey League. NHL Commissioner Gary Bettman and I had become friends, despite his upholding Brett Hull's controversial goal for the Dallas Stars in a Sabres triple overtime play-off loss in 1999. Gary called me after the Rigases surrendered their franchise, and I had a pretty good idea of why he was calling.

Mincing no words, he started right out: "Bob, we want to keep the Sabres in Buffalo, and I want you to buy the team."

I was prepared. "Commissioner, I've been down this road. It's just not going to happen."

"What if someone comes along who wants to move the franchise?"

"I'll tell you what, Gary," I said. "I'll work with you to find a good buyer for the Sabres who'll keep the team in Buffalo."

"OK," he said. "But if you can't find that buyer, will you buy the team yourself?"

"Yes, I will, Commissioner," I heard myself saying, wondering to myself what in the world I was thinking. I guess being an owner of the team for over thirty years meant something. I was also haunted about my refusing the death wishes of two friends to take over the team, and promising to find an owner that would keep it in Buffalo had been weighing more heavily on my mind than I thought.

I went into my dad's office to tell him what I'd agreed to and he just smiled.

My first call was to Larry Quinn, whom I'd always considered to be a good friend. Larry had gone back into commercial development in the city. I told him I was on a mission to find a buyer for the Sabres and wondered if, under the right conditions, he'd return to run the franchise. He quickly said yes but only under the condition that the owner would be someone he respected and could work with. "Obviously, not another Rigas," he added.

"Larry, there could never be another Rigas," I said. He laughed and responded, "Well, let's go find somebody, then," and the search was on.

Most of the legitimate buyers were interested in moving the team to Hamilton, Ontario, or Las Vegas or Sacramento or Seattle or God knows where. A lot of the other interested parties were bottom-feeding pretenders looking for a fire sale.

One local buyer had emerged. Mark Hamister, a Buffalo business guy with a mini conglomerate of holdings, including nursing homes, rental units, and an arena football team, had secured a promise of some equity financing from a friend of his that would later crumble. He had even installed himself in the Sabres offices as the heir apparent. Mark was a nice enough young man, and he was civic minded; he served as the chairman of the Partnership, Buffalo's fanciful name for Chamber of Commerce. The only problem I had with him as an owner was that I didn't believe he had the financial wherewithal to survive in a small market in the National Hockey League, especially given the rumors that the NHL was looking at a work stoppage when the players' agreement ran out in a year's time.

After a search, we came up with a great candidate for owner. Tom Golisano from nearby Rochester, New York, was the consummate entrepreneur. He had founded and chaired a company called PayChex, a third-party provider of payroll services. A political activist, he had run unsuccessfully for governor three times. We'd been invited to dinner at his home several years before and had found him to be a most interesting and engaging host. While he wasn't known as a hockey fan, he did have a deep interest in western New York—and deep pockets as well.

Larry went to see him and a deal was struck, with Larry agreeing to run the club for him.

I know that Norty would have been happy because he and I felt bad that John Rigas had fired Larry when the Rigas family took over.

The National Hockey League was happy; they would now have financially stable, local ownership in Buffalo.

The fans were happy. Tom Golisano's first move was to lower prices, and his second move was going to work to assure that the team would be competitive.

And I was the happiest of all. After what seemed like many years of work, I had helped to secure the future of the Buffalo Sabres and had kept the faith with two dear friends to whom I'd made a promise.

A promise made is a debt unpaid.
—Robert Service

COFFEE RICH PARK

S ix-thirty a.m., Sunday, September 17, 1972; my phone rang.
"Hello."

"We'll name it Coffee Rich Park, and we'll pay $1 million for a ten-year contract," the familiar voice on the other end of the line said.

"Fine, Dad. Talk to you later," I said as the line went dead.

An hour later I woke, wondering if I'd dreamt it or if my father really had just called me about paying a million dollars to name something. Anyway, I knew I'd have to wait a few hours to find out. Sunday was one of my dad's summer golf days, and "old milkmen" always get up and out early.

Actually, milkman was kind of a misnomer. When he graduated from college in 1935, my dad had borrowed $5,000 from his father to buy a dairy named Wilber Farms in our hometown of Buffalo, New York. That was really a misnomer, too. There were no farms. They had a small processing plant and three milk routes, two served by trucks and one by a horse-drawn wagon.

By the time the Second World War ended ten years later, in 1945, the dairy had grown and my father had discovered technology to manufacture nondairy toppings, putting us in the frozen food business.

With the addition of several products, our company, now named Rich Products Corporation, had grown from first year sales of $28,000 to $57,000,000 in 1972. It has continued to grow and is selling $3 billion a year as I write this tale today.

After graduating from college and serving in the army, I had gone to work for my father and had started our Canadian company while getting an MBA. In 1972, I was heading up sales and marketing for North America. Our most popular consumer product was a nondairy creamer known as Coffee Rich.

Like any consumer goods company, we were always on the lookout

A panoramic view of a sellout crowd at Buffalo's War Memorial Stadium.
Courtesy of the Buffalo Bisons.

for unique ways to promote our company and our wares. Being very closely held, we were especially watchful for bargains. Among a diminishing breed of Buffalo-based companies, we were also always sensitive to the economic setbacks our community had suffered and we were motivated to find ways to invest locally.

I went over to my dad's house after lunch, as he was coming home from the golf course, and got the rest of the story.

The Buffalo Bills had been playing football for eleven years in an old inner city facility named War Memorial Stadium. The team had been a start-up franchise in 1960 for the American Football League, which had merged with the National Football League in 1970. With seating for 47,000, the refurbished WPA project was not only shabby but three thousand seats short of the 50,000 seat minimum dictated by the NFL post-merger mandates.

Not wanting to lose the Bills, our county of Erie had agreed to build a new 80,000-seat stadium for the team in nearby Orchard Park, New York.

The large new facility, complete with skyboxes, would probably put enough distance between the stands and the field that the hometown fans wouldn't be able to pelt the visitors or the refs with snowballs, which had been a popular winter pastime in the old place, known lovingly as the Rockpile.

The new playpen for the Bills would not be cheap. The total cost was $22 million, a substantial amount—even though today, given the cost to build new stadiums, it sounds like chump change. The county had been

Erie County's model of the new football stadium.
Provided by the Buffalo Chamber of Commerce.

able to find most of the required funding but was coming up about a million dollars short.

Faced with the deficit, the Erie County Legislature had thought up a unique idea to close the financial gap. They decided to sell the naming rights to the stadium and recruited the local chamber of commerce to set up a process to find some bidders.

Selling naming rights for commercial purposes was a totally new concept at the time. A year before, Schaefer Brewing Company was given the naming rights to a new $6 million stadium that was under construction in Foxborough, Massachusetts, for the New England Patriots. Those rights were part of a package that gave the brewing company "pouring rights" for the stadium.

My dad had heard from one of his golfing pals that, despite "an exten-

"We'll name it Coffee Rich Park, and we'll pay $1 million . . ."
Courtesy of Rich Products Corporation.

sive six-month national advertising program," the chamber had not received so much as an expression of interest from anyone. The Bills, having negotiated away the naming rights in their lease agreement (probably believing the rights had no value), had remained mute on the subject.

"This is embarrassing for our community," my dad said, looking for some golf to watch on television.

"So what shall we do?" I asked, now realizing that my dad had given me the punch line at 6:30 that morning. Still, I wanted to verify.

"We'll offer to buy the naming rights for $1 million, paid over ten years, to call the new stadium Coffee Rich Park," he said, paraphrasing our earlier one-sided conversation. "That is, if you think it's a good idea," he then added gratuitously.

Of course I thought it was a good idea. I'd begun my career thinking that my father knew nothing but soon realized that he was always about two moves ahead of everyone else. Armed with that new respect, we had become true friends and partners. I came to love working with him. While we may have disagreed on some issues, no one ever knew it—those discussions always took place between the two of us behind closed doors. This was his deal, but I was ready to do his bidding as he had always supported my projects no matter how offbeat.

"How shall we proceed?" I asked, fully knowing that he had a plan.

"Well," he said, "I want you to be the point man on this. Let's start with a meeting with the owner of the Bills, then the legislature's leadership, and then the head of the chamber. After that, you might want to call a press conference."

"And the lawyers?" I asked, anticipating his answer.

"No, only after you've drafted our offer."

My dad was from the good old school where business people made deals before lawyers were engaged.

"We've got to move quickly on this," he added. "The chamber has a deadline of October 13 for proposals, and the legislature then has a deadline of November 7 to approve a proposal and select a name."

"Don't worry, Dad," I said, "I won't need that long."

The next day, I set up all the necessary meetings for us, starting with Ralph Wilson, the owner of the Buffalo Bills. While I'd met him a few times, I knew him mostly by his reputation of being focused, proud, and at times extremely stubborn. About five years younger than my father, he was from Detroit and had some diversified business interests that included transporting new automobiles, an insurance company, and, I believe, a couple of radio stations.

A small minority shareholder in the Detroit Lions, he had bought a start-up franchise in the fledgling American Football League for the princely sum of $250,000. A charter member of "The Foolish Club," as he and his cofounders would come to be known, he had first wanted to put his franchise in Miami. After rejection by the Orange Bowl Committee, he decided on Buffalo.

Anyway, I offered to come see him, but he opted instead for a meeting in my father's office, the following Friday, September 22.

The meeting date arrived, and Mr. Wilson brought along his vice president of operations, Bob Lustig, and a young friend of mine, Joe Russo, who also worked for him. I thought the meeting went quite well. We said that we would buy a suite and advertising and would help promote the team if he wanted us to, and we floated the name "Coffee Rich Park," though we were prepared to use other corporate names as well.

We all shook hands, and I went ahead with my meetings with the leadership of the legislature and the chamber and set up a press conference for Tuesday, September 26.

I was in my office Monday afternoon when the phone rang. It was Joe Russo, calling to tell me that his boss had decided he didn't like our name.

"Joe," I said, "he said everything was fine. I've set up the press conference for tomorrow morning."

"I know," Joe said, "but he changed his mind."

"Well, I've gone on the line with the legislature and the chamber and am not going back on my word," I told him. "We did say that it was the name we preferred but would consider derivations and will say that again at our press conference." *Not a great telephone call*, I thought. Oh well; I still had a lot to do to get ready for the press conference.

We had agreed to hold the conference at the chamber's offices. The county legislature was there in force, as were the chamber officials, writers from both of our newspapers, the wire service, API and UPI, reporters from all the radio stations, and reporters and cameramen from all three local network television affiliates. My father skipped it, as did everyone from the Bills.

I hit all my copy points, including our pride in being the only company to come forward and our excitement in being able to fill the economic gap in the legislature's budget for the ballpark.

The "question and answer" session that followed the presentations was surprisingly brief. In retrospect, I don't think the local media knew what to think.

The overall media coverage was overwhelming, though. Besides front page headlines by our papers and great placement by the electronic media, I was pleasantly surprised to see how the national press was picking up the story as well.

I'd been part of a group of friends who bought an NHL expansion franchise in 1969 that came to be known as the Buffalo Sabres, and I thought I knew something about professional sports, but what happened next took me by surprise.

The story went not only national but international as well, with not only the sports people but the mainline press becoming interested.

I took a lot of the calls that came in, but mostly we just sat back and watched while a lot of writers simply ran with the press release or the wire service stories. Here are a few of my favorites:

From Chicago: "Future Headlines: Bills Creamed at Coffee Rich. Maybe we should get a food company to name Soldier's Field so we could write something like 'Bears Crumble at Sara Lee.'"

From Philadelphia: "Coffee Rich Park doesn't sound that bad; it could have been Preparation H Stadium."

Larry Merchant, one of my favorite sportswriters, called from the *New York Post* and said, "I've got two questions for you. Are you under psychiatric care, or are you on illegal drugs?"

Buying some time, I told him, "Neither, but I'll tell you what, Larry. The phone is ringing off the hook, and we're recording the opinions. If you call me back in a week, I'll give you the results."

In a week, he actually called for results of my fictitious phone poll.

"OK, Larry," I told him, "I have it right here. Let me see . . . 238 for our name, 180 against it, 5 held no opinion, 3 obscene phone calls, 2 heavy breathers, and 1 bomb threat. Pretty typical week for our switchboard, I must say."

Larry got a real kick out of the call and actually ran with it in a very humorously supportive article.

In the meantime, our sales people were calling in from around the country to report that Coffee Rich sales were going through the roof.

By the way, it didn't take Ralph Wilson long to weigh in on our proposal. The day after our press conference, September 27, he issued a release that said he was totally against our name—something about "all his hard work" and "our crass commercialism." *Like pro sports are some pure form of classical art and culture*, I thought.

Anyway, off we went. The debate was raging, the press was delighted, and we had to put on another shift to keep up with Coffee Rich sales. I even got an invitation to appear on the *Today* show.

Then came another lull and then a great shot in the arm from an unexpected source. I had known our newly elected County Executive Edward V. "Ned" Regan for many years as the older brother of a friend of mine. Their father had died early, leaving Ned in charge of the family and their business, wholesale liquor. Ned was "Kennedy handsome," although he was a Republican. While I'd always thought of him as a bit of a dilettante who belonged in a college teaching job, I had agreed to work on his election team; I actually put up a bunch of his posters in neighborhoods where a bunch of his blue blood supporters were afraid to go.

So, now newly elected, I ran into him on Buffalo's trendy Elmwood Avenue, walking his bicycle on a Saturday morning while I was getting coffee.

He looked at me and said, "Oh, I'm glad I ran into you. I've reviewed all the facts and decided to vote against your buying the naming rights of the new stadium." Biting my lip, I just shook my head. "What are you thinking?" he asked.

What I was thinking was that there were two things I disliked: people who deliver messages just because they meet you by chance instead of calling for a meeting and people who pontificate while walking their bicycles.

While that's what I was thinking, what I said was, "Well, Ned, I'm thinking that it doesn't really matter what you've decided. It's not up to you. It's the legislature's decision. And I'm also thinking you'll regret your position. Oh, and have a nice day."

I think that was our last conversation. Ned would go on to become the Comptroller of New York State, responsible for a multibillion dollar investment fund. He spent a good deal of time pontificating to investment bankers. He later became president of Baruch College in New York.

As I had predicted, he was lambasted for his stance. To his credit, he would go on to change his position and even sue the Buffalo Bills on behalf of the county for violating our naming agreement . . . but I'm getting ahead of myself.

My prediction about his regret was based on a life's lesson I'd learned in Pro Sports 101. A preponderance of voters do not like public spending on private-use sports facilities. By throwing himself into the debate and recommending against a million dollars of new private-sector funding, our fledgling county executive was creating a controversy that would haunt him for the rest of his term.

Anyway, the county executive went public with his opposition on October 16, creating a miniature furor. It began to look like the momentum for our name, Coffee Rich Park, might be waning. We called another press conference and announced that while we would leave that proposal on the table, we would also be willing to increase the amount to $1.5 million paid over twenty-five years and call the building Rich Stadium. Everyone seemed pleased. Even Ralph Wilson was widely quoted in the press as saying, "I can live with that name." (Yeah, right!)

It looked like everything was moving ahead; then Ralph Wilson changed his mind again. Three weeks after the chamber's deadline, he proposed to match our offer and name the place Buffalo Bills Stadium. The only stipulation he added was that he would have the right to resell the name.

After discussion, and Wilson's refusal to drop the resale rights, on November 8, the Erie County Legislature voted 16–4 in favor of Rich Stadium and authorized their attorneys to work with ours to draft a lease agreement. We were very excited and thought this was a financial win for our county and a public relations win for our company. Everyone seemed happy. Ralph Wilson . . . not so much. In spite of his statements that "he could live with the name," he was apparently brooding.

The negotiations produced a lease agreement that was to be voted on by the legislature at a meeting on May 16. A few days before that, the head of the legislature called me and said that Wilson had requested time on their agenda, and he invited me to attend as well.

"Do you want me to speak?" I asked him.

"Not necessarily," he said, "but I think you should be there."

I said, "OK," and called my dad to give him a briefing.

"This doesn't sound good," he said. "You think they'll cave?"

"I'm not so sure, Dad. I know a lot of those guys. They're pretty independent, and they don't like being preached to."

The meeting came, and there was Wilson with his operations guy, Bob Lustig, and one of his attorneys, a tough guy named Ralph Halpern. *This'll be interesting*, I thought as I took a seat in the back of the room by myself.

The agenda item was called, and the lawmakers recognized the owner of the Bills, who had asked for time to speak. He got up and spoke for a half hour, reminding the legislature how much he had done for the community and how he was upset by their selling the naming rights and how much he disliked the name Rich Stadium. Then, as if sensing defeat, he again made an offer to match our offer and, in a new twist, he offered to call the building Erie County Stadium. *Oh boy*, I thought, *game, set, match*. Then he called on Halpern, who lectured the body for another half hour on how illegal their action would be. During questions and answers, one of the legislators asked Wilson again if he would rescind his resale clause, and he refused. Then they called on their own attorney to comment on the legality of their lease agreement, and he refuted Halpern on all points.

The president of the legislature then called on me to speak, catching me somewhat off guard. I stood up and simply said something to the effect of, "You asked for an offer. We responded. You asked for modifications; we agreed. We have dealt in good faith. We trust you will do the right thing," and sat down.

The twenty-member legislature, bless their hearts, stood by their guns, admonished Wilson, and voted 19–1 to approve the lease and accept the name Rich Stadium.

If I had waited for a congratulatory handshake from Wilson, I'd still be sitting there today. He and his people left in a hurry.

The first thing I did when I got back to my office, after congratulating my dad, was draft a handwritten note to Wilson wishing him all the best in his first season in the new building. He never wrote back.

It soon became apparent that, like Wilson, neither of the two area newspapers were calling the stadium by its rightful name. I made appointments to visit with both their editors and listened to their lame excuses why they chose to call the building something else.

They both promptly reversed their fields, supposedly after receiving calls from a dear friend of ours Armand Castellani, the then-chairman of Tops Friendly Markets and perhaps the largest newspaper advertiser in western New York. Armand told them both that he looked on the selection of the name Rich Stadium as a victory for all of us in the consumer goods business.

In the meantime, the Bills had coined their new address, One Bills Drive, and had started using it as the stadium name on all of their press releases, tickets, and eventually programs. Word was getting around that they were also advising the press not to call the place Rich Stadium. Then, on the eve of their first exhibition game, the sheriff's department got a call that something strange was going on at the main gate. They responded late at night and flashed their spotlights on two workmen who, under cover of darkness, had been removing the eight-inch bronze letters that read *Rich Stadium*. This caused the county to go for a restraining order against the Bills, which they were granted, to allow the erection of the two signs.

The story made great newspaper copy the next morning and occasioned a 7:00 a.m. visit to my office from my father.

"Now it's time to bring in the lawyers," he said.

Not a good start for the Bills. In the first game in One Bills Drive, Herb Mul-Key returned the opening kickoff for a 102-yard touchdown to lead the Washington Redskins to a 37–21 victory against the home team. Off the field, on August 20, we filed a lawsuit against Ralph Wilson for tortious interference with a favorable contract.

While we didn't know whether the case would reach trial or settle out of court, we felt that we were on good footing. Besides being well-documented in the press, we had a lot of great witnesses. I'm also a copious, almost compulsive, note taker, and reading my journals, I felt very good about our legal position.

The legal process, believe it or not, had some humorous aspects. The Bills were represented by a legal legend from Buffalo, Frank G. Raichle, who was a friend of my dad's and who had also represented our company on occasion.

Raichle called my father early on, noting the conflict and saying that he felt obligated to represent the Bills. I know that this was upsetting to my father, whose feelings were hurt. Not so for me. It made me angry. In my early thirties, probably with more nerve than common sense, I was looking forward to taking on the old legend.

I studied the documents, pleadings, clippings, memos, letters, and my own notes for hours getting ready for my pretrial deposition. The big day came and Frank Raichle himself actually showed up at our lawyers' offices along with his associate, Ralph Halpern, carrying his briefcase. My adrenaline was pumping like before a sports event. After I was sworn in, Raichle and I jousted back and forth on definitions of sales, marketing, advertising, and public relations. Oftentimes, Raichle would feign anger and even disgust. Rather than get intimidated, I stayed relaxed and wondered how many thousands of people this old master had deposed. Supported by my notes, I refused to budge, let alone roll over.

While having lost a few steps to age, Raichle still had a mind like a steel trap, which had made him our area's most respected trial attorney.

In one of my favorite exchanges, Raichle got angry at me for referring to my notes and asked angrily, "Who wrote those scripts for you?"

"They're my own notes written after every event, Mr. Raichle, and I've produced copies for you that have been numbered as evidence."

"Well why don't you put them away and just answer my questions?" he asked.

"Why should I, Mr. Raichle?" I shot back. "Do you want the facts or a memory test?"

"I ask the questions here," he yelled at me. "I want the truth."

"The facts are the truth, Mr. Raichle, in spite of it not being what you want to hear."

Raichle asked for a fifteen minute recess.

A long, draining two days ended, and we wrapped up. The court stenographer left. Ralph Halpern packed up their papers and said, "Are you ready to go, Frank?"

"No, you go ahead, Ralph," he said. "I'll see you back at the office."

For some reason, I just sat across from him at the table until we were the only ones left in the room. To this day, I'm not really sure why I didn't leave too; maybe I wanted to chat with him or maybe I respected him and didn't want to leave him alone. I'm glad I stayed.

We sat looking at each other for awhile before he broke into a smile and said, "Nice going, young man."

I smiled too, thanked him, shook his hand, and we walked together to the elevator without saying anything more.

That was the last real conversation I would have with Raichle, though I would see him many more times and we would exchange greetings. I heard that he had died after a long illness in Buffalo General Hospital, in 1986, at age eighty-seven.

The lawsuit was settled out of court, and the circumstances themselves had a degree of humor to them. We were ready for court, and I was bolstered that our attorneys, who called to compliment me on weathering the two-day verbal assault in depositions, were very, very optimistic about our case. Then one day, out of the blue, Ralph Wilson made an appointment to see my father. He initiated the conversation, saying that it was too bad that this "disagreement" had become a lawsuit. Here I have to rely on my father's account, as Wilson had requested that the two meet privately (without you-know-who).

My father told him that the lawsuit could go away. All he had to do was agree to use the stadium name on tickets and programs and not influence others not to use it.

"That's all?" Wilson asked.

"That's all," Dad answered.

"OK," he said. "I'll get my lawyers to draft up something right away."

"There's no need to do that, Ralph," Dad said. "Your word is good with me."

"It is?" Wilson asked.

The two generals shook hands, and so ended the Battle of Orchard Park.

Our relationship, although always somewhat strained, improved dramatically—as did the team's performance after the promotion of Bill Polian to Bills general manager. Polian turned around a team that finished two consecutive 2–14 seasons. Under his leadership they would go to four Super Bowls in a row, a feat that may never again be accomplished. Their team, led by Hall of Famers Jim Kelly, Thurman Thomas, and Bruce Smith, never managed a Super Bowl win. If they had, they'd be remembered as a dynasty.

Back in the front office, Bill Polian rebuilt local relationships as well. Even I was surprised when he signed a broadcast rights agreement with a radio station that we owned, 97 Rock. He went out on a limb for us, and our people worked extra hard to warrant his trust.

The Buffalo Bills playing in Rich Stadium became a great source of pride for our community, but Rich Stadium wasn't only about football. Some other great happenings took place in the venue as well. Rich Stadium hosted an incredible list of live concerts between 1974 and 1997. A few years ago, the folks at 97 Rock listed their choices as the top twenty-five concerts held there, and here they are:

Date	Headliner	Opener #1	Opener #2
July 06, 1974	Eric Clapton	The Band	
July 26, 1974	ELP	James Gang	Lynyrd Skynyrd
Aug 11, 1974	CSN&Y	Santana	Jessie Colin Young
Aug 25, 1974	Chicago	Doobie Brothers	Ozark Mountain Daredevils
July 12, 1975	Yes	Johnny Winter	J. Geils Band/Ace
July 20, 1975	Eagles	Seals & Crofts	JudyCollins/ Dan Fogelberg
Aug 08, 1975	Rolling Stones	Bobby Womack	The Outlaws
July 10, 1976	Peter Frampton	Johnny & Edgar Winter	Todd Rundgren/ Natural Gas
Aug 07, 1976	Elton John	Boz Scaggs	John Miles
June 19, 1977	Blue Oyster Cult	Lynyrd Skynyrd	Ted Nugent/Starz
Aug 20, 1977	Yes	Bob Seger	J. Geils Band/Donovan
July 04, 1978	Rolling Stones	Journey	ARS/April Wine
July 28, 1978	Fleetwood Mac	Foreigner	Bob Welch/Pablo Cruise
Sept 27, 1981	Rolling Stones	Journey	George Thorogood
July 03, 1982	Foreigner	Loverboy	Ted Nugent/Iron Maiden
Sept 26, 1982	The Who	The Clash	David Johannsen
July 04, 1986	Bob Dylan & Tom Petty		Grateful Dead
June 19, 1988	Van Halen	Scorpions/ Dokken	Metallica/ Kingdom Come
July 04, 1989	Grateful Dead	10,000 Maniacs	
July 18, 1989	The Who		
July 16, 1990	Grateful Dead	Crosby, Stills & Nash	
June 06, 1992	Grateful Dead	Steve Miller	
July 25, 1992	Guns 'N Roses	Metallica	
June 13, 1993	Grateful Dead	Sting	
July 14, 1994	Elton John	Billy Joel	
Oct 08, 1997	Rolling Stones	Blues Traveler	

As for Bill Polian, he was actually only around for the first three Super Bowl losses. The owner of the Bills shocked the football world by firing Polian in February of 1993. Quickly snapped up by Carolina, he built a fine expansion franchise there before being hired as president and general manager of the Indianapolis Colts, which he also turned into a winner.

Throughout his outstanding career, Bill Polian has won the NFL Executive of the Year award five times, in 1988, 1991, 1995, 1996, and 1999.

As for purchasing naming rights to sports venues, I wish that my friend Larry Merchant was still alive to see what a prevalent practice it has become and what some companies are paying. He might have had a little different take on my "dementia."

The last time I looked, seventy-one major sports venues' names had been sold to commercial interests ranging from A to X, Air Canada Centre in Toronto to Xcel Energy Center in Minneapolis. Naming rights are even being marketed in minor league sports venues. I'm told that our original naming rights lease with the county became a model for many of the subsequent naming deals.

Last year, *Forbes* published their list of the most expensive sports naming rights fees, and here are some of them:

Citi Field	New York Mets	$400 million
Barclay's Center	Brooklyn Nets	$400 million
Reliant Stadium	Houston Texans	$300 million
Phillips Arena	Atlanta Hawks & Thrashers	$182 million
Prudential Arena	New Jersey Devils	$105 million
Citizens Bank Park	Philadelphia Phillies	$100 million
Minute Maid Park	Houston Astros	$100 million

One can only imagine what the Meadowlands will command in naming rights for the football palace where both the Giants and the Jets will play. Could we be looking at the first billion dollar naming fee? Experts feel that it is entirely possible. Kind of puts our $1.5 million deal in perspective, doesn't it?

Back to Orchard Park; it was widely reported that our company didn't renew our naming rights in 1998 because of this escalation in naming fees. This isn't quite accurate. The lease the Bills held with the county actually ran out in 1998 as well, and in 1997, one of Wilson's "preconditions" before he would renegotiate, no doubt thinking of us, was that the county would give up future naming rights to the stadium. To tell you the truth, this was just fine with me.

Shortly thereafter, New York State Governor George Pataki recommended that the stadium be renamed Ralph Wilson Stadium, and Wilson accepted and signed a new lease.

So be it. There's a lot of water over the dam now, and we all cheered for the ninety-year-old owner of the Buffalo Bills as he was inducted into the National Football League Hall of Fame. As he sat on the dais, I tried to guess what was going through his mind. Maybe he was trying to think of how he could prevent people from calling his building "the Ralph."

TEAM HANDBALL

I'm an Olympic junkie! Summer games or winter games, either is fine. All events; in fact, the more obscure the better. Bring on the luge, Greco–Roman wrestling, the pentathlon, racewalking, or table tennis; it's all the same to me.

I tried to go as a participant in ice hockey in '64, but I got cut before the team left for Innsbruck.

I went as a spectator once to the Summer Olympics in 1972, with my soon-to-be ex-wife and another couple. That didn't work out so well, either. Without some kind of VIP passes and/or a lot of scratch, it was tough to get into the more popular events, so we ended up watching a lot of games on late night German television.

One of my most vivid memories was a boy's night out at the Hofbräuhaus. I remember some late night beer drinking with some young guys who turned out to be the Australian water polo team. At around midnight, I turned to one of them and said, "Hey you guys are great. It's a shame you got knocked out of the competition. I'd have loved to watch you play."

"Oh, we didn't get knocked out, mate," my new drinking buddy said. "You can watch us play this morning at 9:00 a.m. against Hungary."

I couldn't believe it. In quest of Olympic gold in a few hours, and they were pounding down lagers with the tourists. I love Australians!

Soon it was closing time, but I had a half-full stein still in front of me. What's a guy to do? I tried smuggling it out and got caught by the bouncer, who grabbed the ill-hidden stein and unceremoniously poured its contents down the front of my pants. I confronted the ruffian, who proceeded to knock out my front tooth in one of the shortest bar fights in history. (Actually, it was just a cap on a tooth that had previously been knocked out during my career as a hockey goalie playing without a mask.) I look back on that night now and laugh, thinking about my squash-playing friend, Joe Hahn from Detroit, who used to say, "I've had my nose broken five times, twice by friends and three times by total strangers."

Two days later, as we had planned, we left the Olympics after the first week for a motor tour of Bavaria. En route, our car radio was abuzz with the breaking story of a Palestinian terrorist attack at the Olympic Village. Two Israeli athletes were killed while resisting, and another nine Israeli athletes and coaches were taken hostage and eventually transported to the Munich airport where the terrorists had demanded a plane to fly them all to an unspecified Arab country. At the airport, a rescue operation went terribly wrong, and, within twenty-four hours of the Olympic Village break-in, as the world looked on in horror, eleven Israeli athletes and coaches and seven terrorists were dead.

The story was sickening and left the four of us stunned and happy to be away from Munich as we contemplated the inevitable retribution that would follow this unfathomable crime committed against unarmed athletes on one of the world's most visible stages.

As we drove through the Alps, I thought a lot about the crowds we'd encountered, the long lines, the difficulty in securing tickets, the cost of food and lodging, and now this inexplicable act of violence. Maybe it wasn't the Olympics I loved in person, but rather the Olympics on television. Yeah, that was it; the close-ups, the instant replays, the commentary, the "up close and personal" profiles of the athletes, the introduction to new and/or obscure sports; that's what I really loved.

One of the most fascinating games I watched was called team handball. Apparently designed to keep Eastern European football (soccer) players in shape during their long winters, it was like basketball, played indoors, but with a smaller ball like a volleyball that you could only dribble three times before passing or shooting. Also, instead of basketball nets or hoops, you shot at a goal that was ten feet wide and six feet seven inches high and protected by a goaltender. I'd never seen it played before. With seven players on the court for each team at any given time, the action was fast, furious, and very physical. The Eastern European domination of the sport was so overwhelming, I wasn't surprised that many other countries, like the US, didn't even bother fielding teams.

Anyway, our trip concluded, I soon got divorced, and I entered into a new phase of my life as a recycled bachelor. I didn't really think about team handball until six years later in the spring of 1978. By now, remar-ried, I was reading a news article one night about how New York Governor Hugh Carey had approved a new statewide athletic event replicating the Summer Olympics to be held every year in Syracuse. It would be called the Empire State Games. The state was to be divided into six regions: Adirondack, Central, Hudson Valley, Long Island, New York City, and Western. Competition for men and women would be divided into two categories, high school and open.

I scanned the list of sports, and sure enough, there it was—team handball. "Yes," I said out loud.

"What?" my bride asked.

"My shot at the Olympics," I said.

"That's nice, dear," she said, going back to the television show she was watching.

Ignoring me already, I thought. *That's a bad sign.*

The US didn't even have a team. I'd put one together, play in the Empire State Games, and use it as a springboard to the Olympics. My plan was ready to be hatched.

The next day I called the newly appointed western region coordinator, Herb Mols, who'd been a little league baseball coach whose team I'd played against in third grade, and I told him of my plan.

"OK" he said. "I've never heard of team handball, and don't think that anyone around here plays it, but if anyone turns up, we'll have to schedule tryouts."

Better still, I thought, *no competition*. The Western region basically included Rochester to Buffalo and all points west. It was time to select my team, but where to turn? My tennis and squash pals were in shape; that would be a natural place to start.

I went over to the Buffalo Tennis and Squash Club after work on a recruiting mission. The reception to my idea was completely underwhelming—with one exception. My pal Jimmy Klepfer signed up. The scion of a family automobile dealership, Klepfer Buick, whose showroom was in Buffalo's inner city, Jimmy was a real gamer, a good athlete, graced with boundless enthusiasm and a well-honed self-deprecating sense of humor.

Even as their neighborhood suffered loss of revenue as many residents migrated to wealthier suburbs, Jimmy's sales grew exponentially, always making him eligible for Buick's most prestigious dealer motivation trips. Every spring would find him jetting off to another exotic destination like Hawaii, Tahiti, or Paris, all of it on Buick's dime.

One day I asked him, "Jimmy, how do you continue to build car sales in such a struggling neighborhood?"

"It's all in my closing line," he told me, smiling.

"What do you mean?" I asked.

"Well," he said, "customers come in and I show them our cars, wait for them to choose their favorite, tell them the price, and then listen for them to give me the setup line."

"What's that?" I asked.

"After I've shown 'em the car they like and given 'em my spiel, I wait for them to say, 'I don't know, man. I've got my home mortgage payments to make.' Then I take a deep breath and give them my closer."

"And what's that?" I persisted.

"I look 'em in the eye," he said, "and I say, 'Hey, look, you can sleep in your car, but you can't drive your house.' Works every time."

I had my first player, and with Jimmy, I knew we'd have fun. Being practical, I knew that my next recruit should be a goalie. I'd decided early on that I wasn't going to get in that goal. It looked like a horrible position. Not only were the scores always high, but it looked like the goalies would take one right "in the mush" an average of twice a game. Who could I possibly get who would stand up in this kind of firing squad? I had an idea.

Dennis Gorski was one of our Erie County legislators, a good friend, and an ardent athlete who'd donned the "tools of ignorance" and been a baseball catcher growing up. As they say in the business, he was from good political stock. His father, Chester, known by his nickname, "Chet," had been a Democratic congressman for our area, and it was clear that Dennis aspired to higher office. I thought about the Empire State Games' connection to the governor's office and felt that I could use that as an added inducement to sign him up as our goaltender. Also, his heritage was Eastern European, so maybe team handball would be in his blood. To top it all off, Dennis had been a captain in the Marine Corps who had fought in the Battle of Hué in Vietnam and gained a reputation for being cool under intense enemy fire. The man's credentials for the job were impeccable, I thought.

I went over to see him in his office, thinking that it's always easier to say no to someone over the phone. My strategy worked. He didn't say no, but he really didn't say yes either. He asked who else was on the team. Thinking quickly, I said, "You'll have to come out to our first practice to find out."

"So when and where will that be?" he asked.

Keeping my thinking cap, on I said, "The time, place, and date is 'to be announced.' So, will we see you there?"

"I'll think about it," he said.

Back in the office, I called Jimmy to tell him we had our goalie, not totally sure how the "devil may care" car king would get along with the serous military veteran.

A week went by and on Friday afternoon I got a call from Herb Mols. "Got your team together?" he asked.

"Yup," I lied, "we're shaping up nicely, thank you."

"That's good," he said, "because I just got a call from the captain of a team handball team in Rochester. Hard to understand, sounded Eastern European. Said they'd been playing together for years and wanted to represent our Western region."

I'd never liked Coach Mols that much, I thought, believing I detected a little 'ha, ha, ha' in his voice.

"Well I guess they'll have to challenge us then, Coach Mols," I said.

"That's just what they said," he answered, laughing, then turning officious, "but that's not what the rules say. We have to hold open tryouts."

"Fine then," I responded, seeing my dreams of being a US team handballer in the Olympics going up in smoke, "let's set it up."

"I have," Herb said. "I've reserved the basketball court at Erie Community College for you two weeks from tomorrow. I thought you guys could have a scrimmage and kind of work it out, who plays, between you. By the way," he added, almost gleefully, "they've got their own goals and will bring them."

I was screwed.

I called Dennis and Jimmy to make sure we had at least three warm bodies, then stewed on it over the weekend. What was I going to do now?

Opportunity knocked at a strange place on Monday. I was having lunch at the company cafeteria by myself, and a young protégé of mine from Distribution, Jay Rich, asked me if I wanted company and pulled up a chair.

Jay is a great guy. While we are not related, he and his dad before him worked at our company with my dad and me. They are German and we're English but we all decided years ago to adopt each other. People don't even ask if we're related, they just take it for granted. Jay also had four brothers at home, or, more accurately, two in college and two in high school, all redheads, all big, and all great athletes. Jay had played football and had captained his lacrosse team at Lehigh, his six-foot-five-inch brother, Howard, was the current lacrosse captain at Purdue, and their third brother, Paul, was a six-foot-six-inch basketball captain-elect at State University of New York at Geneseo; their younger brothers, Jeff and Russell, played football in high school. I told Jay about team handball and my personnel dilemma.

Jay said, "It sounds like fun; would you mind if I came over to the scrimmage?"

"Great, Jay," I said.

"Paul and Howard will both be home for the summer by then. How 'bout I bring them along, and maybe Jeff, too?"

Bingo, I thought. "Wonderful," I said. My problem was solved. Knowing the boys as I did, I sealed the deal with the magic words: "I'll bring the beer."

"Would you mind if they wanted to bring a few friends to play, too?" Jay asked.

"The more the merrier," I all but giggled.

I spent some time the next few weeks working out and reading about team handball. I discovered that teams consisted of twelve players, a head coach, and an assistant . . . and either one or two medics because of the roughness of play. If a defender was in front of an attacker, he could do just about anything but "depants" him. Full frontal contact was not only allowed but expected. Hitting someone from the side or the back was illegal, drawing a whistle and a penalty shot from seven meters (twenty-two feet). Games were very high scoring, with both teams often scoring over twenty goals a game. I decided not to share this research with Dennis.

It didn't really seem that tough, except for the goalies. There were some intricate offensive patterns deployed that seemed to involve weaves, give-and-gos, and setup picks. It was also clear that there was a lot of contact, and overall fitness was important.

The big day arrived, and we met in the college parking lot an hour before scrimmage time to talk through the game. Howard and Paul arrived together. As they climbed out of their car, I realized how big they both really were. In addition to the four brothers Rich, they had brought along a couple of their pals, both good athletes as well. Paul Brown, a lefty, had played baseball for Geneseo; Tom Keterer had been an all-Western New York soccer star who went on to play for Syracuse.

While waiting for Dennis and Jimmy to arrive, they noticed the outdoor basketball courts, went to the trunk of their car, got out a basketball, walked over to the court, and started an impromptu dunking competition. I realized that I was the only one there who couldn't dunk. *Great*, I thought to myself, all of a sudden realizing I was going to have to fight for a spot on my own team.

Just as Paul won the contest with some double turnaround thing, four cars pulled up, disgorging some middle-aged, athletic-looking guys—most in shorts with black socks—talking in strange Slavic tongues that I didn't think I'd heard before. *Must be the enemy*, I thought.

We all went inside, with me now hoping that they'd brought a ball so we could have a game and an extra ball so we could have a warm up.

Noticing we were without a ball, a well-built, handsome, athletic-looking guy brought one over to us to use and introduced himself. His name was Brian Fitzpatrick, and he would turn out to be the star and spokesman of their team. Brian had the build and the look of a young Frank Gifford, star running back for the New York Giants. Over the next several months, we got to know him well and found out that he too had been a running back and outstanding linebacker who captained his high school football team. After graduating from Villanova, he coached an undefeated high school football team.

So all of us got to touch a real team handball for the first time.

Sizing up the competition before the game, it was clear that they knew the sport, but our team was a lot younger, more athletic, and in considerably better shape. We decided, therefore, that we would have fast changes and play short shifts to try and tire them out.

Not really knowing the rules, we agreed that it would make sense to have Brian, or whoever of their players was between shifts, to serve as ref as long as they would take their time after a play stopped to inform us neophytes of the nature of the infraction.

This was going to be interesting, I thought, looking over at the door just in time to see Herb Mols and a mini-entourage arriving.

Jimmy Klepfer knew Mols too, and he came over to me and said, "Look, the Western New York sports czar has taken time out from his busy schedule; probably looking forward to seeing us get our asses kicked." The old coach was smiling like a Cheshire cat as the scrimmage began.

Herb didn't have to wait long. The Eastern Europeans moved the ball up and down the court, did some intricate offensive plays, and put three quick scores on the board. Every time we mustered up some offense, a penalty would be called and explained, and we'd have to give up the ball and go back on defense.

The novelty was wearing off, and our guys were starting to get frustrated. I was wondering if we'd made a mistake. I could just imagine what our goalie was thinking. In spite of some great saves, we were down 4–0, and Dennis had already taken a direct shot to the mush and another painful hit about three feet lower. I noticed that the guys from Rochester were also playing much more physically than we were. Apparently our young guys were playing by basketball rules, which greatly limited the contact that was part of team handball. My complaints to Brian were followed by his repetitive rejoinder, "No, that's legal, that's legal."

The first quarter ended, and coach Mols, no doubt having seen enough, left. I said to our guys, "Keep your cool, we're learning, and they'll get tired."

The second quarter started, and something happened that turned the game around. We were on offense, and one of the Rochester European guys elbowed Paul in the nose—on purpose or by accident—and no penalty was called. There were three Rich brothers on the court at the time, and their faces turned as red as their hair. Their nonverbal communication said it clearly: "Mess with one of us, you mess with all of us." All of a sudden they looked more like the Hansen brothers in *Slap Shot* than the Rich brothers.

They not only set an example for the rest of our team but also established the tone for the rest of the game. In spite of some great plays by Brian Fitzpatrick, we tied it up with the next four goals then took total control.

The Europeans who'd started the rough stuff were obviously better at giving than receiving. Our quick changes were also taking their toll. As the half wound down, I noticed that many of them were bending over, holding on to the front hems of their shorts, fighting for breath. We also noticed that they were starting to argue with each other in their Slavic tongues, and they took their heated exchanges into the halftime break.

We all looked at each other at the break, confident in our knowledge of exactly what was going on. Two minutes into the halftime intermission, I yelled over, "Brian, would you mind if we get the second half started? A bunch of our guys have dates tonight." The muffled laughter from our sideline huddle was spontaneous.

The second half was a mismatch. The superior conditioning and athleticism on our team was more than obvious. If it had been a prizefight, the referee would have stopped it. We even stopped counting our goals. Halfway through the fourth quarter, a couple of the Eastern Europeans, brothers it would turn out, got into a fist fight and actually walked off the court. Brian looked over at us and kind of shrugged his shoulders and sheepishly asked if we'd mind calling the game a little early. I think he was wishfully thinking that he'd like to switch teams.

After the game, we shook hands with anyone from Rochester who was willing and walked out to the parking lot where, as promised, I had a cooler full of cold Budweisers in the back of my station wagon. The Rochester guys got in their cars and left, with the exception of Brian, who joined us for a couple of cold lagers. Before he left, we set up scrimmages for the same time next week and for two weeks later as well.

The next week, only half of their team showed up, and the week after that only three guys made the trip, Brian and two Eastern Europeans: one was a little guy named Bodo who dressed in sweats and the second was some big guy in shorts and black socks whose name we couldn't pronounce and whose accent we couldn't understand. This guy couldn't run a lick, but he had the hardest shot we'd ever seen. Even the guy who owned the goals was a no-show, but it didn't matter; Region Six's Empire State Games Handball Team had chosen itself.

So there we were, on our way to Syracuse for the very first Empire State Games. I like to think of our selection process as a true example of survival of the fittest, or what is called, I believe, "natural selection."

Now let me attempt a little amateur "up close and personal" on our team. We had twelve players—only three of whom had ever played an actual game of team handball. We had among us seven captains: two captained in lacrosse, one in basketball, one in football, one in soccer, one in hockey, and one in the marines. Nine of twelve of us were from Buffalo, and the other three were from Rochester. Eleven of twelve had names we could pronounce. Five of twelve of us had the last name "Rich," and all of us loved drinking beer.

We had an informal vote and elected Brian Fitzpatrick our captain, me the player coach, and Jimmy Klepfer our team doctor, trainer, and mixologist.

The big day came, and we packed up assorted spouses or squeezes for our two-hour drive east on the Thruway to Syracuse University. I brought my three children, ages nine, eleven, and twelve, for what would be their first college weekend. They were excited, and so was I.

Our team met at the registration headquarters at 2:00 p.m., as planned, and ran into Herb Mols who looked shocked to see us there. We drew our uniforms, light blue shorts and maroon short-sleeve shirts

(Western region's colors) and blue and gold sweat suits (New York State's colors). They were very nice. It was at registration that we received our first bad news. We were to be billeted in college dorms, three to a room, but they didn't allow children or beer. This would never fly. Tom Keterer, who had attended Syracuse and knew the area, suggested an alternative housing plan. I made a call, and within a half hour we were comfortably tucked into a block of rooms adjacent to the pool at the Holiday Inn at Carrier Circle.

Our trainer suggested that the pool would be excellent for hydrotherapy, declared that his quarters would serve as our training room, and enlisted Paul and Howard to help him fill his bathtub with therapeutic ice—for keeping our beer cold.

We called our first team meeting poolside to address our first major nonissue: should we march in the parade and participate in the games' opening ceremonies? The vote was unanimous to skip the event and participate instead in a team building exercise at one of the local watering holes that Keterer knew. An amendment to the motion determined that no one was allowed to appear there in our team sweats.

A rather late night turned into a very nice community outreach where our young single players made many new friends among the locals. Everyone commented on how secure they felt having our team doctor with them from start to finish. Reports were that our team's congeniality rivaled that of the Australian water polo team at the '72 Olympics in Munich.

The first round of games were to be played at a local high school gym, with the finals moving to the beautiful Carrier Dome. Our first game came early the next day. We had drawn Long Island, and they were good. Most of them played in a program at Adelphi University under an Eastern European handball legend by the name of Laszlo Jurak, who was there as their coach. The refs seemed brutal and we were getting penalized to death. In retrospect, they were good and proper calls, they were just different. We were down by five at the half before we really got into the flow of the game. In the second half, we pulled within two before we ran out of time. Brian Fitzpatrick teamed up with Howard and Paul Rich to be the best players on the floor, while Dennis Gorski really found his groove and made some huge saves.

The teams shook hands at the end of the game and Laszlo Jurak was extremely complimentary, offering his advice and counsel on how we could refine our game. He would turn out to be a good friend over the years to come.

Under the strict supervision of our trainer, the team moved one of our coolers of beer to a pleasant grassy knoll by the backdoor of the gym where we could critique our past performance, and maybe even talk about the game, while we made our social plans for the evening.

The next day, after another night of strict training, we were able to redeem ourselves against Adirondack with an easy victory.

We were getting stronger for our match against New York City, but not strong enough. We lost a one-goal overtime game to them. Like Long Island, they were good young athletes who beat us on handball experience. We came to find out that many of their players had learned the game under Laszlo's tutelage at camps that he ran every summer at Adelphi.

The next day, we literally buried the Central Region with speed and ball control. Paul Rich was really picking the game up quickly with a lot of coaching from his linemate, Brian, who turned out to be an incredible ball hawk. Paul was absolutely dominant and turned out to be a natural goal scorer, greatly feared by opposing goaltenders.

I noticed that old Laszlo had started showing up at our games, apparently to scout Paul. I also saw our new star being interviewed at the end of our game by a reporter from the Buffalo *Courier-Express*, who had covered our game with a reporter and photographer.

We had a surprising 2–2 record with one game to go as we gathered for our postgame lagers at our usual spot on the back lawn. It was there and then that we saw the last team we would be encountering.

Playing for Hudson Valley, they were actually all cadets from the US Military Academy at West Point, mainly off-season football players led by a coach who was ex-army. They were 2–1 and had actually double-timed from the dorms to the gym, in formation, led by their drill instructor/coach.

Hudson Valley shoots on Western goal—save Gorski! *Author's photo.*

Their path to the gym took them right past where we were lounging, many of us barefooted and shirtless, wearing shades, drinking beer, and eating pretzels with some of our new groupies. As I saw them coming down the road, I thought, *This is going to be good*, knowing how totally irreverent our team was. I wasn't disappointed.

One of the Riches started it out with a nice greeting as they sprinted up to us: "Hi, fellas, how 'bout a cold lager before your game?" he said. A couple of them smiled, but their coach didn't.

He yelled, "Inside, men" as the comments continued.

"Yeah, inside men," a couple of our guys mimicked in unison. My favorite comment was directed toward the coach as he held the door open for his men.

"Hey General, there's no defense for the bomb!" someone yelled.

Dennis Gorski was silent, but I knew that as an ex-Marine he was finding some humor in this spontaneous, light-hearted army hazing.

Having finished his interviews, I noticed that the Buffalo *Courier-Express* writer was taking it all in with a smile on his face as he accepted a cold beer. Ironically, several years later the *Courier* would close and that young reporter, Mike Billoni, would accept a job first as head of marketing and next as general manager of a minor league baseball team we would buy, the Buffalo Bisons.

Hudson Valley, a.k.a. West Point, won its game that afternoon, setting up our game the next day for the bronze medal. Believe it or not, the game attracted a near sell-out crowd at the gym that had been mostly vacant all week, thanks in part to a lead story in the *Courier* about us. In the story, Billoni referred to us as "the Bad News Bears." There was also a comical piece about us in the Syracuse *Post-Standard*. I think our team's late-night "outreach" program also brought in some fine-looking female fans as well. I couldn't believe it; we were actually the crowd favorite.

The General, as we called him, saw no mirth in the situation at all and called in some heavy artillery. During the first quarter, punches were even thrown, resulting in a few bloody noses. The "Bears" just had too much momentum going. Brian and Paul's practice together over the week paid off. While our scoring was fairly balanced, it was Brian and Paul's spec-

Bronze medalists and groupies. Players from left: (front row) Dennis Gorski, Bodo, and Big Black Socks Guy; (middle row) Jimmy Klepfer; (back row) Paul Rich, Tom Keterer, Howard Rich, Brian Fitzpatrick, Bob Rich, and Jeff Rich. *Author's photo.*

tacular alley-oop goals that the crowd would remember. Our goalie was a rock; he even took two in the mush, but he won one for the corps— Oorah! Semper fi! We beat Hudson Valley by five to win the bronze.

After handshakes with the General and his men, the refs asked us to line up on our goal line to receive our medals from one of the Empire State Games officials. Guess who it was? You got it, our old friend, Herb Mols. I was standing at the end of the line next to our trainer, Jimmy Klepfer, as Herb bestowed our medals tied to red, white, and blue ribbons, which he put around our necks after a handshake. When he got to our trainer, Jimmy pumped his hand extra enthusiastically and said, "Oh, thanks so much for believing in us, Coach Mols. Say, when you get home, why don't you stop by our shop, and I'll put you in a Buick? Make you a heck of a deal." Jimmy looked at me and winked. I laughed.

After the brief medal ceremony, we returned to our familiar post on the lawn, many of us still wearing our medals around our necks. Our postgame confabs had been growing exponentially, and we'd had to greatly increase our provisions of beer. This time there were about fifty people on our lawn, including several cadets and an expanding number of groupies. The "Bad News Bears" were livin' large.

POSTSCRIPT

We would return to the games two more times to collect two silver medals. In the meantime, Laszlo recruited Paul Rich for the US National Team that he coached in 1979. They toured Eastern Europe with stops in Hungary, Romania, and the Czech Republic. They won a lot of games, and Paul was their star player. The excitement of their tour was heightened by the announcement that the United States would play team handball for the first time in the Olympics to be held in Russia in 1980 and that Paul Rich's name had been penciled into their lineup.

All of the "Bears" were thrilled. In only three short years, we'd actually placed someone on the Olympics-bound US Handball Team. Our joy was short-lived as word came down that our president, Jimmy Carter, had announced an Olympic boycott to protest Russia's invasion of Afghanistan.

Undeterred, Paul came home to lead our team to a second silver medal in the 1980 Empire State Games. If he was upset about Russia, the big redhead kept it to himself.

In 1985, the New York State Powers That Be decided to move the games to Buffalo for two years. Probably recognizing me as a former games athlete, they asked me if I'd chair the games, and I said yes. Luckily, I had a great committee—it turned out to be a massive undertaking. Hosting 7,500 athletes and welcoming over 100,000 visitors to western New York was a daunting task, to say the least. Led by a pal of mine, Peter Ruddy from M&T Bank and my vice chairman of the games, our IT guys designed a new software system for scoring that we donated to the games, and which I believe is still in use today.

On the very afternoon of the opening ceremony, we got word that long-time coordinator Herb Mols had died suddenly of a massive heart attack. It was a shock to all, and it was a loss to our region of an amateur sport giant.

I thought about Herb a lot that night as I sat on the stage and watched the opening night parade and ceremonies, the very event that I'd chosen to avoid as a team handball player/coach seven years earlier in Syracuse.

POLO

I used to love squash—not the vegetable you eat at Thanksgiving, but the sport you play. It's kind of like handball, but with racquets and a smaller ball. I started taking lessons when I was ten from a professional named Harry Conlon. His son, Harry Jr., a few years older than me, was my hitting partner and hero and would go on to win the US Championship. I was there. He was incredible. He fell asleep in his chair an hour before the finals, not tired, he just wasn't nervous at all.

Under the Conlons' training, I won the first ever Buffalo Junior Squash Championship at age eleven against a kid named Phil Oppenheimer. It was my first trophy, and it was tiny, but I still have it. Actually, I think there were only two of us in the tournament. My dad was in the audience. I was proud. Phil cried when he lost.

The next year, they put me on the University Club C League team. I hadn't yet turned twelve. My first match, I beat a forty-year-old guy named Red Murray from the prestigious Tennis and Squash Club. He did not cry, but he didn't think it was funny either. They passed some age requirement, and I was off the team. Just as well; I always felt uncomfortable in the locker room with all those old naked guys.

At fourteen, I concentrated on team sports and just played racquet sports for fun and to stay in shape. After college I pursued squash with a vengeance, playing every day I could after work. I won another city championship and two doubles titles playing with one of my childhood pals, George Ostendorf. While we did well at home, we always seemed to struggle in the National Championships. I think we left our game on the barroom floor.

I continued to play, singles and doubles, into my forties. The game took on added meaning for me as I got older. It became a brief respite from the daily business world, a gentlemen's game where two guys would dress down to white shirts and shorts, walk into a small white court, close the door, and play a game against each other where the rules were clear cut and well-defined. You and your opponent shared the motivation to win. There's no lying, cheating, or excuse making. There are no ties, only wins or losses. You are alone and have no one else to blame but yourself if you lose. I found it to be a great break from the more complex "game of business" where the "opponents" had a wide variety of motivations and could use an arsenal of tools, many nefarious, to accomplish their own personal goals. Lying and cheating, or at least shading the truth, seemed to be acceptable—or at least tolerated. Not so in the game of squash racquets.

Then, in the late seventies, I faced a new competitor: Father Time. I felt it in my legs first. My city ranking fell to seventh, and I could feel a lot of the young guys breathing down my neck. It was time to retire from competitive squash, so I did.

I needed newer, younger legs and/or a new sport. Maybe the answer was in the equestrian world. I'd ridden at summer camp and didn't especially like horses, or any large animals that looked down at me for that matter, but they could provide me with "new legs" and speed.

The city of Buffalo is blessed with a wonderful old indoor riding facility called the Saddle and Bridle Club. Its stables and riding ring offer a great place to get away from Buffalo's notorious winter snows. I called over there to inquire about riding lessons and membership. The lady told me that they had beginner's lessons on Monday, Wednesday, and Friday at 5:00 p.m., and that I could ride and sign up for membership later. She also reminded me that I must wear a helmet when riding.

So Monday came and I put on a pair of jeans, my army boots, and an old hockey helmet and headed over there for my first lesson. Mercifully, they put me on an old steed that looked very similar to the horse that Lee Marvin rode in *Cat Ballou* or Don Quixote's Rocinante. I cautiously guided him onto the ring and joined twelve classmates who were forming up around our instructor in the center of the ring, who was on foot.

I was quick to realize that I was the only male in the class. I was also, in fact, the only one out there who wasn't wearing braces on my teeth. My classmates were all eleven- or twelve-year-old girls. Lesser men would have been embarrassed and quit, but I wanted to learn to ride, and this looked like the only game in town. The others giggled when I rode up to join them, but pretty soon they just kind of accepted me as "one of the girls." Years later I would see many of them again as very attractive twenty-somethings, all with straight teeth and lovely smiles. Most of them told me they had given up horses for men.

My first lesson went pretty well, I think. The only thing I didn't really like was the way my classmates shrieked or squealed when they went over the foot-tall jumps. Oh, and I didn't like the mandatory mucking of stalls either. Here I was, a four-time city squash champion one day, shoveling horse manure the next.

When I went down to Florida to visit my parents over my children's spring break, I really wasn't too sure what kind of riding I wanted to do. I still didn't like horses very much, but I was intrigued with some of the games you play on them. I thought fox hunting looked like fun, as did showing horses. Either way, you had to learn to jump over three- or four-foot fences, so I signed up for some jumping lessons at a place called The Show Barn in a newly developed golf and equestrian town called Wellington.

I'd graduated myself to private lessons, which I scheduled at seven in the morning to free up the rest of my days to be with my children. I remember my instructor as an attractive, soft-spoken, and patient young professional named Brad, who I believe was dating the daughter of the woman who ran the stables. Brad taught me a lot. It all seemed pretty basic: collect your horse or get him under control and lined up with the jump; guide him on, standing up a little in your stirrups and dropping your hands to give your horse his head as you approach the jump so he can get a good take off; then let him rise up under you as he goes in the air—kind of fun and maybe not as hard as it looks. Brad was an incredible teacher who saw the smallest of flaws and helped you correct them.

Things were going pretty smoothly by the second week. I had just completed a double-jump of two three and a half foot fences placed fairly close together—what they called a double oxer—and was turning for the backstretch. I looked around to see Brad waving me over to where he was standing by the fence near the barn. I cantered over, and he looked at me and said quietly, but rather emphatically, "Get off the horse."

"What's the matter?" I asked, surprised to say the least. "Did I do something wrong on the jump? I thought I went over them clean."

"You did," he answered, "but on your last four jumps I caught you watching those guys practicing polo in the field next door. Jumping demands 100 percent concentration or you can get badly hurt. So give me the reins and go on over there."

Just like that, my new sport found me. I couldn't believe that Brad had noticed. I was, in fact, intrigued by the polo players' practice moves; I would later learn that what they were doing was called "stick and balling."

"Brad, I could do both jumping and polo, you know," I said.

"No you can't," he said, "It's got to be one or the other. You've learned how to ride now, so go over there and either love it or get it out of your system, but I don't think you will. I believe your jumping days are over."

And he was right.

I didn't go talk to those guys, but I did call a special friend when I got back to western New York to tell him of my interest in trying polo. Norty Knox was perhaps the best athlete I ever knew. In addition to being close to a scratch golfer, he had won the world court tennis championship many times in singles and in doubles with his older brother, Seymour. He had also been an accomplished horseman and polo player who captained the United States against polo powerhouse Argentina.

I had known Norty forever and was proud to serve with him on the HSBC bank board that he chaired, as well as on the boards of the Buffalo Sabres of the National Hockey League and the Albright–Knox Art Gallery, which bore the name of his father and family.

He seemed excited that I wanted to learn the game and invited me to come out to his family's Ess Kay Farm in East Aurora for some "stick and balling" when the grounds dried out. I told him that I didn't even own a horse and he said not to worry, they would find a mount for me. I couldn't have been more excited.

The big day came, and it was mystical. Norty turned out to be a wonderful coach. He claimed to be rusty while knocking balls out of mid-air, bouncing a ball repeatedly on the end of his mallet, and performing a few dozen other tricks. His old polo coach, Louis Smith, known as a "high goaler," was there and he was very helpful as well.

One day, after many training sessions together, Norty invited me to join him at a club called Myopia in Hamilton, Massachusetts, to watch his son Norty Jr. play. While there, he surprised me and told me that he thought I was ready to own my first polo pony and that he had just the right horse in mind, a handy, older, smallish bay mare that he owned with his son. The horse was named Half 'n Half. I tried her and loved her. I told them she was great, but I couldn't accept a gift and insisted on buying her. We struck a deal and just like that, I was really into polo.

Next, I bought some tack and an old used two-horse trailer. Then I needed a groom/trainer. I remembered a girl who had been my first riding instructor at the Saddle and Bridle in the beginner's class. Her name was Jennifer Rice. She was in her early twenties, six feet tall, blonde, and very attractive. More importantly, I'd noticed that she was passionate about horses and outworked everyone in the barn. She could talk for hours about anything in the world as long as it had hooves, a mane, and a tail. I remembered during one of our talks that she had expressed an interest in giving notice and finding a horse job that would get her out of Buffalo for the winters. That really suited me well, as I had planned to move my horse to Florida for the winter, join a polo club, and try to get on a team. Jennifer signed on, and we were in business.

Polo games are divided into six 7½-minute periods called chukkas. A good horse can run for about 7½ minutes, so in order to play a full game, you need at least six healthy polo ponies. The term pony is really a misnomer. It derives from the fact that most polo horses are a little on the small side and are very handy or agile like American quarter horses. The Argentineans, or "Argies" as they are affectionately nicknamed, actually breed horses to play the game. Small Argentinean mares are the gold standard of the polo pony world.

Anyway, Half 'n Half was soon joined in the Knoxes' barn by my second horse, a larger chestnut gelding named Billy. What he lacked in smarts he made up for in speed. I liked to ride him, and Jennifer and I were on our way toward building a "string of ponies."

I traded in my two-horse trailer and bought a new Chevy Silverado twin cab dually to pull an eight-horse stock trailer. Jennifer loaded all our stuff up, and, as the first snowfall of the early winter hit western New York, Jennifer, Half 'n Half, Billy, and her dog, Saucy, were on their way to a new winter home in Lake Worth, Florida.

I had done some homework and found a rather old and modest polo club called Gulfstream Polo on Lake Worth Avenue, not far from the Sunshine State Parkway and only fifteen minutes from the West Palm Beach Airport. It looked like it would serve our purposes well.

The club had five separate polo fields, a club house, and a club barn ringed by members' barns. Many of them had extra stalls and took in "boarders." I did some scouting and found a nice barn on the property, a little off the beaten path, in a hammock of tall Australian pines that gave shade from the blazing Florida sun. The owner, Davey Rizzo, was from Long Island, where he played polo at a famous club called Meadowbrook in old Westbury, New York. In addition to renting stalls, Dave also bought and sold horses, so I knew that he could be helpful to me as I kicked off my career. He also played on a few teams, and he would become a great teacher as well. He had a lot of pals from New York, mostly Runyonesque characters, who would always stop by to visit on their trips to Florida. Dave Rizzo's barn was never boring.

Now, let me tell you some things about polo. There are four riders on a team and each wears a number 1, 2, 3, or 4 on the back of their shirt and on at least one sleeve. Usually, the least experienced player plays number 1, a good defender plays number 4, a strong rider plays number 2, and your superstar plays number 3. At that position, number 3 is like the captain; they must intercept attacks and turn the ball around and move it up field.

A polo field is roughly three times the size of a football field, three hundred yards long and one hundred and sixty yards wide and takes up about ten acres of land. There is a goal at each end designated by two ten-foot pylons, usually red or orange, twenty-four feet apart.

The object of the game is to outscore the other team by striking a hard white plastic or wooden ball, a little larger than a tennis ball, as often as possible through the opponent's pylons for a goal.

In some ways it's like playing soccer or golf on horseback while galloping down the field with someone trying to knock you off the ball or, sometimes, off your horse. To make matters worse, the ball often bounces, making the rider adjust to hit it in the air. In good polo, the ball literally never stops moving. To say it is difficult is an understatement.

It is also exceptionally dangerous. With no disrespect to horses, they have brains approximately the size of a pig's and have survived for centuries based only on their ability to do one thing: flee from danger. They have no offensive tools like the sharp claws and teeth of a lion or tiger, although a good swift kick from one of the shoed hooves can and has incapacitated or killed many an unwary groom. Because of the nature of the beasts, any kind of sport involving horses is dangerous.

Like amateur golfers, polo players have handicaps and are rated at the end of each season. Unlike golf, the higher the handicap, the better the player. Handicaps range from a high of ten, held internationally by only a handful of superstars, down to minus one, where most beginners start out. To put it in more perspective, 95 percent of polo players are plus one or less.

Handicaps are very important, as they add up to determine the level of polo that is being played. Let me explain: low goal polo is generally determined by adding up the team's handicap to eight or less. For example, in an eight goal league, the four team members' handicaps added together cannot exceed eight. You can get there any way you want: four two handicappers; a seven goaler, a three goaler, and two minus ones; a nine goaler, two zeros, and one minus one. Whatever combination you create, you can't exceed eight in total. In a game where an eight goal team plays a seven goal team, their game starts with the eight goal team at zero and the seven goal team at plus one on the scoreboard.

The same calculations hold true for medium goal polo, with teams allowed 9, 10, 12, 14, or 16 total points and for high goal, where the total is usually somewhere over 16 and up to 25. I think this is done to allow a low goal sponsor or patrón to play, usually in the number one position. Polo is an "open sport," which means that one or all players may be paid professionals and still compete with amateurs. There are very few unlimited goal games played, and they are always great international draws.

The system actually works well for rookies like myself who are trying to break in and are automatically handicapped at minus one. It behooves a newby to get to the practice field as often as possible and to show some enthusiasm and as much athleticism as possible. This is where team patróns and their pros usually turn to look for someone whose handicap might lower the team's handicap from nine to eight and make them eligible for an eight goal league.

Anyway, that's what I did the first day I arrived, and I got tapped by a team called Windswept Farms to play number one for them before I'd even played my first game.

Practice was fun. My string, by necessity, was growing exponentially. We soon added Melody, a carbon copy of Half 'n Half, Abra Kadabra, a grey whose specialty was taking the bit in her teeth and running away with her rider, Snow Bird, a black and white Appaloosa who looked like she'd been sitting in a snow drift, and finally, Valentine, whom I bought for my wife, Mindy, and borrowed for our games. She was a quick but skittish pony who hated to touch the white chalk lines on the field. Her saving grace was that she could run really fast.

You had to be very careful in choosing your livestock, knowing that players were always trying to improve their string by selling off their worst ponies and upgrading. Also, horses are easy to buy and tough to sell, and the bad ones eat as much and require as much care as the good ones. Taking all that into consideration, I thought my string was shaping up pretty well. Using Jennifer's experience, we had put together a rather interesting equine agglomeration. Grazing together in the field they were a colorful herd, kind of a United Nations string of ponies.

I felt that we were ready for our first big test—a practice game. While league play in Florida starts the first week in January, there are many players around who like to get in some practice, so the club posts a signup sheet for people to designate how many chukkas they'd like to play. I signed up on the Monday before Christmas for three periods in the game the following Wednesday morning at 10:00 a.m.

Game day arrived, and the only one more excited than me was Jennifer. Per our plan, we would trailer three horses to the field: Melody,

Billy, and Half 'n Half. Jennifer had gone to the barn before dawn to get them ready. When I arrived, the horses were standing tied to the trailer. As is custom, their ankles were all wrapped in cloth bandages (mine are red) and their tails are tied up with matching tape. Jennifer had added two touches of her own, I guessed, from the world of show horses. She had intricately braided their manes and tied off the braids with red ribbons in sharp contrast to all the other ponies down there, whose manes were buzz cut. She'd also bathed the horses with some kind of fragrant bubble-bathy shampoo. I could smell it from twenty feet away. *Oh well*, I thought, *at least she's gotten into it.*

We drove to the field, and I was immediately thrilled to see who else had signed up for the practice game. It was literally a "who's who" of some of the greatest old veterans in the game. There was Les Armour and Joe Barry from Texas, Butch Butterworth, Tommy Wayman, Jules "Tiger" Romfh, and Juan Carlos Harriott, a former member of Argentina's national team and a good friend of Norty Knox's.

At 39, I was the second-youngest on the field, the youngest being Jules Romfh's pretty daughter, Nancy, who was in her first year of Miami law school. Yes, women do play, and some play exceptionally well like Nancy, who grew up on a horse. She would go on to become a very close

Team at rest. *Photo by Arnold Lee.*

friend to Mindy and me. I was particularly pleased to be in this game, as I knew that these veteran players would give me some good mentoring.

Polo matches have two mounted referees to call penalties and generally keep the peace. One of the refs blew his whistle to call the players to the center of the field to line up for a "throw in," which is kind of like a center jump in basketball.

I had been assigned periods one, three, and five and had decided to start with Melody, a veteran. *Here goes nothing*, I thought, mounting up and riding to the front of the line as our number 1. Everyone said hello to each other and shook hands with their counterpart in the lineup. Nancy was my opposing number 1. As we lined up, someone, I think Joe Barry, the old Texan, said, "Boy, you smell nice."

Embarrassment number one, I thought and responded, "Thank you, thank you very much," as everyone else laughed.

Nancy shook my hand and said, "Don't listen to them. I think you look very pretty."

Ah ha, a wise guy, I thought to myself.

The ref threw the ball in, and the game was on. The first period was somewhat uneventful. While the action was pretty fast, I felt that all of these old friends were holding back a little, maybe just easing themselves and their horses into the pre-Christmas game. There was not much bumping. I did actually touch the ball a few times and managed to hit a ball out of the air on a penalty shot to avoid a goal. Melody was great. Believe it or not, you could tell she knew the game and even pulled up once when I was about to ride in front of a player with the ball, which would have been both a foul and dangerous as well.

It was a hot morning, and the horses were sweating heavily. Melody was giving off a particularly strong perfume smell. Halfway through the period, I noticed that she was getting all lathered up as the shampoo seemed to be coming out of her pores. At one point, I looked around to see soap bubbles coming out from between her hind legs. Now this was embarrassing! Mercifully, the whistle blew to end my first period, and I tried to slink off the field, which is kind of hard on horseback. Les Armour rode past me and said, "Nice period, Bubbles."

When I got back to the trailer, I dismounted and gave the reins to Jennifer, who said, "Nice period, boss."

"Thanks, Jen," I said, taking off Melody's saddle. "Could you please walk her to cool her down and then spray her off with a hose? When we get back to the barn, I'd like you to buzz cut all of the horses' manes and, by the way, please no more pregame bubble baths," I added.

For my next chukka, I chose Billy, who seemed to be raring to go. Everything went well until about the six minute mark. I was going to goal when my saddle just kind of rolled over, dumping me unceremoniously on the ground, still holding my mallet and the reins. Nothing was bruised but my ego, and fortunately Billy didn't try to run away. Play was stopped, and Joe Barry and Tiger Romfh dismounted to help me adjust and tighten up the cinch on the saddle.

"You might want to try safety straps on your saddles once you've tightened the cinches as much as you can," Tiger advised me.

"Thanks," I said, "I will," as I formulated another postchukka note for my groom.

Half 'n Half was excited, taking the field for my third and final period. You could just tell that she loved the game and was happy to get back to it. Riding her, I actually found myself feeling safe, secure, and ready.

I got the ball a lot, and three minutes into the period I took a nice lead pass, dribbled almost half the field, fending off a check from Nancy, and actually scored a goal, my first.

"How pretty do I look now, Nancy?" I asked her as we rode back up field side by side, setting the tone early for our friendship. She laughed.

The others on the field seemed to share my excitement and were very congratulatory back in the centerfield lineup before the throw in.

When the period ended, I smiled all the way over to the trailer, not knowing that the ups and downs of that first game would symbolize, in a nutshell, the fortunes of my entire polo career.

My first season of Florida polo went pretty well. I learned a lot by watching and playing as often as I could, and I even got to a place where, if left unattended, I could actually dribble the ball the length of the field and score. While I started scoring pretty regularly, I think I was more skilled at blocking shots—probably a throwback to my old hockey goal-tender days. Anyway, Windswept Farms won the eight goal title, and my teammates seemed happy.

After a light summer of weekend polo around New York State at places like Skaneateles, Gilbertsville, and East Aurora, we returned to Florida at Thanksgiving to find my handicap had been raised from minus one to zero.

That season, '82–'83, I was determined to become a sponsor and put together my own team. I started by hiring a young professional, Brian Pritchard, a five goaler, to play number 3 for us. Brian, a young guy in his twenties, was known to be focused and driven. He played the game hard and wasn't always the most popular guy at the club. Our first addition was a young local doctor, Sandy Cardin, who anchored our team at number 4. Sandy rode and played the game with such reckless abandon that he had been nicknamed "Doctor Death." Finally we added my friend, Jules Romfh, to play number 2. Jules, a.k.a. Tiger, was a "cowboy." He grew up with, and loved, horses—and riding them fast. A sprightly sixty-one-year-old, his only concession to age was his rather impaired hearing. The young referees, all of whom knew Jules, made a point of blowing their whistles extra hard on play stoppage and even waving their arms to make sure that they got his attention.

All in all our team, clad in navy blue shirts with white embroidered sashes and red block letters spelling Buffalo, did pretty well on the field and we even won the second half eight goal league competition. While we played pretty well, we didn't make any friends. Brian played very rough and always seemed to be pushing the envelope on what was fair or improper. Doctor Death rode hard with not much regard for safety—his or his opponents'—while Tiger, obliviously, went flat out in his own world of semi-silence. I don't think the other teams really liked playing us.

As for me, I continued to work on the basics of riding, stick work, and position play while getting a major education on team sponsorship. First, I learned that the team takes on the characteristics of its pro. Brian's aggressive play literally dragged the rest of us into several rather ugly confrontations on the field. Secondly, I learned that sponsors, or patróns as they are called in the polo world, are somewhat like feudal lords constantly doing battle with the other neighboring feudal lords. The collegiality that existed on and off the field between all the players seemed to have a dark underside, as if we were all not really playing games against each other but were going into mortal combat. Third, I learned that everyone was doing deals constantly. Players, pros, patróns, and grooms always seemed to have something going on, whether it was horse trades, team changes, or whatever; it seemed that there was precious little loyalty in the games and very little fun. And the grapevine was always on overload. It was like a giant soap opera, which I titled *As the Mallet Turns.*

At the end of the season, I was approached by a very interesting polo legend in the making, Jimmy Bachman, about a deal for the next season. His informal nickname, the "King of Low Goal Polo," belied the fact that he was arguably the most knowledgeable horseman and best polo player at Gulfstream. He was like a horse whisperer and could get the best out of any horse he rode. His handicap ranged between six and eight in any given year. He was always being approached by the best players in the game and would often sell them a horse he was riding at the time. People

The "rookie sponsor" with Jules Romfh (2), Brian Pritchard (3), and Sandy Cardin (4) collecting hardware from Jules' daughter and Nancy's sister, Julie. *Photo by Arnold Lee.*

Jimmy Bachman demonstrates the art of "the ride off." *Photo by Arnold Lee.*

The race is on. *Photo by Arnold Lee.*

who know the game say that the horse is 80 percent of your success. Those same people who knew Jimmy say that if he had held onto his best horses he would have been a ten handicap, for sure, but selling horses was who he was.

Jimmy Bachman was a real cowboy and looked the part. Slight of build, he was a chain smoker whose sun-wrinkled skin made him look much older than forty. He had grown up on his father's horse ranch, and while his friends were on summer break learning how to play baseball, young Jimmy was in a corral breaking wild horses, as many, I would learn, as ninety in one summer.

I would often go sit in the stands when Jimmy was playing games to watch and learn. He was absolutely incredible. He was as one with any horse, even the most ill-tempered beast. A mythological centaur, half man and half horse, it was hard to tell where the man left off and the horse began.

While I'd watched him several times, I hadn't gotten up the courage to talk to him, and he'd certainly never had any reason to talk with me.

Anyway, Jimmy said that he'd been watching me and wanted to know if I wanted to play with him the following year and put together a sixteen goal team as well as an eight goal team. I was flattered but also intimidated. Sixteen goal is fast and tough. It was the highest goal competition played at Gulfstream, and the Club's best player wanted me on his team!

"Thanks, Jimmy, but do you think I'm ready?"

"Sure," he said, "but you're going to need some more horses." *Ah ha,* I thought. I might be dumb, but I'm not stupid.

"Sure," I told my new captain. "Sign us up. Who else are we going to get?"

"Just leave that to me," he said. "You just do some riding this summer and stay in shape. I've got you and me in a tournament in Gilbertsville [New York] in August. It'll be a good tune-up."

I was pumped.

A word about conditioning. People have asked, why get in shape for polo when the horse does all the work? Well, I've played a lot of sports, and polo is the hardest and takes the most conditioning of any of them. It's extremely physical for horse and rider and very dangerous as well. The expenditure of energy combined with the stress of a sport where you could be severely injured or killed is indeed draining. Playing under the unrelenting Florida sun, it was not unusual to lose over five pounds per game. The bumping is also constant, and after a match, something always hurt.

Back to Buffalo, we turned our horses out for a few months of rest before we started working them again in July.

I went to Gilbertsville in August and met the rest of our new team. Jimmy had signed on a five goaler from Toronto named Dave Offen to play number 4 for us. Dave was a tall, quiet horseman who loved the game and could hit the ball a mile. Rodger Rinehart, a two goaler, was our number 2. He was from a great polo family. His dad played, and his older brother, Owen, was a nine goaler on his way to becoming a ten goaler. Rodger was extremely shy, but he was a great player who stayed extremely calm under fire. Jimmy's horse sales had been brisk, and as a result he had been knocked from seven to six, and I had been elevated to a one. All together, we totaled fourteen (6 + 5 + 2 + 1). This meant that any sixteen goal team we played in the league had to spot us two goals. I'm sure that Jimmy had thought this through. At Gilbertsville, playing together for the first time, Jimmy literally put on a clinic for the crowd, and we lost in the finals by a goal. I thought we'd played great, but Jimmy hated losing and wasn't happy. We had some good chemistry, though, and it was obvious that we were going to win some games.

Jimmy felt it too, and he called me in September.

"They've got a fourteen goal league in Boca Raton," he said. "I've been looking at the schedule, and we could play in it as well as the two leagues at Gulfstream and not miss any games."

"Think we should?" I asked, knowing the answer.

"Yeah, man," he said enthusiastically, "but you're going to need some more horses."

I called my accountant and had him set up a new company, appropriately named Horsepower. I was proving the old adage that polo is not a sport but an addiction for which there are only two known cures: death or bankruptcy.

Now up to ten horses, we'd outgrown Davey Rizzo's barn, so job one for me at Thanksgiving in Florida was to find a landlord with more stalls to rent. I found the perfect situation in a barn owned by a great guy, my age, from Skaneateles, New York, named Peter Winkelman. He played around New York State in the summer where he received the descriptive nickname "Winkelman Down" for obvious reasons. Peter was actually a pretty good player and an excellent horseman. We hit it off well and struck a deal where I rented one half of the barn and he kept the other. I also hoped that our friendship might lead to Skaneateles for some summer games.

Peter's barn was also conveniently located next to Jimmy's barn "the Polo Farm," which was good for advice and consultation when he wasn't showing, trying, trading, buying, or selling horses—which was always. Subtracting his six goals from our team, we added up to eight goals. Jimmy had lined up several different zero goalers to fill in for us and play number 1 on our eight goal team; I moved back to number 4.

Jimmy had a great eye for two-legged as well as four-legged talent and could always find young guys rated zero, just starting to play, who

Dinnertime at the barn. *Photo by Arnold Lee.*

you knew would soon be high goalers. These guys were called "cheap players" as you didn't really pay them anything, making them bargains.

One of my favorites, twenty-year-old Tiger Kneece, became a regular on our team. Totally focused and fearless, I wasn't surprised to read that Tiger, a few years later, had become a success as a professional high goal polo player.

In Florida, most of the leagues are divided into a first half and a second half. I think it's done to give all teams the chance to make midterm corrections to be competitive. Playing as Palm Beach National, representing my father's golf club across the street from Gulfstream, we didn't need time for any corrections. We simply won both halves of all three leagues we played in, plus several tournaments as well. Dominant is an understatement. We absolutely annihilated our competition. I hardly remember losing any games at all. It was the best team I've ever played on in any sport.

In polo, rather than spread out across a field like football or soccer, you literally form a line and ride to goal, backing each other up all the

Mindy joins Palm Beach National for another trophy; Roger Rinehart (1), David Offen (2), Jimmy Bachman (3), and me (4). *Photo by Arnold Lee.*

way. Dave Offen, who usually played back or number 4, was steady and so dependable that when he got the ball the rest of us could automatically start up field knowing, as the long hitter he was, he could get the ball to us.

Jimmy, our field general, was not only a magician with the ball but knew when to slow a game down or speed it up depending on the situation and the team we were playing against. Often when Rodger or I had the ball, Jimmy would yell, "Leave it, leave it," and we would ride past the ball to goal, taking our defenders with us and opening up the field for our number 3. Jimmy then had room to either dribble or lay a pass in front of us. It worked, but I heard that high-pitched command from Jimmy Bachman so often in a game I began to think that "Leave It" was my new name. In fact, when I would call Jimmy on his barn phone and he was busy showing horses to prospective buyers, I would often leave a message to call back "Leave It," and he always did.

Contrary to what you might think, there are well-defined rules in polo, enforced by two mounted referees. A third referee in the stands casts a deciding vote if the two on the field are in disagreement, as is often the case. Most fouls revolve around a player being blocked from his right of way to the goal. A player with possession of the ball can have his mallet hooked or be bumped and ridden off the ball, but his path cannot be blocked. Violation of this rule leads to some of the sport's most serious injuries—or worse. (The most serious mistake you can make in polo, by the way, is to cut in too close to another horse's back legs. Norty Knox used to say, "Do that and you die. Literally." The reason is apparent when you look at the physiognomy of horses. Their front legs are thin and fragile compared to their muscular hind legs where their power comes from. In polo, putting your horse's front legs in contact with another horse's hind legs can be disastrous. I lost several polo friends who made that mistake.) The best defenders I know establish a good forty-five degree angle to bump or ride an opponent off the ball without cutting in front or riding into a horse's powerful hind legs.

An infraction leads to penalty shots of 60, 40, or 30 yards, depending on where on the field the penalty occurred. The penalized team can line

Jimmy could "go like hell and stop on a dime." *Photo by Arnold Lee.*

up to block the two longer shots but must move behind the goal line, but not behind the goal, for the shortest penalty shot. This leaves the goal unprotected, making the shot like a chip shot in golf or, more aptly, like an extra point attempt in football.

The action is so fast and furious in polo, causing "the line of the ball" to change so often, that penalties are common and a big part of any game. Jimmy seemed to be a master at frustrating the opposition and "drawing penalties." When penalties occur, the team that was fouled gets to choose whoever they want to take the penalty shot. With the choice of Jimmy or Dave, we seldom missed a penalty. Sometimes, when we had a big lead, Jimmy would designate Rodger or me to take the shot, probably to keep our heads in the game—or, in my case, maybe for some comic relief.

Our championship season came to an end in April, and my father threw a party for our dream team and our friends at the Palm Beach National clubhouse. It was a great event, an informal pig roast. I remember the bartenders, wait staff, and the band all dressed in royal blue replica polo jerseys with white numbers and Palm Beach Polo patches. It was a nice gesture by my dad, especially when you consider that the new business his sponsorship brought in probably would not have paid for the cost of the pig.

In retrospect, I think all of us on the team knew that we'd been part of something special that would be hard to duplicate next season. Gulfstream's polo committee made sure of that by elevating all of our handicaps. This made our fourteen goal team an eighteen goal team, effectively taking us out of all the leagues we'd played in.

Jimmy rebuilt the team with a changing combination of players, but the magic was gone. We dropped down to two leagues and struggled to be competitive. Our eight goal team had to be totally reworked, and we barely managed to win half of our games.

As often happens, you seem to have to work harder on losing teams in any sport, and polo is no exception. Playing games on Friday and Sunday, I found myself limping to planes on Sunday night to get back to work in Buffalo. Then, after four days to heal and think about what I was doing, I'd find myself saddling up on Friday morning to do battle again, wondering why I was putting myself through it. After all, everyone else I was playing with or against stayed in Florida and rode at least a little every day. Besides, they all seemed to be getting younger every year.

Then I'd put on my white jeans and team shirt, smell the polished leather of my boots, snug down my helmet, pick up a mallet, and climb aboard one of my horses who was anxious to run. Gliding over the manicured lawns, smelling the fresh-cut grass mixing with the scent of orange blossoms from neighboring groves under the cloudless Florida skies, it all came back to me as to why I was out there. If there is a greater adrenaline rush in any sport ever played by mankind, I'd like to know about it. The fear of loss, let alone injury, faded to nonexistence. It was all about riding hard and winning games.

The long first half of our season was winding down for me and my horses, which now numbered twelve. I was in my Buffalo office in February when Jimmy called and told me that we had a playoff game that Saturday to get into the sixteen goal championship. I had just called Jennifer for a status report on my string and found out that five of my ponies were out with a variety of injuries, leaving me with seven horses ready to go.

I told Jimmy that I was short and asked if he had a horse I could borrow. Unfortunately his string was decimated too—not so much by injuries as by late season sales.

"You're in luck, though," he said. "I just tried a bay mare who's the fastest horse I've ever ridden. Why don't you come down Thursday night, and I'll get you a few periods in a practice game on Friday to try her out?"

"Fine, Jimmy, I'll be there," I said, calling my wife, Mindy, to see if she wanted to join me.

Unfortunately she had a meeting of a bank board on Friday and couldn't come down until late that afternoon.

"I really wish you wouldn't do this," she said with an ominous tone. "You know, I've always had this premonition that if you play in a game without me there, something bad will happen. That's one of the reasons I come to all your games, and the thought of my not being there frightens me."

"Don't worry, honey," I told her. "It's just a three-period practice game, mainly to try a new horse. I'll be fine." Famous last words.

I left for Florida by myself and showed up at the barn at 9:30 a.m. to help Jennifer get a couple of horses ready for our 10:00 a.m. practice game. It was a beautiful "bluebird" morning in south Florida with no clouds and a gentle breeze out of the east. We had what the thoroughbred horse racers would call "a fast track."

My first period went well, and Jimmy brought the new horse over to our trailer for me to try. He had signed up for a few periods too, and he told me to play number 1.

"When I get the ball," he said, "drop her head and go to goal. I'll get the ball in front of you. She's like greased lightning."

I mounted the horse, and she felt quite normal. We lost the throw in and went on defense. Then Jimmy intercepted the ball, so I took off up field as Jimmy had instructed. He let go a forehand smash that went over my head and landed about thirty feet in front of me. I dropped the horse's head, and she blasted off like she was shot out of a cannon, completely leaving our opposing number 4 in the dust. As I cocked my mallet in the air to hit a forehand, I thought to myself, *Jimmy was right, this is the fastest horse I've ever ridden*. It would turn out that she was also the clumsiest. I struck the ball and continued toward the opponents' goal, my horse now in warp speed. All of a sudden, with no warning, she caught a toe and went "ass over tea kettle," projecting me into the air over her head. I saw the ground coming up fast and barely had time to tuck my head in before crashing full speed to the ground on my left shoulder. Then I was somersaulting once, twice, three times, head over heels down the field. I never lost consciousness; I remember the whole thing. It seems now like it was in slow motion and I was doing cartwheels. All of a sudden, I stopped. I was lying flat on my back, looking up at the sun. I thought to myself, *I'm still alive*! I sat up slowly before anybody got to me, somewhat dazed and trying to feel what hurt the most.

One of the refs reached me first, jumped off his horse, and told me to sit still for a moment and catch my breath. The other ref grabbed the reins of my horse who had, I later heard, also done a few somersaults. Happily, she never landed on top of me.

I remember being very relaxed as I managed to get to my feet and assure everyone that I was OK. Everyone, that is, except for a doctor who had been watching the game. He reached under my shirt and declared that I had at least a badly separated shoulder and should get to a hospital right away. I felt a little woozy and don't know or remember to this day who drove me to the Wellington Hospital. I do remember telling Jimmy before I left that I was fine and would be ready for the game tomorrow—oh, and I didn't think I'd be buying that horse. I remember Jimmy nodding and saying, "Yeah, right."

The emergency room doctor did a thorough exam and confirmed that I had a grade 3 separated shoulder, a broken collar bone, and three broken ribs. He asked if I'd gone unconscious and whoever drove me over there told him that I'd never lost consciousness. The doctor still wanted to keep me there under observation for a few hours.

I later found out that my mount had broken her jaw, but I never heard whether she had been put down. I didn't ask and I didn't want to know.

Jennifer squared things away at the barn and came over just before dinner to give me a ride home. I managed a shower and lay down gently on the couch to close my eyes just before Mindy walked in the front door as white as a sheet. She was happy to see I was alright. She was mercifully gentle and only said "I told you so" a few weeks later.

We flew home the next day to see my favorite orthopedic surgeon and friend, Doctor Steve Joyce, in the emergency room of Buffalo's Millard Fillmore Hospital. I remembered when I had seen him after one of my first falls, and he'd told me facetiously how happy he was that I'd taken up polo so he would have a chance to work on some compressed fractures.

After an examination of an injury he'd probably seen on hundreds of athletes, Steve said, "Good and bad news. You won't need surgery, but we're going to have to put you in traction to get that shoulder bone to come down. I'll fix you up with a device that will immobilize your arm for awhile that you must wear twenty-four hours a day—in the office and at home, awake or asleep. By the way, no riding for awhile, and did I tell you how lucky you are?"

By then reality had kicked in, with some major league pain as well. Steve said that was natural after trauma, prescribed some pain medication, and he told me to go home and go to bed and come back to see him in a week.

I did what he said, and it was a week I'll never forget, spent lying in bed with the upper left side of my body in excruciating pain. My ribs were the worst. I was tempted to buy a gun and put it on my bedside table so that if I felt a laugh, cough, or a sneeze coming on, I could shoot myself. I never thought about the fact that "nurse" Mindy might shoot me for ignoring her premonition.

The body's an amazing thing and slowly, ever so slowly, I healed, went back to work, and planned to take my children to Florida for their spring break.

The first day I arrived, our sixteen goal team was playing, without me of course, and I went over to Gulfstream to watch. Jimmy saw my car drive up and came over to say hello. "You've got to get back in shape, bud," he said. "There's an opening next year at Wellington in the twenty-three goal league, and I think we should put together a team."

Now it was my turn say, "Yeah, right."

While I didn't say no, a voice in the back of my head was telling me that my riding days were over. Later in the vacation, I tried some stick and balling. It went OK, but I had definitely lost my confidence when other riders came close, and I think my horses knew it.

Football coaches teach their players to go at full speed into a block or tackle. The person on either side who lets up gets hurt. I knew that I'd be that person. I'd lost my nerve.

Summer came back up north. I'd left my horses turned out down south with Jennifer. Jimmy called every couple of weeks to see if I'd made up my mind about a twenty-three goal team.

Then the calls stopped, I got a tearful call from my pal, Nancy Romfh. Jimmy Bachman was dead. He'd been playing at Myopia, had just finished a chukka, said he didn't feel so well, slumped over in his saddle, and died of a massive heart attack before his teammates could lower him to the ground. Myopia was the club, ironically, where I had purchased my first polo pony.

Jimmy Bachman was one of the living legends of the game, playing in his prime, at the young age of forty-three, who literally died in his saddle with his boots on, leaving a wife and two daughters.

We went to his farm in Virginia for his funeral and met up with many friends from the polo world, including the other two members of our dream team, Dave Offen and Rodger Rinehart. We stood together quietly on a practice field that Jimmy had built on top of a windswept hill. We bowed our heads as the last eulogy was spoken. We watched as our friend Jimmy Bachman's ashes were buried appropriately in the middle of one of the goals that he had built.

When I got home, I called Jennifer and told her to sell my horses.

BOOK 2
BASEBALL

A DAY AT THE BALLPARK

Baseball is a game for all ages. An old-timer once told me that the calendar year begins on Opening Day. Yet it is also the game of our youth and all of our happiest memories of summer.

It wasn't opening day, but as always when I drove to the ballpark, I thought about Buffalo Bisons home openers many years ago when I was growing up. I would hand my principal from PS 22, Rebecca Shepard, a note from home, then watch the hands of the clock both move agonizingly slowly toward twelve, when I would jump up, grab my coat, and rush for the curb. I would sit impatiently and watch for my dad's big Packard convertible to drive down Buffalo's Huntington Avenue to pick me up. Together, we'd drive five miles to the ballpark for the Bisons Opening Day.

How proud I'd been, sitting together in that big front seat, just me and my dad, heading for the game together. No matter that it was probably the only game we'd watch in person together that season, it was just the two of us, pals and baseball fans for a day. My dad was the most important person in my life, and I knew he had given up all his meetings and appointments and phone calls to be with me, just me, for the afternoon. It told me that we were friends and that I was important to him. He never brought along anyone else, and I never invited a friend from school. This was our day.

So much had changed since those days. Now I was a dad myself, with four children of my own that I loved to take with me to Opening Day. And I, who couldn't even hit a curveball growing up, had become the owner of Buffalo's professional baseball team. How'd this all happen?

I liked my reserved parking spot in the backyard of a house the city had condemned right next to the old stadium. Clyde, the squeegee man, exchanged a nice greeting with me for my dollar and, as usual, promised me that my car would be safe and that he was off drugs. I hoped that both were true.

A small crowd was already beginning to queue up at the Dodge Street

111

entrance of the stadium, enjoying the tunes on our sound system. "Free Bird" was blasting in contrast to the hymns that had been played and sung in the local churches earlier. It was 1:00 p.m., and some worshippers still dressed in their Sunday best were walking past our gathering crowd, no doubt enjoying the tunes that mixed with the wonderful smells of our ballpark as the concession stands began to cook hot dogs, hamburgers, fries, pizza, and, of course, Maddy's famous ribs. Maddy was a local who served her specialty in a nearby restaurant and asked if she could set up a stand in the park. She used to tell me that her secret ingredients were "love and soul." How could I say no?

As I walked toward the turnstile, I noticed some guy with a picket sign. A one-man picket! While I couldn't read his sign, I did recognize him; he was an usher in one of the upscale churches on the other side of the city who religiously brought a glove to the games and ran over anyone in his way, large or small, to get foul balls. It got so bad that for several games we had to assign an off-duty policeman to watch that he didn't hurt anyone or that someone didn't hurt him. Now I could see his sign. It was "Ladies' Day at the Park," sponsored by the Women's Personal Care division of a large consumer products company. They were handing out free hygiene products to the women, and he was picketing because he wasn't getting free tampons. *What a kook*, I thought. I guess every team has one. He yelled something at me as I walked past, and I ignored him. I noticed some members of the gathering crowd were starting to taunt him.

I saw the familiar face of Larry the peanut man, a ballpark neighbor with a handlebar mustache, hawking his wares. "Get 'em here, Buffalo, the peanut with . . . the *talented taste*," he said, emphasizing the last two words, "talented taste." I could never resist.

"Hi Larry, I'll take a bag," I said. We shook hands, and, knowing the price was seventy-five cents, I reached into my pocket for a dollar and tried to give it to him.

"Oh no, free for you, boss," was what he always said.

"Thank you, but no, Larry," I said, handing him the bill and adding, "keep the change." As he thanked me, I thought that I wasn't really his boss. He was an independent business man, and while our lease with the city gave us the rights to the plaza surrounding the stadium, Larry was an institution with a family to feed, and I had told our concession folks to look the other way.

The gates opened, and I gave my ticket to the ticket taker to tear when my turn came and walked through the turnstile with the other fans. Even though I owned the team, I always made a point of turning in my game ticket when I entered the park, figuring that if I took freebies, who else would? And where would it end? It was easier to pay my own way.

I greeted our general manager on my way to my seats next to the home team dugout on the third base line and asked him to assign a security guard to our "picketer" to make sure that he didn't get punched out by one of the fans who didn't like him or his message.

I always love walking into a ballpark. I see it as a perfect patch of green in a setting of gray, brown, and black concrete, metal, and asphalt—a rural retreat in an urban world where adult pressure gives way to a children's game. It's a simplistic world where you know who's on your side and who's against you by the uniforms they wear, and there's a minimum amount of adult supervision in the form of three black-clad umpires.

As I settled in, the home team, the Buffalo Bisons, were taking batting practice. They wore their white pants and pullover white polyester jerseys with red and blue numbers and trim, which replicated the look of our parent club, the Cleveland Indians. I made a note to look into button-up jerseys for next year—much classier, I think.

From my seat I could see our most famous vendor, the Earl of Bud, dressed in his customary white tails, like the ones Cab Calloway wore in *The Blues Brothers*, and a red cummerbund. The Earl of Bud was loosening up on the visiting team's dugout on the first base line, practicing his now-famous Pee Wee Herman dance routine to the strains of "Tequila" by the Champs. In real life, his name was Earl House. He was, at the time, the only black fireman in South Buffalo. He didn't sell you a beer, he presented you with a special cold beverage and a "Thank you sir, this Bud's for you." A game wasn't a game without a beer from the Earl of Bud. He told me that on a good day he could sell thirty-five cases. Avoiding the customary rule

Nobody serves suds like the Earl of Bud. *Courtesy of the Buffalo Bisons.*

of demanding boring uniforms for our concession folks, our vendors were encouraged to design distinctive costumes that would add to the fun of a trip to the ballpark and build their personas and sales. The Earl of Bud was joined by other character vendors like Conehead and Zorro.

Opening my bag of peanuts, I hoped that it would be a good day. It was a gorgeous June day in western New York, a gentle breeze blowing in from right field and temperatures in the high seventies. I was wearing shorts and a T-shirt. Much maligned for its severe winter weather, a popular joke asks, "What's summer in Buffalo?" Answer: "Two weeks of bad ice skating." Ha! That couldn't be further from the truth. Our summers are spectacular. Tempered by the cool water of neighboring Lake Erie, we enjoy low humidity, very little rain, and temperatures usually in the eighties. As a good piece of trivia for you, our weather bureau has never recorded a temperature of one hundred or higher in our city's history.

In addition to the good weather and "Ladies' Day Promotion," we had booked an appearance of The Famous Chicken (Ted Giannoulas), who was one of my favorites. Minor league teams live or die by their promotions, and I was sure that The Chicken would outdraw last week's "Unemployment Day," where anyone showing their unemployment card got in for free; about twelve friends of mine came into the park with bags over their heads.

I settled in to watch batting practice and noticed that our 300-plus pound batboy, Butchy "The Butcher" Palmer, in his ill-fitting Bisons uniform, was practicing shagging balls off the back screen. It was a seemingly easy feat that he never truly mastered—to the delight of the hometown crowd.

John Fogerty was just finishing up his classic "Centerfield" on the speaker system when someone with a bullhorn shouted out, "Hey, Bob, real owners wear coats and ties!" I recognized immediately the leather lungs of Frank "Fremo" Vallone, a rotund regular who, along with his bullhorn, had become an institution at Bisons games. He would sit behind home plate providing social commentary and harassing everyone from the mayor and other attending dignitaries to the visiting team. But Fremo saved his best stuff by far for the umpires; he was merciless. The league president asked us to confiscate his megaphone, but we refused, risking threatened fines that never came. Fremo was also famous as the host/owner of a popular nearby Elmwood Avenue watering hole called Merlin's, where fans and ballplayers from the Bisons, and visitors as well, would always congregate for cold beer and hot chicken wings.

I liked Frank; he was from the west side of town where I worked and would sometimes stop by my office to chat. I turned and gave him a wave. He was seated in his usual spot not far from two local old-timers who loved the game and had been nicknamed by Fremo "Tennessee Red" and "Meathead."

"Hi, boss!" I looked back to the field to see our manager, "Dirty Al" Gallagher, who had walked over from the batting cage to say hello. Actually, like Larry the peanut man, I wasn't really his boss either. In minor league baseball, the manager, coaches, trainer, and players all work for the major league parent team.

Dirty Al chews tobacco and watches batting practice. *Courtesy of the Buffalo Bisons.*

"Hey skip, how are you?" I said, using baseball slang for the manager, skipper, or skip for short.

"Good, good," he responded, spitting tobacco juice and looking dumpy, unkempt, and unshaven as usual. He had a wrinkled uniform and a wad of tobacco the size of a baseball in the side of his jaw. I liked Dirty Al. He was a "what you see is what you get" kind of guy. He got immediate attention from our minor league players based on his having played in the "Bigs" for many years, mostly with the San Francisco Giants as a gritty third baseman. He got his nickname because of one of his many superstitions: When the team was winning, he didn't like changing anything, including the clothes he was wearing. During a streak, he also refused to take a shower.

Apparently he still had the same superstition, and as the season progressed and we mounted a winning streak heading to the playoffs, I was approached by a committee of our players asking if I would talk with him before they left on a road trip. We'd been winning, and he smelled so bad they didn't want to ride on the same bus with him. (I said I would, but knew I wouldn't. I just hoped they wouldn't take matters into their own hands and lose a game to get him to take a shower.)

Minor league managers, like players, were never very well paid, and I later found out that Dirty Al slept on the massage table in our trainer's room to avoid the cost of a hotel room.

I could write a book about Dirty Al. One of my favorite Dirty Al stories came from a guest appearance that we arranged for him on a syndicated sports talk show with former Buffalo Bills punter, turned sports announcer, Paul Maguire. Paul was probably best known for a record ninety-yard punt he made in the Houston Astrodome shortly after it opened. After the game, one of the sportswriters asked him about his booming blast, and he shrugged it off and quipped, "I had the air conditioner at my back."

Back to Dirty Al's guest appearance: Our people forgot to warn him that Budweiser was one of Paul's major sponsors and that he liked his guests to arrive early so he could get to know them over a couple cold ones, which they would also continue to drink on breaks throughout the show. Forgetting that Al also had a love of longneck Buds, we forgot to send along a handler to watch out for him.

The big night came, and a bunch of folks from the Bisons front office gathered in my living room to enjoy together our manager's coming introduction to Buffalo.

The show started, and there they were, the two ex-big leaguers, one in football, one in baseball, sitting together comfortably in the overstuffed armchairs that made up Paul Maguire's set. They were looking equally relaxed and equally red-faced. Unshaven, Dirty Al was dressed in what looked like a powder blue leisure suit with some kind of open-collared Hawaiian shirt, a chaw of tobacco in his jaw, and a "dip cup" in his hand.

This was not looking good. We viewers drew a collective deep breath as Maguire asked his guest the first "soft ball" question. Dirty Al answered and was slurring so badly we could hardly understand what he said. Our marketing director buried his head in his hands and said, "Two Irishmen with an unlimited supply of beer; we're in serious trouble!"

"Just think of it as great television," I said facetiously as we all slouched down in our chairs like Dirty Al.

After they came back from a commercial, it got worse. Al was intermittently mumbling and spitting tobacco juice into his dip cup. Nice image for the little leaguers at home; hopefully they all had gone to bed. If Paul Maguire ever noticed the impaired condition of his guest, we couldn't tell. If he understood the answers of his guest, he was the only one.

Mercifully, the final segment arrived. Maguire asked Dirty Al a prolonged question, and there was no response. The cameraman zoomed in for a close-up, and there he was, his dip cup fallen out of his hand, our manager, our fearless leader, Dirty Al Gallagher out like a light. He had either fallen asleep, passed out, or died, but he was definitely unconscious. The camera refocused on the host for some prolonged closing comments, and the show ended. It was to be, to the best of my knowledge, Dirty Al Gallagher's last appearance on Buffalo TV—live or not-so-live.

I asked our manager if our team was healthy that day, and he said yes. I wished him luck, and he trotted back to the batting cage as our fans streamed in to the strains of Creedence Clearwater Revival on the sound system.

I smiled to myself and thought of Garrett Morris's *Saturday Night Live* portrayal of Latin baseball player Chico Esquela, who repeated the phrase, "*Beisbal* has been berry, berry good to me." *Me too*, I thought, *or at least, berry, berry funny*.

Growing up, baseball was my nemesis. I couldn't hit a curveball—probably still can't. And I certainly never saw myself as a player, let alone an owner, but that's what I became.

This story began in the fall of 1982 with a call from Buffalo's four-term mayor, Jimmy Griffin. He wanted me to buy the Buffalo Bisons.

Buffalo had had a baseball team for almost a hundred years, playing mostly in the Triple-A International League in a cozy little inner city ballpark named Offerman Stadium. They were always popular and drew well. Playing in a league just below the Majors, people identified with the players; they were youngsters trying to make the bigs and oldsters trying to get back there once again, or at least just stay in the game and get a paycheck a little while longer. The problem started when the stadium was torn down—actually, it was knocked down by a wrecking ball in 1960 to make way for a new inner city grammar school, which opened in 1964 .

The Buffalo Bisons moved to another inner city stadium built as a Works Progress Administration (WPA) project in 1937. The home of the Buffalo Bills, first known as Civic Stadium, was later renamed War Memorial Stadium but was soon nicknamed "the Rockpile" by the citizenry known as Buffalonians. It would go on to house the old Buffalo Bills of the All-America Football Conference before it folded in 1949. Later, War Memorial Stadium was home to the new Buffalo Bills of the American Football League, which folded into the American Football Conference of the National Football League. Jack Kemp led his team to two AFL Championships there, and O. J. Simpson started his professional career there before . . . whatever. Eventually, the footballers would leave for their brand new 80,000-seat stadium in the suburb of Orchard Park.

The stadium was not built for baseball, and even renovations left it with a "short porch," or a short right field wall that was about 260 feet away from home plate.

So the old Bisons played on in front of fewer and fewer fans until the race riots of the late 1960s did them in. A three-day period of summer civil unrest scared even the heartiest Bisons booster from returning to the venue.

As for the team, they went on a midseason road trip in 1970 and never came home, bussing instead to their new home of Winnipeg, Manitoba, where they became the Winnipeg Whips, finished their season, and disappeared into oblivion.

A feisty Irishman, Buffalo Mayor Jimmy Griffin was a huge baseball fan. In 1979, he called upon a bunch of his cronies to ante up $90,000 and purchase a franchise in the Double-A Eastern League. Playing as an affiliate of the Pittsburgh Pirates, the team limped through four years before they ran out of cash and credit.

As popular as Hizzoner was among his pals, I think his phone calls to his cronies for a "cash call" probably went unanswered; and that's when I got the call.

Why me? To this day, I'm really not sure. While we'd become friends, the mayor and I had a stormy relationship. He was a First Ward Democrat and I, as a rock-ribbed conservative Republican, always felt that we were on the verge of an argument. He knew that I was a "Buffalo guy" and had experience in pro sports as the youngest investor in the start-up Buffalo Sabres of the National Hockey League. Or maybe it was just like Warren Buffett says: "A fool and his gold are invited everywhere."

Anyway, I hadn't been in the stadium in nine years. We talked, and I agreed to take a look at it, think about it, and get back to him.

The trip to the park certainly didn't seal the deal for me. I went over

Yankee Stadium it's not! Buffalo's War Memorial Stadium under a sheet of snow. *Courtesy of the Buffalo Bisons.*

there on a Saturday and got the watchman to cage his German shepherd and let me in for a look-see. Even covered in a mantle of beautiful new fallen December snow, it was easy to see the place was a dump. Mayor Griffin had said that all it needed was a good clean-up, paint-up, and fix-up, which the city would supply. Moreover, he promised that if I'd step up and buy the team, he would go to work immediately on building a new downtown stadium for the team.

If the stadium wouldn't convince a prospective new owner to buy the team, neither would the books. The first-year attendance was abysmal, and the next three years were progressively worse. The place was a dump, and the fans stayed away in droves. With no money to spend on improving things, the community owners could only hope to cut costs, which they did. In a great sports town used to watching their football team play the Dallas Cowboys and their hockey team play the Montreal Canadiens, there wasn't much interest in watching their baseball team compete against Eastern League powerhouses like the Reading Phillies, the Glens Falls White Sox, or the Lynn Pirates.

A check of previous newspaper stories wasn't very encouraging, either. Mainly overlooked by the writers because of the team's poor performance on and off the field, there were only a few passing comments about the Rockpile. Said one writer, "War Memorial Stadium looks like it was named to memorialize a war that was fought within its confines." Another writer, referencing the once-combustible neighborhood that caused the team to leave town a decade earlier, called the venue "more shabby than intimidating."

So what to do: Buy or don't buy? Based, in part, upon some experience in marketing products and the mayor's promise to build a new stadium, I decided to roll the dice and go for it.

The acquisition was largely overlooked by the press as the refurbishing and marketing jobs began in earnest. Six and a half months of work would lead us to a wonderful Sunday afternoon in June with a giant crowd returning to a stadium that was now beginning to feel like an old friend. Sitting in the June sunshine, watching our young prospects sign autographs for their adoring younger fans, some of whom may have been getting the first autographs of their lives, and our large stuffed Bison mascot, Buster, hugging some youngsters, I felt that I had made a good decision for my hometown, for my company, and for my family. What's more, I knew in my heart, if not my head, that the best was yet to come. How right I was.

THE NATURAL

Now what kind of promotions would bring the people of Buffalo back to a decrepit old stadium to watch their Double-A baseball Bisons play?

That was what I was thinking about in my office in the spring of 1983 when my assistant, Elaine Gallagher, told me that our team's newly appointed marketing director, Mike Billoni, was on the phone.

I picked it up and prepared for his customary greeting. "Hi ya, chief," he said. I'd been trying for two months to get him to stop calling me that, but he couldn't. Maybe it was from his many years working as a sportswriter for the Buffalo *Courier-Express*. It's like he thought I was Perry White, editor of the *Daily Planet* from the Superman universe, and he was cub reporter Jimmy Olsen. "Hi ya, chief. I've got some good news for you."

"I hope so, Michael. You know we've only got a month 'til Opening Day."

"I know, I know," he said. "I got a call from a guy from Hollywood. They want to shoot a movie at the Rockpile," he said, using our affectionate name for our home field, formally known as War Memorial Stadium.

"Who is he?" I asked.

"Says his name is Mel Bourne," Mike said.

"Does he have a brother named Sid Knee?" I asked.

"What?" he said.

"Never mind, Michael. Who is he?"

"Says that he's a set designer for Woody Allen."

"Yeah, right," I said, "probably one of those X-rated porn guys who wants to do *Debbie Does Buffalo*. Why don't you ask him who the stars are? That'll shut him down fast."

"OK, chief, I'll call him back and let you know." Man, I hated it when he called me that! A half an hour later, Michael called back to report on his conversation with Mel Bourne. "He said they don't have any women actors signed yet, chief."

"See, I told you so, Michael," I said.

"But they do have the male lead," he said.

"Who is it?" I asked.

"Robert Redford," Mike said, adding, "Mel said they heard about our stadium from an old catcher in the South Atlantic League, and he's flying in 'cause he wants to see it for himself. What should I do?" he asked.

"Send him a limo!"

"Right, chief, I'm on it," he said.

Mel's visit was arranged for the next day, and I went over to the Rockpile to greet our visitor. As I waited for the limo to arrive, I stood at home plate and looked over the park. She looked like an old lady dressed up for disco. All the seats were brightly painted a rainbow of colors to designate the price of the sections. Reds, greens, yellows, blues, and oranges prevailed. Our sign painter, who Michael called "Crazy Kevin," because he worked day and night regardless of the weather, was putting the final touches on a Pepsi sign. We were hoping that the paint, like the field, would be dry by Opening Day, now less than a month away.

Robert Redford's first practice at War Memorial Stadium.
Courtesy of the Buffalo Bisons.

I was shaken from my reverie by the blare of a siren from a motorcycle police escort that Michael had ordered for the limo, obviously ignoring Mel's request for a quiet visit. "Under the radar," I think he called it.

The limo pulled up to home plate and a sprightly, older guy with gray hair jumped out, perfunctorily introduced himself, and began his tour.

"Ideal, perfect, wonderful, marvelous!" I'd never heard such adjectives connected with this place. "This is just what I've been looking for!" he gushed. I wondered if he and I were looking at the same place but figured that beauty was, in fact, in the eye of the beholder. When we returned to the limo and Mel Bourne seemed to come back to earth, I asked him the name of the movie.

"It's called *The Natural,* based on a novel written by Bernard Malamud in 1952 about baseball in the thirties," he said.

Ah ha, I thought, putting two and two together, *that's why he wanted an old stadium.* I'd read *The Natural* in school. It was about a great baseball player who took a bribe to throw a championship game—a story of lost innocence.

"Kind of a dark piece, isn't it Mr. Bourne?" I asked, with Michael looking at me like I'd lost my mind. "A very sad ending, I remember."

His excitement unabated, Mel Bourne just smiled and said, "Oh we've fixed that." *The wonderful world of Hollywood*, I thought. "I want to bring our director here next week to see this beautiful field. He'll make the final decision. Will it be available?" Mel asked Michael.

"It's not going anywhere," Michael quipped.

"Who's the director?" I asked.

"Barry Levinson," he said. "You may remember him from *Diner*." I did indeed. It was one of my favorite movies. "Good deal. I'll see you guys next week then," he said. "And, oh, Michael, I don't think we'll need the police escort," he said.

"Right, chief."

Hey, wait a minute, I thought I was Chief. Oh well, the draw of the bright lights trumps all, I guess.

"Oh and could you bring along a local contractor?" Mel asked, almost as an afterthought, as he climbed into the limo.

Mel was as good as his word and returned a week later, not only with Barry Levinson but also an entourage of men and women with notepads, cameras, and portable Dictaphones. We introduced the director to our chosen contractor, Bill Lenz. "Walk with me, Bill," he said, and the circus began.

"See those seats? They should be gray. Paint them!"

"Check," said the guy with the clipboard.

"See those signs? They should be from the thirties. Cover them!"

"Check."

"The facing on that right field press box must be modified to look like the owner's office. Build it!" Levison said, pointing.

"Check."

"That centerfield scoreboard is too small and too modern and electronic. We need one twice its size that people run manually, where the operators look out from the inning holes. Design it!" Levinson said.

"Check."

I looked at Billy Lenz, who was carrying a clipboard of his own and shaking his head, taking notes and smiling like he'd just found a pot of gold.

"Where's the tunnel going into the home team's dugout?" Barry Levinson asked.

"We don't have one," Michael intoned.

"We need one right away," Levinson said.

"Dig it?" Billy jumped in.

summer turning the clock back at War Memorial Stadium, and here's how it was captured by the camera lens of Fritz Fernow: Above, in a unique cross between advertising eras, billboards touting classic American products are set-up in left field, eventually in place of current-day ads. At right, a giant hand-operated scoreboard, identical to those used in major league stadiums during the '30s, is constructed around War Memorial's electronic scoreboard. After weeks of work, the scoreboard's 15-ton frame is finally completed and pressed into operation by the film crew.

sun-parched bleachers to underground cave-ins.

"The toughest part of the job was digging the tunnel behind the team dugout for the camera crews," said Bill Lenz, project manager for Huber. "We had a couple cave-ins while we were digging and trying to shore up the structure. Nobody was hurt, but it took lots of Yankee ingenuity to get it right."

"We looked at 70 different stadiums around the country and none of them were close to what we wanted," said Mark Johnson, producer of the film. "This one has all the character we ever dreamed of."

War Memorial's interior has essentially remained unchanged since the stadium was built in 1935 under a Federal Works Project Administration program. The city did add several thousand seats to the facility in 1960, but the wooden seats and steel posts that were installed as part of that covered addition, fit right in with the stadium's Depression-era design.

All totaled, the stadium's refurbishing called for 5,000 gallons of flat grey paint for the bleachers, a giant 15-ton scoreboard with hand operated tally cards, a few additional seats, and a host of 1930s advertising billboards.

"The scoreboard was another headache at times," Lenz added. "It was built around the old structure and we had to shore up all the old bleachers so they would be able to hold the 15-ton load. We even had to dig underneath the stadium and shore up the dirt underneath to handle the weight."

The massive scoreboard stretches more than 50 feet high and 120 feet wide, Huber said. It contains eight backside levels where technicians were stationed to change score cards during filming. The scoreboard, topped off by a giant billboard ad proclaiming Sears, Roebuck & Co. the "store of the future," hides the stadium's regular electronic scoreboard from view.

The entire remodeling project was completed in less than two months and provided plenty of summer work for 40 Huber construction workers and another 30 subcontractors. Now that the filming is completed, all the props will be removed except possibly for a few new seats. Then the stadium will return to its familiar flavor.

"Some of the stuff looks so good they may just leave it up," Lenz said. "It's a shame the scoreboard has to come down. Everybody really loves it."

The new "old" scoreboard. *Courtesy of Rich Products Corporation.*

"Right!" the Director ordered.

"Check."

"Excuse me, Mr. Levinson," I felt duty bound to interrupt. "We've got a baseball season to play here, you know."

"Oh yeah, right," he said. "Mel, take care of it."

"Check," Mel answered.

This is going to be a memorable summer, I thought to myself, thinking we'd found or been found by the promotion we'd been looking for.

Barry Levinson spent the rest of his time at the park walking around looking at camera angles with a young, dark-haired guy who turned out to be the cinematographer, Caleb Deschanel. Meanwhile, Mel and I talked about what arrangements would have to be made so that the Bisons and the fictional NY Knights could coexist in the ballpark for a season.

We had a lot to discuss. For example, I had a feeling that Danahy Insurance or any of our other advertisers would not want the wall signs they'd bought and paid for covered up by a Burma Shave ad. In short, Hollywood agreed to pay for all of their changes and create portable canvas covers for all the wall signs painted with period ads. They also agreed to remove any changes they made and to turn the building back to us the way they found it.

We entertained a few more visitors from the movie's producers, TriStar Pictures, like Mark Johnson and Patrick Markey, and helped them line up some wonderful locations as well as lodging for the stars. Finally, they went public at an on-field press conference.

Thanks to the beautiful old Buffalo architecture, the locations chosen in addition to War Memorial were outstanding, like the hotel (the Ellicott Square Building), Doc's Soda Shop in Chicago (Parkside Candy) and Wrigley Field (All-High Stadium).

We also helped them secure the Masten Avenue Armory next to our park for construction of their local sets. Other scenes were to be shot in California in the fall.

Housing was easy; I was surprised to see how many of our friends were willing to move out and turn their houses over to "the stars" for the summer.

As we worked on preparing the ballpark, Knights Field in the movie, opening our own season, and helping the producers with endless details, the cast began to fill in—and a blockbuster cast it would be. Supporting Redford as Roy Hobbs the superstar ball player would be Glenn Close as Iris Gaines, his love interest; Robert Duvall as Max Mercy, the unrelenting beat writer; Kim Basinger as Memo Paris, the niece of the Knight's owner; Barbara Hershey as the mysterious Harriet Bird; Wilford Brimley as Pop Fisher, the lovable manager of the Knights; Darren McGavin as the gambler Gus Sands; Robert Prosky as the Judge, the conniving owner of the Knights; Richard Farnsworth as Red Blow, the sympathetic coach; and Joe Don Baker as the Whammer (loosely based, I believe, on Babe Ruth). Brought to life by Levinson's direction, Deschanel's photography, and the beautiful, Academy Award–nominated score by Randy Newman, *The Natural* would go on to win acclaim and a total of four Oscar nominations as one of the best-ever sports movies. But there was a lot to be done before any of that happened.

Between takes, two great actors, Robert Redford and Glenn Close, talk shop.
Courtesy of the Buffalo Bisons.

With the cast rounding out nicely, Patrick Markey called to tell me that they would soon be having a local casting call for extras, including baseball players and coaches, vendors, ticket takers, policemen, faces in the crowd, etc., etc. I told him that we'd do anything we could to help.

He thanked me and said that they were looking for someone to play Redford's Roy Hobbs as a twelve year old. He had to be a good looking boy, of course, and a good athlete and left handed. We had just the kid for him, the son of a pal of mine. My friend was a hockey player who'd followed me through Williams College, and his son was a youngster by the name of Paul Sullivan Jr. Young Sully read for the part and got it immediately.

Then the casting hit close to home. My son Bobby was working at the ballpark as a soft drink vendor for the summer. He called me one day at my office all excited.

"Dad, Dad, some woman came up to me in the stands today and asked if I wanted to read for the part of the batboy in *The Natural*," he said.

"Great, son," I said, "go for it, and good luck."

Two days later, I arrived at home to see him in a frump. "What's the matter, pal?" I asked him.

"I read for the part of the batboy," he said frowning, "and I didn't get it. They want me to play the part of Robert Redford's son."

"Bobby, are you kidding? That's great," I said. "Congratulations. Why are you so down?"

"Because I didn't get the part I read for," he scowled.

"Buddy," I said, "you just won the lottery. Forget the batboy; you're going to be Robert Redford's son in the movie. What fun!" Trying to put it in terms a fifteen-year-old might appreciate, I added, "Think about all the girls you'll meet who'll ask you who you are and what you've done, and you can say, 'Oh, perhaps you saw me in *The Natural* as Robert Redford's son?' Bobby, this will be a great experience." I think, at least for the time being, he was mightily unconvinced.

Hollywood has very strict rules that demand that minors like my son be accompanied on set at all times by a guardian. So, whenever Bobby would be called for a shoot, I'd accompany him only to sit with him sometimes for hours of inactivity and listen to him complain on the way home about the pittance that he was receiving as an extra. "Hey bud, you got paid more than I did today," I'd always say to him.

I remember well one seminal scene he had to rehearse for where, at the end of the exciting climax, Roy Hobbs crunches an inside fast ball that clears the stadium and goes from dark to light, where it is caught in a wheat field by his son, Ted Hobbs. Seeing as how Bobby hadn't played much baseball, I brought home a fungo bat from our clubhouse, used by coaches for hitting fly balls, and a dozen baseballs so we could practice after work. After a week, he was doing pretty well. They posted the scene to be shot in South Dayton, New York, the next day.

I drove him out there in the morning, and we waited all day for the sun to begin dipping in the west, creating what they call in the business "the magic time," when the setting sun makes everybody look good.

"Hurry up, hurry up everybody," Barry Levinson shouted through a megaphone. "We don't want to miss this light. Bobby, get out there."

Dressed in trousers of the period, a checked shirt with suspenders, and an old-fashioned cap with a fifty-year-old baseball mitt, Bobby took his place in the wheat field.

Levinson called "Action," and they put a ball in some kind of cannon and launched it to my son, actually well over his head. As Chris Berman would say, "he went back, back, back," then tripped over one of the wheat field's furrows and went "ass over tea kettle." His suspenders broke, and his hat fell off, and the ball landed about ten feet away from him.

"Cut," yelled the director, "we don't have time for this. Leave the hat off and the suspenders." I cringed, wondering how I'd rehab my son after the end of his short movie career.

"Barry, how 'bout using this fungo bat?" I suggested and gave it to one of his paid baseball advisors to use in place of the cannon.

"Fine," he said. "'The Catch,' take two, and action." The guy hit the ball and Bobby faded back, settled under it, made the catch, smiled, and threw the ball in as directed. A sigh of relief came from my heart.

Then take three, take four, take five, all the way to take eleven, and Bobby, my son a.k.a. Ted Hobbs, son of Roy Hobbs, a.k.a. Robert Redford, went ten for ten after that first fielding error. It stands today as my proudest moment in sports.

By the way, the last time I would see that cannon was about a week later when they were practicing using it for the dramatic climax, when Roy Hobbs's Herculean blast knocks out the lights. They had it super-charged, and some special effects guy waved everyone back from home plate, yelled "Fire in the hole," and triggered the fuse.

I've never heard a blast like that, and I wondered if the baseball had survived. Wondered, that is, until about fifteen minutes later when we got a call from some old guy in the 'hood about ten blocks away asking us if there was a game going on today "'cause somebody just hit a ball through mah new picture window." Hollywood meets Buffalo!

Bobby's spirits picked up dramatically one night after shooting a shot at the armory. It was a scene where Glenn Close leaves her seats at the big game to give a note to Roy Hobbs revealing the parentage of their son. The scene apparently wasn't working, and Barry Levinson said, "Bobby, when Glenn stands up say, 'Where are you going?'"

Bobby delivered his line. Barry yelled "cut, that's a wrap," and our night was over. As is custom, we headed toward the paymaster's window to get Bobby's thirty-or-so bucks, but were intercepted by an assistant producer.

"No, Bobby," he said, "you've got to go upstairs and fill out some papers. You've got a speaking part now, and you've got to join the Screen Actors Guild [SAG]. They'll have a check for you, and you'll probably get a screen credit in the movie."

We followed his instructions, and, as his parental guardian, I signed the papers as they handed him an envelope. On the way out to our car he opened the envelope and looked at his check. "Oh my God, Dad, oh my God," he repeated over and over. "Look," he said, showing me his check for $4,000.

"I think I better take that, pal, and put it in the bank for you," I said.

"Thanks, Dad. Isn't Hollywood great?" *Yeah, great*, I thought to myself, *a star is born.*

As the call went out for extras, I never realized how many friends I had. Because of the perception that I had some say in the selection process, which I didn't, I was getting calls from everywhere, from people that I barely knew or hadn't seen or talked to in years.

Some of the funniest selections were those that they made to fill in the ranks of the Knights. They selected our official scorekeeper Kevin Lester, advertising salesman Steve Poliachek, and color commentator Duke Maguire, who'd been a prospect in the Baltimore Orioles organization. The best, however, was one of our recent former Bisons, Joe Charboneau.

Joe had been an American League Rookie of the Year a while ago with our parent team, the Cleveland Indians, and was known equally for his off-field antics and his on-field heroics. Whether dying his hair purple or getting a Mohawk, drinking a beer or eating the glass it came in, Joe Charboneau was a classic. Bombing after his rookie year, the Indians sent him to us to rehab his career and maybe put some fannies in the seats.

We had managed to sign a contract for an unheard-of twenty-four game minor league television schedule. The head of player personnel for the Indians, Dan O'Brien, came to town and was sitting with me for our first televised game on a Friday night that turned out to be Joe Charboneau's first and last game with the Herd (as the Bisons are called). In about the third inning, in front of a nice crowd, Joe hit a lazy grounder back to the pitcher, but he chose not to run out. Instead, he kind of shuffled down the first base line.

The Buffalo fans, known to be a rough crowd, didn't like it and booed lustily. Hearing that, Joe Charboneau gave the finger to the left field crowd, another finger to the right field crowd, and a classic double-pump finger to the folks behind home plate and those watching the game at home.

Dan O'Brien was furious. He left his seat and made a beeline to the Bisons dugout. That was the first and last at bat we saw by the colorful Joe Charboneau in a Bisons uniform.

Apparently he'd moved his family to town and never received any offers after the Indians cut him—never, that is, until TriStar signed him to an extra's contract with the New York Knights as a teammate of Roy Hobbs. Watch for him in the dugout scenes. He did some of his best, albeit most conservative, acting ever.

All in all, I believe that the shooting of *The Natural* in Buffalo went very well, and the Bisons and Knights shared the stadium in peaceful harmony. The weather cooperated and gave the producers some beautiful days and nights for filming. The calls for extras turned out some huge numbers for crowd scenes, at least until the novelty wore off and the cool evening breezes of fall began to blow through the ballpark. The Bisons were drawing well, too, and every time we had an upcoming event with low advance sales, I learned that Mike Billoni, now nicknamed P. T. Barnum, would put out the word that Robert Redford was coming to the game and tickets would sell and crowds would come out.

By season's end, both the Bisons and the Knights would make the playoffs. Then both teams packed their gear and took off for their homes, leaving some wonderful memories for all. My hometown had put its best foot forward and was rewarded with many complimentary thanks from everyone involved in the production of the movie. It was a wonderful ego boost for all Buffalonians, who sometimes need to hear from outsiders how great a place Buffalo really is. It seems, unfortunately, that years of declining self-esteem are not easily overcome.

Robert Redford himself provided a fitting ending to the summer when he came out to the final Friday night game of the season, threw out the first pitch, and accepted a handcrafted saddle to take back with him to his ranch in Sundance. His heartfelt thanks to the city for accepting him as a resident for a summer were well received by the locals who had unofficially adopted him as one of their own. Even after the truckloads of movie making equipment pulled out, the memories live on.

I too have fond memories of that summer like playing catch and chatting with Redford on location; arranging a tennis match with Robert Duvall; watching Associate Producer Bob Colesberry stand in for Bump Phillips and run through a balsa wood wall in centerfield; listening to Glenn Close sitting in a dugout harmonizing with a group of extras; and, of course, watching my first born son go ten for eleven in a wheat field in South Dayton.

Finally, that September, Bobby announced to me his plans to quit high school to pursue a career in Hollywood. I suggested that he continue his schooling and wait for that call to come. He went on to complete high school, then college, then graduate school, marry a great girl, have two wonderful kids, and start up a very successful business. He's forty-two now, and he still stays in touch with Glenn Close, his screen mother, and several other members of the cast. Once in awhile, he receives a small residual check. For him, that call never came, but as for all of us, the memories never left.

After the Bisons made their last out of the season that summer, Mike Billoni walked up to me and said, "Quite a season, wasn't it, chief?"

"Yes, Michael. It was indeed quite a season."

MAJOR LEAGUES

Be careful what you wish for, lest it come true.

—Proverb

Baseball is all about "the Dream"—the dream of making it to the Bigs, where the grass is always green and the stadiums are full, where you have your own hotel room on the road, and where you leave the bus and fly to games.

The Dream is the shared glue that holds the game together for everyone; the rookie outfielder from Wisconsin who's been the star on every team he's played on; the old left-handed pitcher from California, trying for a comeback from two rotator cuff surgeries; the utility infielder from New Jersey who's never quite been able to stick "for more than a cup of coffee"; and the slick-fielding shortstop from the Dominican Republic who can run, hit, and field but cannot understand the language. Players aren't the only ones dreaming the dream. How about the grizzly old manager, good on teaching the basics but bad on baseball politics; the young radio announcer, just up from three long seasons in the South Atlantic League; the college graduate trainer wondering if his sports therapy degree is ever going to pay off; and the coaches waiting for someone to fail up top so they get their shot.

So, too, was the Dream part of my life from the time I walked through an empty snow-covered stadium as a rookie Double-A owner until I made my final presentation to the National League Expansion Committee eight years later as the owner of the most successful Triple-A franchise in the history of the game. It was always about the Dream.

Buffalo, New York, has proven itself a big league city. In spite of the economic downturns endemic to the Rust Belt and a few blizzards of legendary ferocity, Buffalo fans have proven themselves to be in a league of their own. Their undying support for the Buffalo Bills of the National Football League and the Buffalo Sabres of the National Hockey League has been unparalleled. Ironically, the city has a history in big league baseball dating back to a seven-year stint in the National League, starting way back in 1879, and two seasons in the Western League (1899–1900), which later became the American League.

Most of Buffalo's baseball history, however, was spent as an eighty-three-year mainstay of the International League, which at the time was truly international. I grew up watching our Bisons play against the Toronto Maple Leafs, the Montreal Royals, the San Juan Marlins, and the Havana Sugar Kings.

Then, almost before I knew it, I was the forty-one-year-old owner of the Bisons, an all-but-bankrupt Double-A team playing in a decrepit old inner city stadium that the community had basically given up on. Any baseball glories for our town were now all in the past tense.

But baseball is all about dreams, with the ultimate dream being a trip to the majors. I felt the dream for my city from the very first day. The challenge was to add the spark and rekindle the flame that seemed to be so dead, especially on a January day walking through the park.

I made a promise, the first day we bought the Bisons, that I would do my best to take the club wherever the fans wanted it to go; back to Triple-A and to the Major Leagues if that was their dream. We kept the faith and worked hard on that mission for eight and a half years, but it wasn't to be.

If being spoiled means always getting what you want, I plead guilty. Baseball was to be the exception. Now as I look back on our quest, objectively for the first time through the eyeglasses of age and experience, I can probably see more clearly why we failed. Wiser now, I'm no doubt better able to take that look back and with hindsight see what went right and what went wrong. What seemed like such a bitter pill then actually now seems like a very lucky break for me, for our fans, and for the city of Buffalo itself.

They say that young men have dreams and old men have memories. These memories, then, fold into a story. This is mine, told in nine innings.

First Inning (1983)

The Mayor's call to bail out the Double-A, Eastern League Bisons in December of 1982 was unexpected but well-timed for many reasons. I'd been part of the "Knox Group" that bought the Buffalo Sabres in 1969. Seymour and Norty Knox were older friends and under their tutelage I'd studied how to run a sports franchise. While they'd been good mentors, I felt that I wanted a shot at running my own team.

The stadium was a disaster. There were some quick temporary fixes that had to be made before we could bring people back and justify construction of a new ballpark, which the mayor had promised.

The people were our jobs one, two, and three. If we couldn't bring them back, it was over. Hiring a great promotions guy was critical, and Mike Billoni was the best. He juggled public relations activities with formulating an ambitious promotional calendar second to no other baseball team. We couldn't rely on baseball alone, we needed event marketing. Giveaways; concert double-headers; characters like The Famous Chicken and Max Patkin, "The Crown Prince of Baseball"; ethnic nights, ladies' nights, children's days—the more the merrier—and, on top of it all, fireworks. Buffalo loves fireworks.

It was great having *The Natural* filmed in our ballpark, but it was only a curiosity that would bring some people out once. We needed a lot of marketing to grow and sustain a customer base.

Michael soon got the nickname, P. T. Barnum, after the legendary circus promoter. There was nothing we wouldn't try. Some of our promotions worked and others flopped badly, but we always tried hard. I think people appreciated that effort.

One of our worst flops, the first year, was Michael's Easter Egg Hunt. The crowd of kids that showed up for the pre-advertised event was so large that Michael decided after the Easter candy was spread around the field that we would have to break the kids up by age: over twelve and under twelve. He sent the older kids out first and then announced over the microphone that it was time for the older kids to stop foraging so the younger kids could have a chance.

Good luck on the big kids stopping their hunt. They continued on and took everything off the field but the bases, which were tied down. This left the younger kids with nothing but grass, dirt, and angry parents.

Undaunted, Mike jumped in his car, drove to the local Walgreens, emptied all of their Easter candy shelves (which he paid for himself), and returned to the park in time to conduct the under-twelve Easter Egg Hunt two innings later.

It was silly stories like this that immortalized Michael but also showed our growing number of fans that we really cared and were all about fan satisfaction.

My second hire was also important. Our stadium was in a decaying section of town. If people didn't feel safe coming to the park, we were finished. We felt it was an imperative to insure the security of our fans as well as our associates and players. Joe Petronella had set all kinds of records working undercover on the streets of Buffalo for seventeen years for the police department, and he was a close friend of mine. Joe signed on to be our chief of security. His first action was to enlist off-duty Buffalo police officers to supplement their pay by working for the Bisons on game days.

The general manager of the Bisons when I bought them, Don Colpoys, agreed to stay on. Don was the baseball coach at local Canisius College, and he had a small group of baseball guys to help him run the Bisons.

One of the first things we had to do was to teach everyone the art of customer service. We started by dressing everyone smartly in team polo shirts and khaki slacks so they could be readily identified. Then we made all of them turn their back on the field and pay attention to what was happening in the stands. This was where our customers were. It was part of trying to "control the controllables." Before the first game, we brought everyone together and said, "Listen, you can't control the weather anymore than you can control what goes on inside the white lines, so focus on the fans. They're the ones who will determine our success, so give them your full attention."

Looking back, this doesn't seem so earth-shattering now, but it was an enormous psychological sea change, especially for some young people who went to work for the Bisons because of their "love of the game."

Baseball was the last thing we could count on to sell tickets. With so many major league games televised, it's all too easy for baseball fans to get their fix while never leaving their couches. While the quality of minor league baseball is excellent, the young players obviously don't have the name recognition of major league all-stars. That's why it's ultimately easier, believe it or not, to sell tickets to an old timers' game, featuring a bunch of fifty- and sixty-year-olds than a minor league all-star game that features the stars of the future.

Success comes by building the entire experience for fans, young and old alike. It takes dedicated staff and painstaking attention to detail to insure that everything is done right. You can probably sum it all up in a fictitious quote from a customer. Let's say it's a middle-aged woman talking with her friend on the phone the Monday morning after a game. She says something like this: "We all had the best time. The seats and restrooms were clean. The children all got autographs; the entertainment was fun. Little Johnny Jr. brought his glove. He almost caught a foul ball, and John showed him how to keep score. Oh, the team, they lost 10–2 to someone, but the food was delicious, the prices were reasonable, and everyone was so nice. I can't wait to go back next week for some of those fabulous chicken wings and to see The Famous Chicken!"

Don't get me wrong, it's great if your parent team can provide you with a winner, but you can't control it so you can't count on it. At the end of the day, it's not the team's performance on the field that will determine the enterprise's success.

We were fortunate our first year to have a very good young team. The Pittsburgh Pirates had been Buffalo's parent team for four mediocre years until Buffalo management had drafted a new affiliation agreement with our Great Lakes neighbor, the Cleveland Indians. They stocked our club with a bunch of good young prospects like third baseman Kelly Gruber, who would go on to star for the Toronto Blue Jays. One of our fielders, Dave Gallagher, led the Eastern League with a .338 average, while our centerfielder, Dwight Taylor, shattered a Bisons record with ninety-five stolen bases.

The team compiled a 74–65 record, and we lost in the first round of the playoffs. Our first-year attendance was 200,531 compared to the prior year of 77,077.

Second Inning (1984)

Our second year was a success, as we were able to raise attendance to 223,433, a nice increase that proved that the year before hadn't been only about the novelty or *The Natural*. Our people had done a lot in the off-season to meet other baseball people and find out categorically what worked and what didn't. Years are made by what you do in the off-season. People with the idea that baseball front offices only work in the summer are simply wrong.

On the field, we went 72–67 and watched several good prospects get called up, like pitcher Jose Ramon, who finished with a 14–6 record. Many critics of minor league sports complain about call-ups. They don't have to be a negative for the club. Rather than complain, we celebrated call-ups and tried to make all of our fans feel the excitement for the player. Call-ups are inevitable. They are also one of the uncontrollables.

One of my favorite stories from the '84 season involved a young prospect the Indians had signed for us by the name of Nehemas "Pookie" Bernstine. We always helped our players find lodging and get acclimated. Wanting to help Pookie get comfortable, I called our longtime soft drink supplier, Jerry Cooper, who was Jewish, and told him about Pookie and asked him if he'd mind inviting him to seder dinner. Jerry was delighted. Only thing was, Pookie was a southern Baptist. No matter; I heard they had a wonderful evening together.

The towns in the Eastern League were very nice; they just weren't very large. We started to hear rumblings among our fans that they wanted to get back to Triple-A as soon as possible. The only problem was finding a team that was available. In baseball, there were twenty-six major league cities at the time, and they were each allowed to have one Triple-A team, playing in one of three leagues: the Pacific Coast League, the American Association, or the International League.

The Pacific Coast League was ruled out geographically. The American Association, as a league of heartland cities, could work, but the natural choice was the International League, of which Buffalo had been a member for eighty-three years.

I called around the league and found out that the only team that might be available was Pawtucket. Owned by a chap named Ben Mondor, the Paw Sox were the longtime affiliate of the nearby Boston Red Sox, and they were alleged to be disgruntled about having to play in an old park that their city would not renovate. I called Ben Mondor and he agreed to meet, so I asked my dad to join me and off we flew to Pawtucket.

It was a long visit with an extremely noncommittal Ben Mondor. We roughed out an offer that he said he'd think about, but I began to think he might just be using us as a stalking horse to get his city to do some renovations.

At the end of the day we departed, and he said, "Thanks for coming, but I'm really surprised you came here and not Wichita of the American Association. I've heard they're available."

We said good-bye at the airport, got in our plane, and buckled up. Before takeoff, my dad looked at me and asked, "Wichita?"

"Wichita," I said and passed the new destination on to our trusty pilot and Minister of Aviation, "Flaps" Czelusta.

Our plane was equipped with a phone. From the air, I called an old friend, A. Ray Smith, the owner of the Louisville Redbirds of the American Association. Considered to be the Bill Veeck of the minors, he had used zany promotions to become the only minor league owner whose team drew over a million people in a season. A. Ray was our mentor, and I called him for two reasons: To see if he'd support our application for the American Association and to find out if he had the Wichita owner's phone number.

His answer was yes to both questions, and we were on our way to Kansas.

We met the Wichita owner, Milt Glickman, just in time to go out for dinner. Milt was an older gentleman who'd made his living in the scrap metal business and who'd also owned the Wichita club for many years. He was married with a daughter and two sons, of whom he was very proud. One son, Norman, was a lawyer. The other, Dan, was a US congressman who would go on to become secretary of agriculture under President Clinton and would later become chairman of the Motion Picture Association.

Dinner was pleasant. We told Milton why we were there, then listened to him talk for a few hours about his love of family, Wichita, and his baseball team and how he never wanted to sell it.

Before dessert was served, Milton excused himself and went to the men's room. My dad leaned over and whispered, "C'mon, son, this is ridiculous; he's never gonna sell. This is a waste of time. Let's go home."

"Not so fast, Dad," I answered. "I've got a feeling. Let's play it out." I didn't know how to verbalize it to my father, but I felt that Milton was an older man reminiscing who had actually realized in the back of his mind that the time had come to sell his team.

Wichita's attendance was low and getting lower, and I had a feeling that after years in the business, this must have been a major frustration to this gentleman. That's the theme I pursued when he returned to the table.

His mood changed—he talked about his dealings with the majors and his inability to get a winning team, his dissatisfaction playing in an old ballpark that wasn't up to standards, and the fickleness of the fans who'd quit on the team.

I made him a cash offer of $950,000, and he said yes and assigned his son Norman to close the deal.

Just like that, we were in Triple-A baseball.

Yup, '84 was a great year. We increased attendance, brought home a Triple-A team, and I met and fell in love with a woman at the ballpark who would become my love of a lifetime.

I had been watching a late season game with a bunch of my bachelor pals and became aware of her dark-brown-eyed presence a few rows behind me.

Mindy Roth had moved to Buffalo and taken a job as an account executive at the city's largest advertising agency. Born in Cincinnati, she claimed baseball as a birthright and loved to go to Bisons games.

She was thin and fit, with short-cut brown hair, a warm smile, and the most haunting brown eyes I'd ever looked into. She was also very bright, with a friendly personality and the most inquisitive mind.

Sabre Rob Ray challenges Canadiens to a game of shirts vs. skins. *Courtesy of the Buffalo Sabres.*

Sabres fans are big on signage.
Courtesy of the Buffalo Sabres.

Silver in the Carrier Dome in 1977. *Author's photo.*

Suiting up for a game of polo takes time. *Photo by Arnold Lee.*

The Beach Boys and surfer girls. *Courtesy of the Buffalo Bisons.*

The Famous Chicken entertains. *Courtesy of the Buffalo Bisons.*

Rocky and me. *Courtesy of the Buffalo Bisons.*

Atlantic sunrise in Islamorada. *Author's photo.*

Our smallest blue marlin. *Author's photo.*

Hot tarpon day. *Author's photo.*

The River Test. *Author's photo.*

Babe the Hunter. *Author's photo.*

London's Tower Bridge. *Author's photo.*

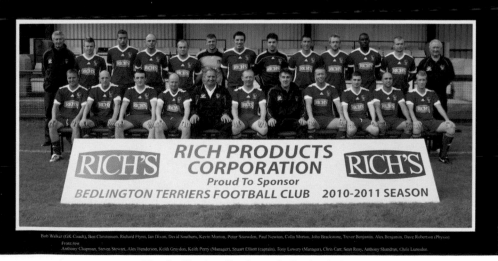

RICH'S · RICH PRODUCTS CORPORATION Proud To Sponsor · RICH'S
BEDLINGTON TERRIERS FOOTBALL CLUB 2010-2011 SEASON

Bob Walker (GK Coach), Ben Christensen, Richard Flynn, Ian Dixon, David Southern, Kevin Morton, Peter Snowden, Paul Newton, Colin Morton, John Brackstone, Trevor Benjamin, Alex Benjamin, Dave Robertson (Physio)
Front row
Anthony Chapman, Steven Stewart, Alex Henderson, Keith Graydon, Keith Perry (Manager), Stuart Elliott (captain), Tony Lowery (Manager), Chris Carr, Sean Reay, Anthony Shandran, Chris Lumsden.

The Bedlington Terriers. *Author's photo.*

Jimmy Bachman sets up for off side backhand. *Photo by Arnold Lee.*

Having become used to the rather shallow life of a twice-recycled bachelor, I felt strangely and overwhelmingly drawn to Mindy. Uncharacteristically, I was almost afraid to talk with her; when we did chat, I'd feel my heart racing and I'd break out in a cold sweat. I think that my malady was pretty easy to diagnose.

Third Inning (1985)

This was to be a banner year that I'll never forget. It was both the one-hundred-year anniversary of professional baseball in Buffalo and the year of our return to Triple-A. Mike Billoni took over as our GM, allowing Don Colpoys more time for his growing Canisius College baseball program. As for me, I was head over heels in love, and Mindy and I became inseparable. She was a great athlete with a wonderful mind for business who had run a children's ski school in Aspen. We shared so many interests it was frightening. We seemed to complete each other's sentences. I knew it was a lifetime contract when, before Opening Day we merged our collections of record albums.

It was a busy year getting ready for Triple-A. We signed a two-year working agreement with the Chicago White Sox. Their owner, Jerry Reinsdorf, made us feel welcome and important by coming into his office on Yom Kippur, the highest of Jewish holy days, for the sole purpose of meeting us.

Over twenty-one thousand people showed up for our opener, which, ironically, was against Louisville. A. Ray Smith came to the game and watched the Bisons beat up on his Redbirds, 7–2. The result didn't seem to faze him. It was like sitting with the master. No one knew the minor leagues like A. Ray, and he delivered advice and counsel with wit and wisdom. For example, in about the third inning one of the batters fouled a pitch off and the ball was caught by a fan nearby, who was absolutely exalted. He apparently recognized our guest, and, after jumping up and down several times and showing off his prize, he yelled over, "Hey, A. Ray, what does one of these balls cost?"

A. Ray yelled back, "About two scotches." A. Ray was also an authority on scotch.

On the field, our team wasn't very good, and ended up at 66–76. The excitement of being back in Triple-A carried the day at the box office, though, and we sold 362,762 tickets. The White Sox came to town for an exhibition game against the Bisons. Our fans loved seeing future Hall of Famers Tom Seaver and Carlton Fisk on the field.

We were on a roll when, in August, the baseball commissioner threw a fastball that took up the pace of the game. The talk of expansion had been simmering on the major league's back burner for several years. In 1984, Commissioner Peter Ueberroth said that expansion was a "front burner item." Then, in August 1985, he turned the heat up in a press conference when he said, "I only favor expansion when there's a city that qualifies under three criteria: local ownership with roots in the community, fan support, and support from the city, county, state, and their politicians." He later added a fourth criteria, almost as an afterthought: a suitable stadium, preferably designed for baseball only.

Bingo! I felt that he was talking about Buffalo, knowing that support from our politicians would soon be manifested in our new downtown stadium that was in the planning stages. We'd been dreaming about it, and now the majors were actually taking about it. We were pumped, and our spirits were bolstered by our fans' reaction to our first concert double-header featuring the Bisons followed by the Beach Boys, which drew 26,696 fans to the Rockpile.

After the season, Mindy and I eloped and headed to Paris for a two-week honeymoon, full in love yet tired from the season, with a lot of dreams to talk about.

We had no sooner returned home in mid-October than I received an invitation from the commissioner's office to come to New York to meet with baseball's Long Range Planning Committee in early November.

Showtime! This was what we'd been waiting for, but we had only three weeks to pull a presentation together. My desk was piled high with Rich Products work. I needed help, fast. Who could I recruit? The answer was obvious. Mindy had quit her job just before we got married, and she had all the skills required. I asked her, and she jumped on the opportunity.

Mindy did a lot of fast research and pulled together a very profes-

Mindy and me en route to Paris. *Author's photo.*

sional and glamorous presentation piece outlining the qualifications of Buffalo as a Major League Baseball city.

Our big day came, and we arrived a half hour early and ran into the Orlando contingent, which had just made their pitch. They told me that thirteen cities had received invitations to appear over a two-day period and none of the presentations were to run over an hour.

Our time came, and we trooped into the meeting room. The MLB was represented by the commissioner, both league presidents, and nine owners. No introductions were needed. We knew them, and they knew us. It was like old home week. Our presentation went well. It was a good back-and-forth session with a lot of questions. Many of the owners had fond memories of dealing with the old Bisons. Their questions ended, and

Commissioner Ueberroth thanked us for coming and asked that we not report to the waiting press that "it went well or poorly." I glanced at my watch to see that we'd been in there for ninety minutes. Any quizzical or skeptical looks on the big league faces were gone. We were in the hunt.

We said our good-byes and went back into the lobby to see the Denver contingent waiting impatiently. All of a sudden, we were surrounded by the press. "How'd it go?" they asked.

Remembering the commissioner's admonition, I said, "I feel great that baseball people were finally able to talk baseball together." I exited stage left, barely able to contain a big grin, thinking to myself that finally, some people were going to take my hometown seriously.

Appreciating the great job Mindy had done on pulling together the MLB presentation, Michael asked her if she would go to work for the team on special projects. This was to be the start of her career at Rich Products.

Fourth Inning (1986)

This was to be another busy year for us. We opened the season with a new record crowd of almost 28,000 fans, which was followed by 35,788 for a Bisons–Beach Boys double-header in June. That concert was memorable for more than the attendance. It was a beautiful, warm, cloudless day with some beautiful suntanned lasses surrounding the stage, enjoying the "good vibrations" and swaying to the beat of "Surfer Girl." From the left-field stands emerged a middle-aged fan running toward the stage to dance with the groupies . . . totally naked. The police tackled him and paraded him in front of the crowd to the security office, still with no clothes on, to the mixed horror and delight of the Bisons faithful. The Beach Boys gave the crowd two hours instead of one, and a delighted Mike Love announced that the band hadn't had a streaker in twenty-five years. I made a note for our head of security to buy a couple of blankets for our next concert.

In July, we broke ground for our new downtown stadium. We went into August with the turnstiles spinning, nine games over five hundred, making a shambles of our division, and play-off bound. The White Sox had a flamboyant first-year general manager/ex-ballplayer/ex-broadcaster, Ken "Hawk" Harrelson. Harrelson came to town for a luncheon with our largest advertisers and season ticket holders. Basking in the glory of an eight-game lead, he spoke for about fifteen minutes then took questions and violated General Manager Rule Number 1. When asked if there were going to be many call-ups, he said, "No, you don't have anyone here we need. There won't be any call-ups. You'll finish the season with a pat hand." He returned to his chair to a standing ovation.

Within a week of Harrelson's appearance, the Sox were floundering and the call-ups began. Our lineup was decimated. We went from eight games up to seven games down, going 15–24 and finishing well out of the play-offs.

Our fans were furious with Harrelson, leaving me no other choice but to dump the Sox. In spite of our late-season collapse, we still drew 425,113 people to the park.

A sad footnote to the season came that December when we learned that our fan favorite, league all-star slugger Joe DeSa, was killed in a car crash following a winter league game in Puerto Rico.

Fifth Inning (1987)

We started off our last year at War Memorial Stadium with a one-year working agreement with the Cleveland Indians. It was a busy year going back and forth between games at our old yard and overseeing details of the new park, which was to be called Pilot Field, after the city had sold its naming rights to Pilot Air Freight.

We had some great bats in the lineup, but our starting pitching was atrocious and our bullpen was worse. Every time a reliever would come in, he'd pour kerosene on the fire. We finished 66–74 but still drew 497,760 fans, many of whom came, I'm sure, to pay homage and a last visit to the old Rockpile, which was slated for demolition.

My three highlights were watching one of our outfielders, Dave Clark, hit .340 with thirty homers and eighty RBIs, the Beach Boys concert that drew an incredible 38,211 fans, all of whom remained at least partially clothed, and a nostalgic stadium farewell event at the end of the season.

The year ended on a very high note. Mindy and I were in an audience at the Winter Baseball Meetings to hear Commissioner Ueberroth deliver his State of Baseball address when, out of the blue, he said, "One of the best baseball experiences in America will be in Buffalo with its new stadium." We were shocked and were then swarmed after the meeting.

A good pal of ours, baseball analyst Peter Gammons, walked up later and shook my hand. "You wrote that, didn't you Bob?" he whispered.

Commissioner Ueberroth's comments would turn out to be spot on.

The Beach Boys' crowd was our largest ever in the Rockpile.
Courtesy of the Buffalo Bisons.

Sixth Inning (1988)

This year started with the legal upholding of a collusion conviction against major league owners. While we were too busy to pay much attention at the time, it would come back later to haunt the sport and our efforts to obtain an expansion franchise.

Mindy and I cut back a lot on our travel to meet major league owners so that we could help get Pilot Field ready for Opening Day. It seems that baseball on or off the field is a never-ending succession of chances to pay attention to innumerable details. In the off-season, we signed a development agreement with Syd Thrift, baseball boss of the Pittsburgh Pirates, that would last for seven years. They were alleged to be loaded with prospects.

Opening Day finally came, and there was our beautiful new home, Pilot Field, finished and ready to welcome a new era of baseball in Buffalo. What had once seemed like mission impossible, four years of planning and arguing, and two years of construction, had now sprung full-born into the heart of our city. It was a special green place, our own field of dreams, waiting to play ball. Built at a cost of forty-two million dollars, it was a two-tiered, baseball-only park, built with off-white concrete panels inlaid with green marble tiles for accent, a teal-green roof, a real grass field, and red seats for 20,000 fans, which we would later expand to hold 21,500. Stadium amenities included Pettibones Grille, a five hundred-seat restaurant, forty skyboxes (all sold out), a press box for eighty-five journalists, a giant four-color video board mounted in centerfield, five TV camera locations, concession stands (with TV monitors) serving everything from traditional ballpark fare to deli sandwiches, sushi, chicken wings, clams, and ice cream sundaes.

Players' facilities included spacious club houses for the home team, visitors, and umpires, two indoor batting cages, a weight room, and a fully equipped trainer's room. There were offices and showers for the managers and coaches, TV replay and interview rooms, a spouse lounge, and even a separate locker room for the batboys and mascots.

It was almost time to cut the ribbon and welcome our fans, many of whom had been partying for hours out on the new plaza. I climbed into the back of a convertible with Mayor Griffin and New York Governor Cuomo, both of whom had been actively involved in making this day a reality, for our reinstated, customary Opening Day Parade through down-

At last, our new home—Pilot Field. *Author's photo.*

town Buffalo. Mindy opted to stay behind at the stadium and look after some final details.

The weather was sunny but kind of windy and cold. *OK*, I thught, *nothing can put a chill on this day.*

I was listening to messages crackling on one of the Governor's secret servicemen's walkie-talkie when, halfway through the parade route, I heard a familiar voice, Mindy's, making a rather unfamiliar announcement. It was one that I'd never heard before: "Buster down, Buster down!" she shouted. *That's strange*, I thought. It wasn't until we got back to Pilot Field that I realized what had happened. Apparently Buster T. Bison, our mascot, already in costume, had pitched in to help some of our guys move a scaffold. Inadvertently, he had touched a live electric wire, and the shock sent him halfway across the concourse. He blacked out for a few seconds but was all right, although we took him to the nearby Buffalo General Hospital for observation. We'd pressed a back-up Buster into action for the day. Out of earshot from Mindy, Mike Billoni whispered to me, "You should have seen it, chief, he really got singed. You could smell the smoke from his burned fur."

"Not now, Michael, please," I said. "We've got a new stadium to open."

We hadn't opened the doors yet as I walked down to our clubhouse to say hello to our new manager, the irrepressible old veteran Rocky Bridges. "Rocky, do me a favor will ya? You know we're trying to get a major league team, and there's a lot of national press here today. Could you please try and say some nice things about the city?" I asked him.

"You got it, boss," he said as we walked out of the tunnel to the sunny glare of the beautiful spring day. The press corps knew that Rocky was always good for a quote and gathered round him with cameras snapping and film rolling. A guy I recognized from *Sports Illustrated* started off the questions.

"Hi ya, Rocky. Kind a cold here for baseball, isn't it?"

Without hesitation, Rocky shot back, "Cold, jeez, it's so cold even Admiral Bird would turn back!" The crowd of sports guys roared as I cringed and tried to smile. *Man*, I thought, *so much for a media assist from Rocky Bridges.*

Outside, the crowd was buzzing. We cut the ribbon and people started filing in. Their responses as they went through the gates and then the concourses and on to their seats were universal. A hush fell over them as if they were entering some sacred high holy place that they never expected to see in their lifetimes. Then they started cheering—cheering everything, the music, the mascots, the players, the no-smoking announcements—everything. The atmosphere was electric.

The national anthem never sounded sweeter, the jet flyby overhead was perfectly timed, and the umpire's call to play ball drew a standing ovation.

Our Opening Day opponents were, appropriately, the Denver Zephyrs, with whom we would be competing for an expansion franchise. Before a sellout crowd, our first of twenty-two sellouts that year, the

Pilot Field brought two opponents together for Opening Day, Governor Cuomo and Mayor Griffin. *Courtesy of the Buffalo Bisons.*

Bisons won 1–0 on the backs of two players: our lefty pitcher Bob Patterson, who pitched no-hit ball through the seventh inning; and our catcher Tommy Prince, who slugged a solo homerun to the left-field power alley in the third.

Sitting in the first row, next to the home team dugout on the first base side with Mindy, the governor, and our mayor, I opted not to wear an overcoat so that I could show the large national television audience how pleasant it was in Buffalo, New York, in the spring. I just hoped the footage of my breath in the cold air, which was getting colder as the shadows lengthened, wouldn't be visible.

The game had everything, including a narrow escape for the home team. In the top of the eighth with one on and two out, Denver's big right-handed slugger, Brad Komminsk, stepped to the plate. With a count of 2 balls and 1 strike, he jumped on a fastball and creamed one down the left-field line. My prayers were answered, and the frigid west winds off Lake Erie curled it just foul by three feet. We retired him after two more pitches and got out of the inning. I tried to applaud, but my hands were too cold to feel anything. My fingers were turning blue.

Our new home provided a mystical backdrop for our magical first year but just like the year before in the Rockpile, our team went into a horrendous swoon in the second half of the season. We were 65–50 in early August and lost twenty of our last twenty-four games to end up out of the playoffs again, seventeen games behind Indianapolis. That year, it really didn't matter; Pilot Field was our draw, and the baseball purists were thrilled that we were now playing an interlocking schedule with the International League.

In spite of our late season woes on the field, we drew a record-shattering attendance of 1,186,651. We outdrew three major league clubs. A. Ray Smith was the first to call to congratulate us.

This number didn't even include two other sold-out, nationally televised events, the National Old Timers' Baseball Classic and the Inaugural Triple-A All-Star Game, both of which drew many guests from the Big Leagues and helped us in our quest to land a Major League club.

As our storybook season came to a close, Peter Ueberroth, who had become a good personal friend of ours, stepped down as commissioner of baseball. While this may have dealt a blow to our major league chances, we will always remember him for another subject. It was Peter Ueberroth who inspired us to start Western New York United Against Drug and Alcohol Abuse. Known as Western New York United, it has served our community for twenty-five years. It is clearly one of the good things that indirectly came from our Major League hunt.

Seventh Inning (1989)

This was the beginning of the Terry Collins years in Buffalo. Terry came over to the Pirates from the Dodger organization and was named our manager. He would be with us for three great seasons. A fine player, Terry kept himself and his team extremely fit. He was an emotional leader who hated losing and drew out the best in everyone around him.

I suppose I can talk about it now, as the statute of limitations on tampering has no doubt expired: Terry Collins was my runaway choice to manage the Major League Bisons if we got the nod. By then we had added a Double-A team in Wichita, a Single-A team in Niagara Falls, and a semipro organization called the National Baseball Congress. Mindy had taken on the responsibility for our baseball operations. We were building our own farm system and agreed that Terry Collins would be a great motivator for these young men. My confidence in Terry was born out, as he would go on to manage the Houston Astros, the Anaheim Angels, and the New York Mets.

That year, under Terry's tutelage, we added winning on the field to winning off the field. The team went 80–62, our highest winning percentage since 1959, yet incredibly we lost our division pennant by five games to Indianapolis, which was fast becoming our arch rival. Off the field, we drew 1,132,183 fans to become the first minor league club to exceed one million in attendance twice.

It was also to be the year of the commissioners. As we were opening in April, the majors chose Bart Giamatti to succeed Peter Ueberroth as

Manager Terry Collins going through the signs with catcher Tommy Prince.
Courtesy of the Buffalo Bisons.

their new commissioner. A gentle man of letters from Yale University, Giamatti demonstrated a fervent love of the game which I'd never seen in Ueberroth. In fact, he penned some of the greatest prose ever on the subject of the game he loved and now ran, like the following, which became my favorite baseball quote. It was quite prophetic as well.

"It breaks your heart. It is designed to break your heart. The game begins in spring, when everything else begins again, and it blossoms in the summer, filling the afternoons and evenings, and then, as soon as the chill rains come, it stops and leaves you to face the fall alone."

Giamatti also said, "There's nothing bad that accrues from baseball." Then he had to spend almost the entire season wrestling with the affair of baseball legend Pete Rose and his gambling on baseball. Assisted by his deputy commissioner, Fay Vincent, whom Rose called "the crippled guy," Giamatti ended up banning Rose from baseball for life.

Mindy and I had a meeting with the new commissioner that summer, and we were encouraged to "follow our dream." We, like everyone else in baseball, were shocked to hear that he died of a heart attack on September 1, less than five months after assuming his job as commissioner of the game he loved so much. The baseball owners moved quickly to install Fay Vincent as commissioner on September 13.

There was no need for an introduction to Fay. He was a senior at Williams College when I was a freshman. He started out college as a brilliant student and a hard-nosed football player. During his freshman year, he was victim of a prank that nearly killed him: One of his pals locked him out of his dormitory room, and Fay climbed out a window onto an icy ledge and fell four stories to the ground. The fall left him with a broken back and some paralysis that he never fully overcame. He was out of college for a year and returned to graduate Phi Beta Kappa.

Fay had gone on to law school and then worked with a Washington law firm before he was hired, ironically, by another mutual friend and Williams College graduate, Herb Allen Jr., to become the CEO of Columbia Pictures. Herb needed a tough guy to protect his image in a beleaguered business, and he chose well.

That toughness would serve Fay well as he started the job as commissioner of baseball, but it would haunt him later on. In his first year, Fay had to cope with the horrific earthquake that interrupted the '89 World Series in San Francisco between the Giants and Oakland, the owners' spring training lockout, and the expulsion of George Steinbrenner over illegal actions during a tiff with Dave Winfield. Great start!

In the aftermath of a collusion settlement against the baseball owners, Commissioner Vincent adopted the image of a strong, tough operator. This would eventually impact his dealings with the minor leagues a year later. That notwithstanding, I considered him a friend and we always stayed in touch.

Eighth Inning (1990)

This would turn out to be the seminal year in our quest. Our trips to spend time with every single owner continued and led to some memorable and sometimes humorous results.

I believe that the baseball owners individually were some of the most interesting and brightest business people I'd ever met. It's when they had to come together to make joint decisions that they got into trouble.

Most of them were quite charming; all of them were extremely competitive. Perhaps the most brilliant was Carl Pohlad, a financier and self-made billionaire who owned many diverse companies, including radio stations, banks, and the second largest Pepsi bottler in the country. He bought his hometown Minnesota Twins in 1984 and won his first World Series in 1987. In spite of his success, when we met him in his office he was upset with the size of his community and its inability to support his club in a less-than-adequate domed stadium. He was also angry with the local politicos for not helping create a new stadium.

Mindy and I finished our Buffalo pitch and Carl sat back, took a deep breath, and said, "I've got a deal for you. Let's trade; you take the Twins, and I'll take the Bisons, even trade."

"Are you serious, Mr. Pohlad?" Mindy asked him.

"Very serious, Mindy," he answered.

"And we could move the Twins to Buffalo?" I asked.

"No, you'd have to keep them here, and I'll keep the Bisons in Buffalo in Triple-A."

"Thanks, Carl, but we're Buffalonians," I told him.

"OK, it was just an idea," he said. "You've got a great team, and I don't know why you'd want to join the major leagues, but I like you both and you'll have my vote."

We left his office shaking our heads in disbelief. I was dying to tell my old college roommate Tommy Roe from Minneapolis this story, but I never could—up until now, that is.

In San Francisco we met with Giants owner Bob Lurie, who'd made a fortune in real estate, and his baseball business manager Corey Busch. They had been fighting with San Francisco for years to help build a suitable baseball-only stadium so that they could move out of Candlestick Park, where the freezing summer winds off the bay made baseball night games all but impossible. Their frustration was palpable.

We pitched Buffalo, and then Bob had to leave for another appointment. We continued to chat with Corey. During lunch, Mindy did another one of her great out-of-the-box things. "Corey," she said, "why don't you move your team to Buffalo?"

"What?" he answered. "Why would we do that?"

"Well," she said, with both Corey and me looking at her like she was nuts, "we've got a great stadium, supportive politicians, and the best fans in the world. The Giants came from New York, so now they could come home to New York and play as the New York Giants in Buffalo."

"Wow," Corey said. "What a great idea. Let's talk about it," which we did during several more meetings over a few months. Unfortunately, it proved to be politically and logistically impossible. Bob Lurie even made a trip to Buffalo to check out our ballpark.

Another west coast meeting that I'll never forget was with Tom Werner, who had just purchased the San Diego Padres from Joan Kroc, the widow of Ray Kroc, the founder of McDonald's. Tom was an enormously successful television producer, whose credits included *Mork and Mindy*, *The Cosby Show*, *Taxi*, *Bosom Buddies*, *Soap*, *Roseanne*, and later, *3rd Rock from the Sun* and *That '70s Show*.

I was amazed at how young he was for all his successes and how excited he was about becoming a part of baseball, which was obviously a passion for him.

As we were finishing a nice lunch, he talked about his player and promotional plans for the Padres and how he had already signed up Roseanne Barr, the earthy star of his series, to sing a national anthem.

"Can she sing?" Mindy asked.

"I don't know," Tom said, "but I don't really think it matters. She's Roseanne Barr."

"Well," Mindy continued, "you'd better be careful. Baseball fans take their national anthem very seriously." Tom kind of sloughed the comment off as lunch ended.

A few months later, the nation heard a report of Roseanne Barr cater-wauling her way through something that vaguely resembled "The Star Spangled Banner" and being booed off the field, but not before responding to the hostile crowd by grabbing her crotch.

It was a performance that nearly ended Tom Werner's baseball career. He would go on to gain even more fame, though, as a producer and boyfriend of Katie Couric. After he sold the Padres, he became a co-owner with John Henry of the first Boston Red Sox team to win a World Series. To the best of my knowledge, they've yet to ask Roseanne to reprise her rendition of the national anthem in Fenway Park.

One of my favorite major league owners was Charles Bronfman, owner of the Montreal Expos. A member of the Bronfman family that owned Sea-gram, Charles was a quiet, understated gentleman with a passion for his family, baseball, and Israel. He almost seemed out of place with the other owners and took an independent course of action, developing players from within and not paying outrageous amounts for superstar free agents.

Along the way, Charles seemed to have become disenchanted with the economics of the game and the collective mentality of the other owners. We had heard of his unsuccessful attempts to sell the Expos to Canadian buyers who would keep the club in Montreal.

His vote was very important to Buffalo's chances, but I also felt we needed a backup plan. After pitching our city, I asked him if he would consider an offer to sell us the Expos. He didn't say no, so a week later I sent him a registered letter offering to buy the Montreal Expos for $90 million in cash. A few weeks later he called me and said, "Bob, I want to thank you for your offer, but I love this team and I love this town and I won't be known as the person who sold them to another city."

"Charles, if it's a matter of dollars, that was just our opening offer," I told him.

"Bob," he said, "I appreciate that. I have a lot of respect for you and your family. Your offer was more than fair and generous. I just cannot sell you this team."

Disappointed as I was, I will always respect Charles Bronfman as a true gentleman.

Second-to-last but not least, I'll never forget my three Bloody Mary luncheon in Cincinnati with Marge Schott, the outspoken owner of the Reds, who we'd known for a few years. In fact, at meetings Marge used to take Mindy by the arm and introduce her to the owners, who she facetiously referred to as "the great men of baseball." Mindy had a scheduling conflict, so it was just Marge and me at the Waterfront, one of those great restaurants overlooking the Ohio River. As we sat across from each other drinking our lunches, I smiled, thinking of Peter Ueberroth's story about owners meetings where he always made sure to get ahead of Marge in the lunch line, as it was her custom to let her Saint Bernard, Schottsy, eat off the buffet table.

Marge, a devout Catholic, was telling me about her beloved husband whom she'd worked with for years in the automobile business. Then she stopped, looked me in the eye, and asked, "Mindy *is* your first wife, isn't she, Bob?"

Trying to think fast and not lie, I thought of a line I'd heard Mindy use on occasion when asked what number wife of mine she was. I looked her back in the eye and said, "Believe me, Marge, Mindy is my *last* wife!"

"Good," she said, ordering another Bloody Mary. "I just love that Mindy."

"So do I, Marge, so do I."

I guess this section on owners wouldn't be complete without a mention of the most famous of them all. While twelve years older than me, George "The Boss" Steinbrenner also graduated from Williams College and had a lot of good friends in Buffalo from his days in Cleveland running American Ship Building. Buffalo, in fact, was always known as a Yankee town.

Steinbrenner was an enigma to me. Most days he was extremely friendly to us and very supportive, but other days he would fly into a rage—like after an expansion article appeared in New York with a quote from me. The writer had asked me, "Are you trying to be another Steinbrenner?" I responded that "there could only be one George Steinbrenner." I thought I was paying him a compliment, but he apparently didn't read it that way. He called me, went ballistic, and then hung up on me. A week later, he called to chat like nothing had happened.

Whether you liked him or hated him, I believe that he was part of the fabric of the game and that he is missed. I've also always believed that when the chips were down, he'd be there for us.

In Buffalo, things were moving along well. We'd added 1,400 new bleacher seats and a stand-up lounge of 5,000 square feet to accommodate our growing crowds. We opened our season and put up some more good numbers, and in May received some great news. The majors were planning to expand in '93 by adding two new teams to the National League so that both the National and American League would have fourteen teams, and, we, Buffalo—the dark horse—had made their list of ten possible cities. Commissioner Vincent also announced that at the owners meeting in Cleveland on June 14, they would announce more details, such as entry fee, down payment, new criteria, time table, and procedure.

I called our Bison folks together: Mindy, Mike Billoni, Jon Dandes, and Mike Buczkowski, to ask the question. "Should we go to Cleveland?" The answer was a resounding "of course," but only under an alias so as not to tip our hand to the other applicant cities.

So after a month of denying to everyone that we would be there, Mindy and I registered in the Cleveland host hotel, Stouffer's Tower City Plaza, as Mr. and Mrs. Roy Hobbs (Redford's character in *The Natural*). Corny, I know, but almost no one figured it out.

Our Bisons leadership team was there, and as we were having morning coffee in our suite to talk about the day, there was a loud knock on our door. We opened it to three muscular looking guys, two of whom flashed Secret Service badges. The third was head of Major League Baseball security. One of the Secret Service guys asked who was in charge, and my brave band of hearties, as one, pointed at me. "Yes sir," I said, introducing myself and wondering if you can get arrested for impersonating a movie character. "Is there something wrong?"

"Well," he said, "we're on duty and we heard that there are several busloads of people on their way here from Buffalo. Do you know anything about this?"

I looked over at Mike Billoni, who was avoiding my glance, and figured it out. Knowing the role of the Secret Service, I figured that out, too.

One of the new owners of the Texas Rangers club was a young chap by the name of George W. Bush, the son of the president, and as a member of his family, these must be members of George W's security force.

"Well sir, the only thing I can think of is that they're Bisons Boosters supporting our candidacy for expansion."

"Is that all?" the officer persisted.

"Yes, sir, I'm sure they're coming in peace, although most of them are probably Democrats."

The three didn't smile.

"In fact," I pushed my luck, "George W's dad is a pal of mine and was our first visitor to our new stadium with Congressman Jack Kemp on April 13, 1988, the day before it opened, and they received a warm welcome. Also, I don't think our fans even plan to enter the hotel."

Apparently they were satisfied, and as they started toward the door, P. T. Barnum Billoni offered them each a Buffalo Bisons T-shirt. They gratefully declined. I thought to myself, if you didn't love Michael, you'd have to kill him.

The owners were locked in all-morning meetings, but I'm sure they heard the arrival of the army from Buffalo at around 11:30 a.m. Five busses pulled up in front of the hotel with horns blasting and discharged Buffalo sports fans of all shapes, sizes, and ages, clad in Buffalo wares, hooting and hollering with all kinds of signs, banners, and noise makers. I was kind of embarrassed but very, very proud.

The noisy rally was going on outside when the owners broke at 12:30 p.m. Fay Vincent held a press conference to report on the new criteria, which were as follows:

Strong and Stable Local Ownership
Commitment to Baseball
Full Government Support
The Ideal Baseball Stadium
Record Sports Attendance
The Perfect Location
A Major TV Market

While he didn't say what the entry fee would be, he did say that they expected to reach a decision on which cities would receive a team no later than September 30, 1991.

As planned, we had a nearby room set up for our own press conference, which we called promptly after the commissioner's press conference and before the sports scribes had a chance to leave the hotel for lunch. I walked in to see the room full, with about sixty-five writers from around the country and a lot of cameras. My spirits had been bolstered walking down the hallway and hearing the familiar chant from outside, "Let's Go, Buffalo."

I knew that we'd pre-empted the other cities and felt like this was our coming out party, our chance to shine. Press from the other potential expansion cities would be there, I knew, but I didn't care. I had a message to bring.

I took a deep breath and jumped in, "Buffalo's here, and we're ready! Any questions?"

"Why are all those people from Buffalo outside?" one guy asked.

"To show their love of baseball," I said. "The others at home had to work today." I got a laugh.

"Why are you here?" another asked.

"Because the commissioner said he'd tell us the criteria, and I thought it'd be rude not to show up."

"Do you know that you're the only prospective owner here?"

"Maybe that's because Buffalo's the only city that's ready," I answered.

Then, as an afterthought, I reached into my coat pocket and pulled out a blank check and said, "I brought this check to make a down payment, but I guess we'll have to wait for another day. Thank you all for coming." I left the room, knowing the gauntlet had been thrown down.

I walked hand-in-hand with Mindy into the sea of Buffalonians in their Boost Buffalo, *Natural*, Bisons, Bills, and Sabres T-shirts, sweatshirts, and jackets. Jon Dandes, from Rich Entertainment, produced a bullhorn. I said simply, "Thank you all for being here. I'm proud of you all and proud to be a Buffalonian!" Then we shook all the hands we could before going back inside, knowing that none of our critics were taking us lightly anymore.

The resulting press was great. "No one comes close to Buffalo," said CBS's Greg Gumbel. "Buffalo would be a logical choice," said Hal Bodley.

Back in Buffalo, our skipper, Terry Collins, was having his second great year. We finished the season 85–61, in a tie with the Nashville Sounds atop the Eastern Division of the American Association. On September 4, we met them in Pilot Field for an epic one-game playoff that would become known as "The Game." We ended up losing to them in an eighteen-inning game that lasted five hours and eight minutes.

National press support for Buffalo was growing. *Courtesy of the Buffalo Bisons.*

Off the field, we drew 1,174,358 fans, topping major league teams in Atlanta, Houston, and Cleveland. We were too busy to be sad about our loss, let alone proud of our accomplishments. We had only weeks left to polish our presentation to the National League Expansion Committee, which was scheduled for September 16 in New York.

Several months earlier, we had amassed a great team of professionals to help do our research and put together the best possible presentation. We used the prestigious Atlanta law firm Arnall Golden, three divisions of Peat Marwick (Real Estate, High Wealth, and Sports), and New York public relations firm Hill and Knowlton, as well as Buffalo's Alden Schutte for advertising. Fearing the emphasis being placed on television, we later added MLB's own media consultants, Kagan and Associates.

Also, still not knowing what the expansion fee would be, I decided to line up a strong ownership group consisting of individuals well-connected to our community and with special qualifications that I knew would get the MLB's attention and approval. Some of our new group were from Buffalo: Seymour and Norty Knox, owners of the Buffalo Sabres; Jeremy Jacobs, chairman of Delaware North and owner of the Boston Bruins; and Bob Wilmers, chairman of M&T Bank. From New York I enlisted Robert Joncs, president of the city's largest minority real estate appraisal, consulting, and development firm; and Larry King, host of the nightly *Larry King Live*. I rounded our group out with Luis Gomez, an insurance executive who all but ran the Puerto Rican Baseball League.

I wanted to put together a strong, diverse group of qualified investors, and boy was I ever glad I did. One afternoon, I was watching a game in our suite when Mike Buczkowski, our talented assistant general manager, came in holding a piece of paper and looking ashen.

"What'cha got there, Bucz?" I asked him.

"Hot off the wire," he said. "Baseball just announced their expansion fee: $95 million."

No wonder he is looking pale, I thought, smiling. The fee didn't surprise me. I knew that they weren't going to be conservative, and I knew we had financial commitments that would cover the fee. What did anger me though showed up in the body of the release. They weren't going to let the expansion teams share in the first year television rights worth about $13 million per team. That certainly didn't seem like a fair way to treat new partners. It seemed to me, in fact, to be downright piggish.

At any rate, the meeting was set to be held at the offices of Major League Baseball's attorneys, Wilkie Farr & Gallagher, on the forty-ninth floor of CitiCorp Center in Manhattan.

Baseball was to be represented by six people, three of whom were owners of National League teams: committee chairman Doug Danforth of the Pittsburgh Pirates; Fred Wilpon of the New York Mets; and John McMullen of the Houston Astros. (John would one day join the list of seven Major League owners who would offer to sell us their team, but only if we wouldn't move it.) They were joined by Phyllis Collins, the legendary vice president of the league, and two lawyers, Louis Haynes, representing the National League, and Tom Ostertag, representing Commissioner Vincent.

The title for our presentation, taken from Robert Redford's movie, was "Buffalo: The Natural for Expansion," and it featured several charts, a fifty-page leave-behind, and a surprise video. The entire thing was supported by some carefully chosen presenters.

We arrived on time for our 4:00 p.m. meeting, which was to last for forty-five minutes. Mindy and I knew everyone in the room, as did our other presenters. After pleasantries, Governor Cuomo (a former Pirates farmhand) kicked it off with a wonderful endorsement, which was followed by an equally impressive testimony by my friend and our county executive, Dennis Gorski, who was pinch-hitting for Mayor Griffin who was on a long-scheduled trip to the "old sod" with his family.

Having repledged their support, they said their good-byes. I then unveiled a large chart titled "Buffalo NY—Check it out," listing MLB's very own criteria. I took out a red marker and checked off *Government Support*.

Next, we attacked our perceived weakness and introduced John Mansell from Kagan, who was well-known to the baseball folks. He did a fabulous job of positioning us as a strong "regional market" with a potential television market larger than our competitors. Backed by well-researched slides, it was easy to see that he'd made his point. After answering questions, he left and the six Major League attendees, laughing, agreed that I was entitled to check off *TV Market*.

That left Mindy and I to double team the last five criteria, checking four off one at a time.

Only one was left: *The Ideal Baseball Stadium*. We dimmed the lights and showed a short but highly impactful video on Pilot Field, narrated by our newest potential investor, Larry King, who we knew had gone to school with Fred Wilpon. The video finished, and I stood up and said, "Well?"

"Check off stadium," they all said in unison, and our well-researched, formal presentation ended precisely at 4:45 p.m. to applause from the Major League contingent. Unlike some of the other cities, we had ended on time.

I smiled at Mindy, who was beaming. I felt like the Russian pairs figure skaters who had just completed twin triple axels and were hoping for 10s from the judges and Olympic gold medals.

The mood relaxed in the room, and we all just started to chat. No more probing questions and answers, just baseball talk between baseball people. After another forty-five minutes, Doug Danforth called the session to a close, and we shook hands all around, receiving more nice comments from our hosts for the precision of our presentation. We met our gang downstairs and walked a few blocks back to our hotel, only to get swamped again by the local, Buffalo, and national press. It went on for an hour, although we tried to keep it short. Even though we felt our presentation spoke for itself, we wanted to be courteous. The only answers I remember giving were "I feel great," "No, I wouldn't change a thing," "Yes, we've been looking forward to this," "There were no surprises," and "It was fun talking to Baseball."

We took our front office out for a nice Italian dinner, and then Mindy and I flew home, arriving at around 12:30 a.m., absolutely exhausted. At the airport, we received word that all three network news affiliates had cameras outside our front door at home. Mindy and I were both worded out. We parked a block away, climbed over our back fence, snuck in the backdoor, left the lights out, and went to bed. There was nothing more to say.

I felt good falling asleep. I believed in my heart that if baseball had made a decision that day, we would have been in. I couldn't have known then that we had in fact peaked and that from there on in, time would not be on our side.

Baseball gives you no chance to rest on your laurels. Mike Billoni's call woke us up sometime in the early morning. Showing he still had a reporter's nose for the news, he'd been snooping around New York and had gotten some intelligence on two of the other presentations. "Denver's went very well," he said, "except for a major problem they have with finding committed local ownership."

"And you should hear about Miami," he said to me. "This guy Wayne Huizenga, the founder of Waste Management and Blockbuster Video, goes in all by himself with no notes and no presentation, sits down, pulls out his checkbook and says, 'Here I am, how much shall I make the check out for, and when do we start?' Can you believe it, chief, just like that? That's crazy, but it's one less city we have to worry about. Talk to you later; bye."

"The old checkbook gambit" left me feeling severely "one-upped." I *could* believe it, and I drew a totally different conclusion than Michael. Given the storm clouds beginning to gather for MLB, I felt that Wayne might be the very type of deep-pocketed owner they were looking for, one who didn't need to call a shareholders' meeting to make a fast decision. At the least, he had sent a message that there was at least one owner out there who was willing to pay cash for whatever expansion fee they set.

All of a sudden, I had a hollow feeling in my stomach that one city had been chosen, and that we were in competition with eight others for the remaining one franchise. Hopefully, I thought, Denver won't get their ownership act together.

In the aftermath of the collusion verdict against the owners, bad things were happening to Major League Baseball. The owners' spring training lockout had set the tone for the 1990 season, which was followed by an umpires' strike. The players' collective bargaining agreement was to run out in January, and talks between the owners and players were not going well. Then came the order from the commissioner's office to the twenty-six big league teams not to re-sign any of their working agreements with the one hundred and seventy minor league clubs.

Minor league owners were frantic, fearing that the Majors were going to dump them and go to their own internal player development.

As the December baseball meetings approached, this was a battle that Mindy and I wanted to avoid, fearing that our involvement could only hurt our relationship with the Majors and negatively affect our expansion hopes. It proved impossible to sit on the sidelines. We owned three minor league teams, and these were our friends.

Seeing some of the turns the MLB seemed to be taking, I wrote a letter to the people of Buffalo, which was published in the *Buffalo News*, for which I was much maligned. I pointed out some of the negative indicators that we were seeing in the sport. We were staying firmly in the hunt, but I did not want people to be upset if we got turned down. I knew that I'd be upset enough for all of us.

Ninth Inning (1991)

An early winter emergency meeting of the minor leagues was scheduled at the Loews Anatole in Dallas to address the problem; Mindy and I made our room reservations.

The first order of business was structure and governance. The minors had hired a college professor as a consultant who was laying out a complex plan for some kind of parliamentary structure. In spite of myself, I all but took over the meeting and argued for a more conventional corporate structure and form of governance that would more resemble publicly held companies and Major League Baseball itself. Our minor league colleagues agreed.

Now we had a structure that transcended our multitude of leagues. What we needed next was some kind of leverage. The minor league owners felt powerless, like little brothers who were being bullied by their big brothers. They had to find their voices and bulk up as well.

We had an idea. A recent unsuccessful candidate for president of the minor leagues was a lawyer named Stan Brand who, besides being a life-long baseball fan, was chief counsel to the House of Representatives.

Mindy and I met first with Stan and then with Stan and our new president, Mike Moore. Realizing that all of our teams were in someone's congressional district, we came up with a plan whereby every affected congressperson would contact the commissioner on behalf of the team or teams in his or her district.

The members of congress obliged, happy to help, and we turned what had looked like a mismatch into a positive discussion, which resulted in a new agreement between the majors and minors. The Major Leagues took a slight increase for providing players; the minors got the security that they wanted, and a family fight was avoided. Both sides learned that the minor leagues had political clout. Stan Brand was elected vice president of Minor League Baseball. As for Mindy and I, we were more than happy to see the issue resolved and to stay out of the limelight as well. To this day, I don't believe that our stridency had any negative impact with the Bigs.

The new player agreement that the owners ratified, on the other hand, had devastating financial impact on the owners. A writer from the *Buffalo News* pointed out that in 1990, there had been only one major leaguer with a contract of three million dollars, while in 1991 there were thirty-three! By anyone's calculations, the salary flood gates in baseball were open.

If Baseball was upset with us, we never heard about it. In fact, a few weeks later, we were notified that Buffalo had made the final short list and that we would be visited formally in a month by the National League expansion committee. The other finalists selected included three Florida cities, St. Petersburg, Miami, and Orlando, as well as Denver and Washington, DC. Based on what I'd heard in the aftermath of the New York meetings, I felt that Miami was a lock, and it was us against Denver for the second team.

While our staff worked to get our ballpark ready for the visitation and for Opening Day, Mindy and I put together an agenda for our visitors. We heard that some of the other cities were going to put on major chamber of commerce-type "dog and pony shows" for the National League, complete with helicopter tours of their regions; we had a very different plan.

We planned to pick them up in a large van and bring them to the park for a reception with our head elected officials and business leaders at our ballpark restaurant, Pettibones, which featured Buffalo specialty snacks like chicken wings and small beef on weck sandwiches. Then, a good tour of "the yard" would end up in our conference room for some straight talk with Mindy and me. Finally, we planned a press conference back in Pettibones before a ride back to the airport.

On the tour, we planned to reference our engineering plan that would allow us to build out our upper decking, taking our stadium's capacity to 45,000 seats. This was easy. Our architects, HOK, who had also built Camden Yard in Baltimore and Jacobs Field in Cleveland, already had the design. The real meat of the day was going to be the conversation in our boardroom.

We felt that we had made our case, and now the agenda was being formed by events in the news every day. Soaring salaries and declining TV revenues were shaping a new dialogue in the Major Leagues between large cities and small cities on how they were both going to peacefully co-exist.

We had retained our contract with the Peat Marwick sports division, and they were running an ongoing financial computer model for us. Every month, they would factor in the newest player signings and TV revenue forecasts to show not only the value of a franchise past, present, and future, but the projected economic condition of the Major Leagues as well. The model sounds complicated, but it's really wasn't.

February's report was bleak to say the least. It started by showing that in the wake of the payment of the collusion settlement of $10.8 million per team, players' signing increases were at 85 percent to date and climbing, with signings in '91 expected to be up by 50 percent over '90; in '93, the average would be well over $1 million per player.

On the revenue side, sports teams always seemed to enjoy increases in television revenue. This did not look to be the case in baseball this time around. CBS was already pressuring the MLB to restructure their contract and decrease their rights fees. The Peat Marwick study projected a marked decline in television revenue per team in spite of the large fees the Yankees had been able to negotiate for themselves.

The study concluded that only five major league teams lost money in

1990 and that, based on their forecasts, only five would make money in 1995. As you'd expect, those five would all be large market teams.

It was apparent that Baseball was going to turn into a battle between the "haves" and the "have nots." Preparing for previous visits had been about compiling information to answer questions about us; now it was time for us to do the asking. We hoped that our future business partners might be able to answer our questions and dispel and/or disprove the forecasts provided by our experts. On Monday, March 25, Chairman Doug Danforth led basically the same contingent to Buffalo as we'd met with in New York in the fall, with the addition of National League President Bill White and chairman of the Philadelphia Phillies Bill Giles, who was replacing John McMullen.

Bill White was a great guy and a friend. He had been a superstar in the majors, famous for hitting a homerun in his first at bat. He played first base for the Giants (in New York and San Francisco), the Cards, and the Phillies during his thirteen-year career. He was an eight-time All-Star and had won seven consecutive Golden Gloves before being enshrined in the Hall of Fame. He went on to an eighteen-year career in broadcasting, calling Yankees games with Phil Rizzuto before becoming president of the National League.

The tour went very well. They were all almost in awe of our beautiful ballpark. We had HOK representatives on hand who did a good job of explaining how we had overbuilt the infrastructure to accommodate the planned build-out. As a new member of the committee, I stayed close to Bill Giles, whom I already considered a friend.

Our people had paid attention to every detail, and I was delighted to see that they had even hung jerseys in the visitors' clubhouse of the three teams represented on the expansion committee: Pirates, Mets, and Phillies.

As we walked up the stairs to Pettibones Grille, Bill Giles whispered to me, "Your park is absolutely beautiful! You want to trade franchises?"

"Thanks, but no, Bill," I said. "I'm a Buffalo guy."

"Well, we all know that," he said, laughing.

In retrospect, I think Bill Giles was kidding. His love of the Phillies is legendary. I did believe, though, that he was greatly impressed with our beautiful new ballpark and our baseball program.

Our reception was pleasant but uneventful. Everyone loved the buffalo wings, of course. Then we went into our conference room meeting.

Mindy and I asked if they had any questions about our application or doubts about our readiness, then we handed out copies of our recent Peat Marwick study, certain that they would have answers for our concerns.

The room got real quiet real fast as we went through the study results and asked where we were wrong. After a long silence, one of the owners said authoritatively, "This just won't happen."

"Why not?" I asked.

"You just have to trust us," the same owner said.

Trust us? I thought to myself. As our guests poured through the study, I glanced over at Mindy, whose eyebrows went up as she took a quick look at the ceiling. I think that it was at that precise time that we knew the dream was over. Catching her glance, I made a small sign of the cross, which only she could see. Mindy responded with a sad smile.

We made a little small talk, thanked our guests for coming, and went next door for our press conference, which was a muted event at best. The visitors were complimentary and, I noticed, all clutching the report we'd given them. Doug Danforth talked about how great our presentation was but sounded a somewhat foreboding note when he said, "It would be great if you had another million people living here." Bill White showed some good humor. When asked by a reporter who came up with the $95 million expansion fee, he answered, "Jesse James" and got a huge laugh.

Before leaving, Doug Danforth said that his committee hoped to have a recommendation for the owners by their next meeting, June 10–12 in Santa Monica, California. And so ended the visit, and so began the wait.

Under Terry Collins, the Bisons got off to a great start, and our fans jammed the building to watch them win.

Then, on June 10 came the announcement that the hunt was over and we were out. The expansion committee recommended that the two new franchises be awarded to Miami and Denver. Doug Danforth stated how pleased he was that Baseball would be going into two new television markets, Florida with Miami and the Rocky Mountain time zone with Denver.

For Mindy and I, it was far from a surprise, but it was still a hugely disappointing end to the eight-year odyssey. I felt that the Major League's logic spoke for itself but still called a press conference for the next day.

I started by thanking everyone for their support and apologizing for our failure to prevail in the "expansion derby." I ended by pledging our continued support for Bisons Baseball. In the question and answer portion, I said that I felt we had been a victim of the changing economics of baseball, which I still believe today. Finally, I believe that Baseball had chosen two television markets over a great baseball town.

Mindy and I went home to dinner, and our eleven-year-old son Barney, who had literally been raised at the park and had accompanied us on a lot of our trips, asked why we were so quiet. "Just a little tired I guess, buddy," I told him. I think we were both dreading the onslaught of negative calls and mail that we were expecting to receive from our Bisons fans whom we knew we'd disappointed.

The next day, as expected, our mailboxes were full. I opened the first letter, which really set the tone for all the others that we received. It was from a mom in nearby Amherst who said, "I know how hard you worked for this and how disappointed you must be. But we're not. We love the Bisons just as they are. You have given us affordable family fun. The Majors were your dream, not ours. Thank you."

I took it into Mindy's office and found her reading a similar note from a guy in Cheektowaga. She had tears in her eyes. I took the letter back to my office and put it in my desk drawer. I still have it today. For me, it speaks volumes about the people in my hometown of Buffalo and why I love the city as I do.

Jerry Sullivan, a sports writer with whom I've not always agreed but have always respected, wrote in the *Buffalo News*, "If Bob and Mindy would only stop chasing the dream for a while, they might find they've already achieved it."

If the fans were disappointed, they sure didn't show it at the box office or the turnstiles. We set an all-time Triple-A attendance record of 1,240,951 that still stands today—and may forever. The Bisons went 81–62 on our way to winning the Eastern Division of the American Association.

Ironically we met our expansion nemesis, Denver, in the best-of-five finals. Terry's team jumped all over them, and we beat them twice at home and only needed to win one out of three games at Mile High Stadium. After our second win, our GM Mike Billoni grabbed a mic, went to the mound, thanked our fans, and told them "We have to go to Denver to finish some business, then we'll see you back here in a few days for the biggest celebration in the history of Buffalo sports!" It was a nice idea, the only problem was that apparently Michael didn't see the dejected bunch of players still sitting in the visitors' dugout with their heads down. Hearing Mike's party invitation, one of them threw his batting helmet against the wall and another trashed our water cooler with a bat. Our GM had apparently given them the ammunition to rally.

Usually our clubs fly commercial, but I called our travel agent and booked a charter flight for our team and invited our front office to make the flight as well as a thank you for their hard work. Mindy, Barney, and I rounded out the travel team.

We lost the first game, 8–3, but were pumped for game two. Maybe fearing the worst, their owner, John Dikeau, a real estate guy, skipped the game to go watch his beloved Colorado Buffaloes play their opening football game. *So much for "dedicated local ownership,"* I thought.

No one could call game two better than our well-loved, now-departed Buffalo baseball historian Joe Overfield in his book, *100 Seasons of Buffalo Baseball.* I'll let his words do the talking.

"In the next game they [the Bisons] were shutout for eight innings without a hit and went into the top of the ninth facing a 9–0 deficit. Suddenly coming to life, the Bisons scored six runs and had the bases loaded with two outs. Late season hitting star Greg Tubbs then lines a double to left. Runs seven and eight scored easily, and it seemed certain that speedy Greg Edge would score from first with the tying run. But a brilliant relay by the Zephyrs nipped him at the plate, at least in the opinion of umpire Scott Potter. The Bisons did not agree."

The last sentence is an understatement. What happened next was ugly. The team stormed the field, as did our general manager, who got in the umpire's face—for which he received a fine and suspension. It was a tough call that replays would later show was a bad call. Sitting in a suite with my family, I forgot myself and kicked a wastebasket. Watching his dad, the way my son always did, Barney punched the wall and broke his hand.

Riding with him to the hospital, I felt totally embarrassed for my act that he had copied. Holding him down on the operating table with Mindy while the surgeon reset the bone in his hand and casted him up to his elbow, I made a promise to myself that I would re-examine my priorities and that never again would any sport consume me or become the dominant pursuit in my life.

Back to the series: our ace, all-star, MVP pitcher Rick Reed, who'd gone 14–4 on the season, took the mound and had to retire in the first inning with a bad back. We lost the game 12–3, and the championship with it, and headed for the plane.

Back on board, I thanked Terry Collins and the team for a great season and apologized again to my son for the example I'd set that ended in his broken hand.

"That's OK, Dad," he said. "I still love you, and I've learned a lesson. Want to sign my cast?"

"Sure, son," I said. "Thanks; I've learned a lesson, too."

POSTSCRIPT

Everything we predicted for Baseball came true, but worse. Tim Muehler from Peat Marwick sports division, himself a huge baseball fan, called to ask me if I would mind if he kept the computer program going, as it was essentially ours.

I laughed and said, "No, Tim, I don't mind—with one condition. I want you to call me if and when the numbers show that an expansion franchise has a negative net worth."

He called me five years later.

BOOK 3
TALES OF THE SEA

ISLAMORADA

I clearly remember the first day I fished Islamorada and how I got there. The year was 1974, long before I met Mindy, and I was going through a rancorous divorce with my first wife in Buffalo. After two months of acrimony and attorneys, my soon-to-be ex and I agreed on a formal separation agreement and a division of worldly possessions. It appeared that we were then moving into an informal process of dividing friends.

I found the whole thing onerous and distasteful and was looking for new pursuits that would get me out of town. It was then that an old pal of mine, Robert Buck, who had moved from Buffalo to Orlando, called to see if I wanted to go fishing. "Now why in hell would I want to go fishing?" I asked Buck. I'd fished as a boy years before, but had moved into racquet sports.

"Well," Buck said, "I figured you might need a long weekend get-away. You could fly to Orlando, and we could drive down to Islamorada in the Florida Keys." I thought about it and figured, why not?

Robert Buck is one of the most creative and off-the-wall people I know. He moved to Orlando and cofounded a company called Presentations South, which designed and built museum displays and attractions for everyone from the Department of the Interior (the Parks Department) to Disney.

Buck is about ten years older than I am. He has graying blond hair and a receding hairline that keeps him from wearing his hair in a pony-tail. His scraggly goatee barely allows you to see the two dimples on his chin. His eyes sparkle as he tells you nonstop stories of his past and present. He is the best storyteller I know, can hold your attention for hours, and can make you laugh until your sides ache.

Buck had been recently divorced, and his dispute ended up in court. Buck tells the story of how his ex had brought in a dozen or so witnesses to take the stand and tell the judge what a lout he was. Buck became par-ticularly intrigued with the testimony against him by one ex-babysitter named Texann Ivy. To make a long story short, Buck lost his house, car, and furniture, but he kept his clothes and his company. He and Texann were eventually married, with me as his best man. We hosted their wedding reception at my summer home in Canada.

Buck met me at the Orlando airport dressed in his customary garb: tattered jeans, sandals, and a sleeveless black vest with an embroidered rebel flag on the back that was open in the front to expose his emerging potbelly. His ensemble was topped off with a dented English Homburg with an eagle feather sticking out of the band. In addition to being the world's greatest storyteller, Robert Buck is also the world's oldest living hippie.

The drive south was fascinating. I became totally distracted by Buck's tales of fishing, the Keys, and life in general. At our destination, Buck told me that the sign on the outskirts of town used to read, Islamadora, sport fishing capital of the world. "Actually," he said, "I've found Islamorada to be a quaint little drinking village with a fishing problem." Leave it to Buck to set the stage for an adventure.

Unbeknownst to me, Buck's passion was the outdoors, and he apparently reads every outdoor magazine he can find, concentrating on the fishing stories. He also orders every fishing catalog printed and had with him a suitcase full of brand-new fishing tackle that he promised to show me when we got to Cheeca Lodge in Islamorada, where we were staying. In truth, I couldn't have cared less about the tackle or the fishing. While I hadn't shared this with Buck, I was really going to the Keys for the sun and relaxation.

Our first stop in Islamorada was Papa Joe's, a great restaurant back then. PJ's had a well-deserved reputation for its excellent seafood bisque and dolphin or catch of the day served any way under the sun. Buck and I both ordered cups of bisque. For an entree, he ordered dolphin Veronique, a concoction made up of white wine, butter, and grapes that he said was delicious. I meanwhile gained his disfavor by ordering a thick New York sirloin strip steak. "We're in the Sport Fishing Capital of the World, and you order steak!" he lamented. It was then that I disclosed to him that I was there for a different sport than sport fishing, and I really didn't think the ladies I was looking for would care what I had had for dinner.

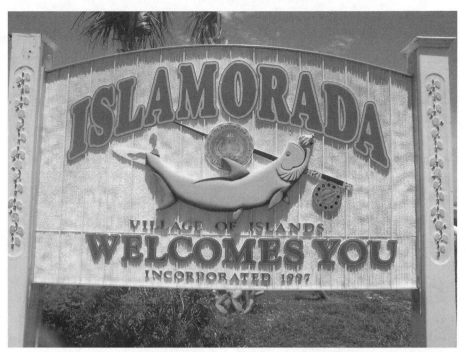

Islamorada: "A quaint little drinking village with a fishing problem." *Author's photo.*

Buck prepped me for fishing the next day. He said we would meet our guide after breakfast at the Islamorada Yacht Basin (now known as the Lorelei). Earlier that week, Buck had asked if I wanted him to hire a young guide or an old guide. Not knowing the difference, I had voted for a young guide. Buck had said that the young guides liked to go out at night, and the old guides got a little cranky. Little did I know then that we would end up with a cranky young guide who didn't like to go out at night.

At 6:30 the next morning, we sauntered into the Islamorada Yacht Basin for breakfast. I'm not big on breakfast, but my mood was such that I ordered the works: O. J., two fried eggs, bacon, hash browns, grits, toast, and all the coffee I could drink for $1.97 including tax (tip was extra). This was certainly a breakfast fit for some ketchup, which I asked the crusty old-timer sitting next to me to pass over. He did. I said "Thank you," and he grunted something inaudible. I looked up to realize that this old-timer was none other than the legendary Ted Williams, Hall of Fame slugger from the Boston Red Sox. I could barely speak, let alone eat my breakfast. Ted Williams had been my first sports hero growing up, and there I was having breakfast with him—kind of—in a greasy-spoon restaurant in the Florida Keys.

When the Kid got up to leave, I nudged Buck, who was wearing his brand-new, catalog-ordered, peach-colored, half-cotton, half-Dacron Orvis fly-fishing shirt with three-quarter-length sleeves, seventy-three pockets, and twelve loops, the purposes of which I'm sure Buck had no idea about. Frighteningly, I wondered that he actually might! Where, I wondered, was yesterday's hippie who'd picked me up in Orlando?

"Buck, do you know who that was?" I asked.

"Who who was?" he answered.

"That was Ted Williams. Don't you know who he is?"

"Sure I do," Buck said, surprising me. "He's an expert old angler who endorses aluminum bass-fishing boats in the Sears catalog. I think he lives around here."

"Wrong, Buck. That was Ted Williams, the Splendid Splinter, one of the greatest hitters in the history of baseball."

"You're both right," said the old Conch working over the griddle without turning her head. "Teddy Ball Game brought his magnificent eyesight and hand–eye coordination to the sport of fly-fishing, now lives here, and has established himself as a premier saltwater fly-fisherman."

Wow, I thought as we paid our check, *where'd that woman learn to talk like that*?

"See I told ya so," Buck quipped as we walked out the door.

"Shut up, Buck," I snapped, as I wondered what kind of day was I in for. (Years later, Ted Williams would pull up stakes and move to north Florida, never to be seen again in his beloved Keys. Some said it was because his eyesight was failing and he couldn't see fish the way he used to. Others claimed it was because he felt his Keys were being ruined by overpopulation. I think that it was for a combination of both.)

As we picked up sandwiches for ourselves and the guide, I wondered why we were the ones getting the lunches. Wasn't that the captain's job? Buck said it was a local tradition. Little did I know how much I was about to really learn about local traditions that day.

We walked out to the dock where our guide, Jim Brewer, was impatiently pacing next to what looked to be an eighteen-foot boat with an outboard engine. He was acting as if we were two hours late. Buck said hello and shook his hand. "Jim, this is Bob Rich," he said, introducing me.

"Hi, Rich," he said.

"It's Bob," I said.

"Yeah, right, Rich. Wipe your feet off and get in the boat." I wondered if it was too late to head to the beach. My greeting was mild compared to Buck's. You see, Buck came whistling down the dock looking like L. L. Bean's grandfather, resplendent in catalog clothes and carrying a new tackle box and an even newer fishing rod equipped with a shiny new reel. After growling at me, Brewer turned on Buck.

"What are you dressed up for?" he asked.

Buck said, "These are all the latest fishing fashions."

"What's that you're carrying?"

"That's my new Shimano rod and Fin-Nor reel," he said. "They're the latest in high technology for catching fish."

Brewer grabbed the rod, grumbled, "F——ing coffee grinder," and spit on the reel, ordering Buck to "get onboard."

I wondered what Jim Brewer had against Fin-Nor's "high technology," but Buck whispered to me, "He's got a deal with Shakespeare, a rival reel manufacturer." In spite of myself, I offered to cast off the lines. Brewer told me to "just sit down." What, I wondered, had Buck gotten us into? Maybe he had turned into a masochist in his advancing years.

As Jim Brewer motored out of the basin in his flats skiff, I guessed that he was about forty years old. He had an athletic build, a full head of dark brown hair, and green eyes. If this were a movie, his part would have definitely been played by James Garner.

What a grump! If this guy were for real, I'd have jumped ship. For some reason, though, he intrigued me. I'd noticed a twinkle in his eye that told me catching fish was important, but Jim Brewer suppressed any sense of humor he might have had. Maybe this would be fun after all; if not, I'd just kill Buck when we got back.

As I settled in for the twenty-minute ride into the backcountry, I realized what a beautiful and totally foreign environment we were entering.

Sitting three abreast on the bench seat of the tiny eighteen-foot vessel with the rising sun at our backs, skimming over the one-foot shallow water of Florida Bay, startling meandering fish and lazing seabirds, I was overcome by the beauty of this strange place. I was also aware that my mixed feelings—of sadness and bitterness for a lost love and a failed marriage—were dissolving in the wake of the speeding skiff. Maybe Buck had been perceptive in bringing me down here. Maybe we'd have a good day in spite of Captain Ahab.

Jim Brewer finally slowed the boat, tilted up the engine, put shrimp on our hooks, unhooked an eighteen-foot fiberglass pole from the side of the boat called the gunwale, went to the back of the boat, and started pushing us up onto a flat with the pole. He ordered Buck to the front end and told me to stand behind him to "throw back up," whatever that meant.

"What do we do, Captain?" I was hoping that by showing some respect, Brewer would stop giving me verbal abuse.

"We're looking for bonefish. Watch for tails, wakes, pushes, muds, or shadows."

"OK," I said, having no idea what he was talking about.

About fifteen minutes into our journey, Brewer whispered to Buck, "There he is at ten o'clock, moving left to right. See the small puffs? Now there's a tail. He's walking toward us."

"What is this strange tongue in which he communicates?" I wondered out loud.

Buck seemed to understand, and after what seemed like an eternity he said, "OK, I see him." Just about that time, believe it or not, I saw the critter too. He had a greenish tint and a rounded snout. He seemed to be moving, then putting his nose in the sand, then moving again.

"Throw, throw!" Brewer whispered.

Buck said, "Watch this, Rich. I'll show you how it's done." Great— now Buck was calling me Rich, too.

Buck threw about two feet behind the fish. "Nice shot," I said just as the fish took off like he'd seen a ghost.

"Yeah, nice f——ing shot," Brewer mocked as we watched the startled bonefish push a wake across the flat as he headed for open water. I had thought the object was to have the bait land as close as possible to the fish, but Brewer explained that "Close only counts in horseshoes, hand grenades, and slow dancing. You've got to get the bait in front of the fish."

"Your turn, Rich. Get up there."

"No, no, Captain Brewer," I demurred. "Please, Mr. Buck, show me how to do it again."

Buck stayed on the bow. Six minutes later, Jim saw another fish. Buck saw it two minutes after that. Buck threw. His shrimp hit the tailing bonefish right on the tail, sending him flying. Brewer strung together six of the foulest words I have ever heard, took a deep breath, and said, "Buck, they don't eat with their ass."

Buck hung his head and whined, "Your turn."

"Thanks a lot, Buck," I said, stepping up to the bow (which, in those days, I called "the pointy end") and hoping that every bonefish in the Florida Keys would go to Cuba, or anywhere away from our boat. But not ten minutes later, just as we slid up to a mangrove island, here came Mr. Bonefish. Brewer positioned the boat and whispered, "Throw, Rich, throw."

My heart was in my mouth and my hands were shaking, but I gave it the old college try. Unfortunately, my release was a tad early and my shrimp, hook, and line sailed off 180 degrees away from the target and snagged in the mangroves directly behind us.

"Great, just f——ing great," profaned Captain Brewer as my target headed for the hills. At that point I thought of an English proverb: "If you swear, you will catch no fish." I had the good sense to keep it to myself.

We left for another location with Brewer refusing to talk to us anymore. We set up and Buck went back to the bow. Once again, a bonefish quartered toward our boat. A cautious Buck threw approximately twenty feet in front of a fish that was only twenty feet away from the boat. (Think about it—that's not easy to do!)

"Leave it, leave it," said Brewer as the fish moved over toward Buck's shrimp. All of a sudden, he was on it. Buck lifted the rod tip as the line tightened and the fish peeled off a hundred yards of line in what seemed like a millisecond. Then suddenly there was a terrible *snap* as the line went limp, leaving Buck standing bewildered and all alone on the bow—but not for long. Captain Brewer jumped up to the bow, grabbed Buck's rod, and quickly inspected the Fin-Nor reel only to discover that the line had gotten caught in a protruding metal part. Without saying a word, Brewer threw the rod and reel approximately sixty feet across the muck and mire known as a bonefish flat. The startled Buck said nothing.

I managed to say, "Good distance, Captain Brewer," as our guide silently stuck his pole into the mud, tied our boat to the pole, and nonchalantly asked, "What did you bring me for lunch?"

The mood relaxed over turkey sandwiches. I complimented Buck on his selection of "high technology." Even Jim laughed, loosened up a bit, and told us some stories about a few bumbling anglers he had fished with. After lunch, Buck's pitiful groveling got the captain to pole over to where his new rod lay half buried in the silt so that Buck could retrieve it without getting his new Orvis cotton/Dacron slacks and Sperry topsider yachting slippers wet. If I'd have been in Brewer's sneakers, I'd have let Ensign Buck sludge through the silt or leave his new rod for the sharks.

"Rich!"

"I know. It's my turn again, right?"

"Right."

This time I didn't care. We'd had a nice lunch, a few laughs, and a couple of cold cans of Busch Bavarian. Our fortunes had turned. Besides, what else could go wrong?

Jim Brewer's instincts were good. In five minutes we were in fish— two of them, to be exact, a pair of big hungry bonefish rooting and snorting in the silt like a couple of bulldogs digging for bones.

We were about fifty feet away, upwind, when Jim said, "Throw now." My shrimp landed right between them and they both dove on it, fighting each other for the tasty morsel that had dropped on them from the heavens. The line came tight, I lifted the rod, and the fish felt pressure and blasted across the flat at incredible speed with Jim Brewer polling in hot pursuit.

Have you ever noticed how often an entire area seems to come alive when you have fish on, almost as if all the creatures in the vicinity are aware of the struggle and want a view of what's going on? That's exactly what happened on this day. It was as if nature had erupted. As I stood on the bow holding onto Captain Brewer's Shakespeare rod, I yelled to Buck and Brewer, "Look, there's a shark, and there's a ray! There's a pelican! And isn't that some kind of fish hawk?"

Apparently the lunch had worn off, as Brewer yelled from the back of the boat, "Goddamnit, Rich, this is no f——ing nature walk! Fight that fish!"

This is a phrase I'll always remember and have often used myself since then. I went on to catch and release that bonefish and two others, all in the eight- to nine-pound range, before the afternoon was over.

As we headed for home that afternoon, with Buck grumbling about what had led to the technical failure of his new reel, Jim Brewer leaned over and whispered to me, "Nice going today, Rich."

I knew then that I had met a special man and a special place, not to overlook a special friend who cared enough to bring it all together for me at a time in my life when I needed a hand.

I got to know Jim Brewer over the next seven months. When word flashed through the fishing community that he had been killed in an airplane crash, I was crushed. He and a friend, Bill Hagley, a novice pilot, had gone out in a small single-engine aircraft to spot tarpon when Bill apparently misjudged his speed and altitude, stalled, and crashed in Florida Bay. Both he and Jim died on impact.

Jim Brewer was a talented and dedicated professional who lived for his sport. How ironic it was that he should perish in the prime of his life doing what he did so well and loved to do best—look for fish. Tragically, he left a wife and three young children: two sons and a daughter. He also left many stories and a rich legacy of a strong-willed young man whose sport was his passion and his life.

Some of us believe that his spirit lives on in the haunting waters of the backcountry. One exasperating day about twelve years after Jim's death, my wife, Mindy, and I were tarpon fishing with one of Jim's protégés, Captain Gary Ellis. It was the kind of day where if we hadn't had bad luck, we wouldn't have had any luck at all. As the sun began to set, I hooked a tarpon that must have weighed 130 pounds. The fish seemed to be hooked solidly. He performed three great jumps in front of the setting sun, then turned, headed right for us, went directly under the boat, and broke us off. Gary yelled, "God damn you, Brewer!" And we knew exactly what he meant.

WHAT'S A GRAND SLAM?

During the '70s, I found solace in the waters of Islamorada in the Florida Keys. Little did I know then how important that place would become to me and how much I would learn there. For example, I learned that a bases-loaded home run in baseball is not the only type of grand slam in sports.

Perhaps my longest friendship in the Florida Keys has been with Captain Gary Ellis. I first fished with Gary in the spring of 1975. My pal Robert Buck and I had returned to Florida for a weekend of backcountry fishing. Our regular fishing guide, Jim Brewer, was booked for the weekend, so he set us up to fish with a young friend of his, a rookie guide named Gary Ellis.

If life were a movie, Gary's part would be played by Tab Hunter, whom many folks mistook him for when he (Gary, not Tab) was younger. If Gary were a cat, he would be about halfway through his nine lives, a few of which I'll tell you about. Born in Sioux City, Iowa, Gary had a few lives before he ended up in Chicago running a Playboy bunny training program. I cannot imagine what Hugh Hefner was thinking. Gary was a handsome young man with blond hair, brown eyes, and a stentorian voice that he had put to good use as an actor and a radio announcer. Putting him in charge of training Playboy bunnies is similar to putting the fox in charge of the henhouse.

The Keys called in 1973, and Gary soon found himself living in Islamorada guiding fishermen.

We met Gary the night before our fishing trip at the bar at Plantation Yacht Harbor, where he kept his skiff, *Mr. Bojangles*, next to Captain Al Flutie's boat. Like Buck, Gary turned out to be a great storyteller and we hit it off immediately.

Our first day fishing together would turn out to be memorable for more than the horrible weather that threatened to shorten our outing. As Gary, Buck, and I headed west out of Plantation Yacht Harbor in his eighteen-foot Mako at 6:30 on Saturday morning, we could see storm clouds behind us blocking the rays of the rising April sun. Gary steered the boat southward for twenty minutes until we reached the ruins of the old Flagler railway bridge pilings next to the new Overseas Highway Bridge that spanned Channel 2, south of Lower Matecumbe Key. Gary explained that we were looking for tarpon as he pulled out two large spinning rods with sixteen-pound test and attached round cork bobbers to our lines about four feet above the hooks, which he then baited with live pinfish. He told us to fling them out and then set our boat up for a drift toward the bridge on the falling tide.

My line hadn't been in the water for five minutes before my cork disappeared. Following Gary's earlier instructions, I reeled down, took up the slack, came tight, and struck the fish three times as hard as I could. The sea came alive as a large silver fish jumped completely out of the water four times and started swimming with the current under the bridge.

It was the first tarpon I had ever engaged. He was beautiful and incredibly strong. By the time we released him, twenty minutes later, we were almost half a mile offshore. Gary estimated that the fish weighed about seventy-five pounds.

Captain Gary Ellis went on to found the Redbone Tournament Series, which benefits the Cystic Fibrosis Association. *Author's photo.*

Gary drove the boat back to the old railroad bridge pilings, and Buck slung his pinfish out while I sat down to watch. As our drift carried us within fifteen or twenty feet of the pilings, Gary took the cork off the line on the Shakespeare rod I'd been using and put a small crab on the hook. "Here," he said, handing me the rod. "Throw this over by the pilings. Sometimes large permit hang out there."

I cast where Gary said and the line seemed to come tight the minute it hit the water. *Great*, I thought. "Gary, I think I'm snagged," I said. "I guess I threw it too close to the pilings." All of a sudden the line seemed to move about twelve feet to the right.

"Strike him!" Gary yelled.

I did, and the hooked fish on the other end took off, this time running in a straight line away from us, up current, with no jumps.

"Tarpon, Gary?"

"I don't think so," our young captain responded.

I held the rod up high while this fish peeled off about 150 yards of line. This time Gary lowered his Evinrude engine, kicked it in, and gave chase. The fight took twenty minutes before Gary pulled out his net and hauled in a beautiful oblong fish in the pompano family, which he identified for us as a permit—my first! Gary told me that unless I wanted the fish, he would like to take it for a barbecue he was having the next day for his client, Paul Newman. I had no problem with that, and I told him that was fine. In those days, catch and release was unheard of, and grilled permit was considered a delicacy. We've come a long way. Today Gary Ellis, like many other guides, does everything in his power to dissuade his anglers from killing any species of fish, let alone a permit.

To put this in perspective, we left the dock at 6:30 a.m. I had made two casts and caught my first tarpon and my first permit. A glance at Buck's watch told us that it was only 7:40 a.m.

Gary looked so excited that I thought he was going to jump out of the boat. As he started the motor, I whispered to Buck, "What's he so excited about?"

"We've got a great shot at a grand slam," Buck whispered back.

"That's nice," I said to Buck. "What's a grand slam?"

Gary overheard me and said, "If a boat catches a tarpon, a permit, and a bonefish in the same day, that's a grand slam. It's a rare feat, and you already have the two most difficult fish, and it's not even eight o'clock. We're going bonefishing!"

Sounded easy enough, but it wasn't going to be. As we headed under the Overseas Highway Bridge at Channel 5, we could feel a cold wind picking up. It was driven out of large dark storm clouds that seemed to be threatening to move inshore. Gary cut the engine, tilted it up, and started pushing us onto a flat while Buck and I rigged up two smaller spinning rods with shrimp.

We had some visibility for about an hour, during which time we saw nothing but a shark and a few rays. Then the rains came, gentle at first and then heavier, as the wind and rising tide turned the flats into mud bowls. We put on rain gear as the heavens opened.

It was approaching 10:00 a.m. and we couldn't see twenty feet ahead of us. I couldn't believe that we were standing out in the rain and Buck wasn't even whining. This grand slam thing must be something special. All of a sudden, a bolt of lightning lit up the sky, followed closely by a loud clap of thunder.

Gary said, "Maybe we better head in for a while and wait this out."

Clear thinking, I thought. I have never liked lightning, from boyhood camping trips to abbreviated golf games. I don't think you can be too paranoid about lightning. For the last several years, in fact, lightning storms have accounted for more deaths, injuries, and damage in Florida than in any other state. Lightning killed eight people in Florida in 1997, injured fifty-three others, and caused two and a half million dollars in damage. As a footnote, my guide pals tell me that you can tell how close lightning strikes by counting. Every second from the sight of the lightning to the sound of the thunder is equal to one mile. It may be so, but I wouldn't bet on it. I also think that lightning jumps around a lot. I'm not proud: lightning, like seasickness, sends me to safe harbor.

On this day, our safe harbor and closest port happily turned out to be the Tiki Bar at Holiday Isle. After stowing the skiff, Gary, Buck, and I headed for the friendly confines of the thatched-roof Tiki Bar where the jukebox was blasting out the Righteous Brothers hit single, "You've Lost that Loving Feeling."

We sat down at the bar, and Buck asked for a menu. The comely young barmaid said that they wouldn't be serving lunch for two hours, but that they did have a two-for-one special on margaritas.

"Sounds good to me," I said in my best W. C. Fields voice.

"I'm in," replied Buck.

Gary just scowled. He must have really wanted that grand slam thing. But in spite of the torrential rain outside, the weather was great in the Tiki Bar. Buck and I made an executive decision that if Gary wasn't going to drink his two-for-one margaritas, then Buck and I would do it for him. By then the luncheon trade was filtering in. We had the makings of a party in spite of our forlorn guide friend glumly staring out into the sheets of rain pelting the flats.

At 1:30 p.m., the rain stopped. Gary jumped off his bar stool and said, "Let's go!"

I said, "Go where?" I was starting to think *nap*, but I said, "OK," not wanting to see this grown man cry if we jumped ship. Buck and I gingerly made our way to Gary's boat.

By the time we got there, we could see another round of storm clouds moving in on us from offshore. Gary drove right to a spot he must have been thinking about at the Tiki Bar. It was a shallow white-sand spit in the middle of an ocean-side turtle-grass flat. We poled up on the edge, where Gary broke up a handful of shrimp and threw them into the water. We waited, hoping the scent would attract our quarry.

After half an hour, it turned very dark and the wind came up again, complete with the morning's familiar sound effects. Gary noted that the tide was falling fast, and estimated that we had about fifteen minutes left before we would have to vacate the flat, which could "go dry."

It was a tough break for Gary: stuck on the boat with two bozos like us and weathered out of a chance for a grand slam. All of a sudden, as if in a dream, the sun broke through the gray if only for a minute. Simultaneously the three of us spotted a single small bonefish heading across the small patch of white sand, apparently attracted by Gary's thrown shrimp.

"Your turn, Buck," I said.

"No, you go ahead."

"Make it good," Gary added. "You're only going to get one shot, and it will probably be our last of the day."

The fish was thirty feet away and coming right at us. I aimed and let it go as thunder crackled in the background. New raindrops dimpled the flat and obstructed our vision. My shrimp landed two feet away, directly in front of the fish. We held our breath. He didn't spook. As another bolt of lightning struck, I watched our bonefish stroll forward and take a long look. "Bump it," Gary said. I did, and, and, boom, he snapped it up. The rain was coming down in sheets as the bonefish ripped off line and headed for deeper water. Seven minutes and two runs later, we had a catch, a release, and a grand slam thanks to a cooperative bonefish that Gary estimated, by the way, to be around seven pounds.

After congratulations all around, and now hardly noticing the rain, we took off for Plantation Yacht Harbor with Gary calling the story in on his radio to the local newspaper while Buck and I sang a special commemorative version of "Mr. Bojangles."

When we arrived at the dock, the rain had subsided. We were greeted by the dockmaster, two other guides, two waitresses, and a leggy young photographer dispatched by the newspaper to get the heroes' picture. As she was setting up to take the picture, Buck ran to his car, opened the trunk, and brought out his infamous Shimano rod and Fin-Nor reel that he had been afraid to bring on the boat. He asked Gary to get the permit out of our ice chest and pose with me, the fish, and Buck's high-tech Shimano rod and Fin-Nor reel, as if these had been our weapons that day. Then he extracted Gary's promise that he would personally deliver a copy of the picture and the article to Jim Brewer. Gary would later report that he made the delivery, that Brewer wasn't fooled, and that his response was unprintable.

During our photo shoot, Linda, the photographer, expressed so much interest in what it felt like for me to complete the Florida Keys triple that I invited her out for dinner. Over the years I've embellished the story by saying that after a good dinner with Linda I was able to turn my triple into an unprecedented Keys quadruple. No such luck. Linda was a no-show at the Green Turtle, leaving me alone with my memories, all the while listening to Buck complaining that his turtle chowder was cold.

PASTIME TO PASSION

It was now 1985. Many years had gone by since the Florida Keys had first made a great long-weekend getaway for a recycled bachelor. I had basically stopped going there during the eighties, as I was extremely busy tending to business, playing polo on the weekends, running a growing professional baseball operation, and, of course, courting and marrying Mindy.

Having been either regaled with, or bored by, my stories of Islamorada, Mindy asked me if I would take her there to see the place. I kind of said yes, hoping that any "ghosts of my past visits" would no longer be around.

We planned our weekend trip and arrived there on a beautiful, warm, and cloudless afternoon in April. After checking into the Cheeca Lodge, we went fishing with Captain Gary Ellis, whom I hadn't seen in about five years. On our boat ride out, it was easy to see that Mindy was as smitten by the beauty of the place as I had been a decade earlier.

While she was an ardent sailor, fishing was not on her list of accomplishments on the water. All that would change on our first stop when she surprised and delighted all of us by catching a large thirty-pound permit, one of the most sought-after and least-caught game fish in the Florida Keys. You could see on her face that she was totally hooked on the new pastime.

Fishing is, by the way, absolutely gender neutral. It affords women the opportunity, if they wish, to compete with men on a totally equal footing. It was something that Mindy and I could enjoy doing together. At that time it was still a pastime for us, not yet a staple sport as it would later become.

We began looking for occasions that we could sneak away to the Keys for some time on the water. For example, when we were still in the Major League hunt and looking for a spring training site for an expansion team, we finished up with a trip to Islamorada to chase "silver," as big tarpon are known. To this day, I don't know how Mindy could land these fish, as she did, since some of them actually outweighed her.

Islamorada was no longer a refuge for a disenfranchised single but rather a favorite destination for a couple in love.

I remember one day in the Keys; it was after we were married and were up to our eyebrows in the Major League hunt. Mindy and I were watching a sunset over Florida Bay. "Have you ever thought what we'll do if we don't get a major league team?" I asked her.

"What do you mean?" she asked.

"Well," I said, "we've worked so hard and gotten so many people excited about it, people would be so disappointed and even angry. What would we do?"

She thought for awhile and then said, "We'll find an island—our perfect island." Little did we know then that we were standing on it.

Something else changed for us in Islamorada. Gary Ellis invited us to fish in a tournament he was running, the proceeds of which would help fund the search for a cure for cystic fibrosis.

"We just fish for fun," I told him. "I don't think we're ready for any tournaments."

"Nonsense," he said. "You'll do fine and you'll have fun and it's for

Captain Rusty, Mindy, and me. *Author's photo.*

a good cause. Get yourself a backcountry guide for two days. You're entered."

"What do you think, Mindy?" I asked.

"Sure, why not. What's the worst thing that could happen?"

Rusty Albury. Oh, no, Rusty Albury was not the worst thing that could happen; that's just the name of the guide I called to fish with us in the tournament. We'd fun-fished with him before and knew that he was good at finding fish.

The first day of the tournament arrived and we literally stepped off a plane and on to Rusty's boat. After a high–speed, forty-minute ride through Florida Bay, Rusty poled us into a school of tailing redfish. We started casting and man, were we awful, bouncing plugs off their tails, spooking fish, pulling hooks—awful.

We were just happy to be out there and even laughed at our own ineptitude. Rusty was not amused.

"Hey, c'mon," he said. "This is a tournament; you can do better than that."

Seeing how much it seemed to mean to him, we tried to get serious. Believe it or not, we caught seven reds and two snook. The next day we caught several fish as well. We went to the tournament "banquet" that night with our grumpy guide and his pretty bride, Therese, feeling pretty good about ourselves in spite of overhearing Rusty telling all his friends about how badly we'd fished.

As we watched Gary handing out "the hardware" to the winners, Rusty told us, "You could have won this, you know, if you'd only slowed down and taken some time to practice." Mindy and I both laughed.

Back in our hotel room, I asked Mindy, "Do you think we could have won?"

"Sure," she said. "Rusty said so, didn't he?"

The inevitable happened; we were passed over by the Lords of Baseball. Happily, the groundswell of disappointment around our failure to get to the big leagues never materialized, nor were we run out of town as I'd feared. Our team went on to draw over a million people for three more years as Bisons fans voted with their feet for affordable family fun. In the meantime, Mindy and I put our personal disappointment aside and converted our pastime of fishing into sport fishing, competing in a lot of tournaments.

Islamorada became "our perfect island." Known as "The Sport Fishing Capital of the World," its front yard, the Atlantic Ocean, offers prime fishing for sailfish, tuna, dorado, and wahoo. Its backyard, Florida Bay, is home to redfish, snook, bonefish, tarpon, and permit. In short, Islamorada has it all as far as saltwater fishing goes, and it is also well located near fishy waters like the Bahamas and the Gulf of Mexico.

I, of course, had to turn fishing into a game, a sport, a competition. Mindy not only went along goodheartedly but also has become an accomplished tournament angler. I hate to disclose that she has beaten me on too many occasions to count.

And Rusty? Well, he's now more than just a member of the team but more a member of the family. We fish together, in shallow water and in deep, and I call him my Minister of Fisheries—among other things.

Fishing has become our passion, and it has proven categorically that for every door that closes, another one opens.

THE 151st PSALM

My favorite fishing day for bonefish started out as an offshore search for a big marlin. Here's how it happened. I had for a long time wanted to catch a big blue marlin and had conferred with friends about where to go for a two-day weekend trip. The consensus was that Bimini's Big Game Club in the Bahamas was the place to go, and Captain Bob Smith was the man to call. I didn't know much about Bimini other than that it was close to the east coast of Florida and that Ernest Hemingway used to base out of there to pen some of his stories and search for big fish. I called Captain Smith and set up a weekend date in June.

The awaited day came, and I flew to Bimini from Fort Lauderdale. The whole flight took about eighteen minutes. Then, a land taxi and a water taxi put me, an hour later, at the dock of my hotel, the Big Game Club, to meet Captain Smith.

Offshore fishing in Bimini was, in a word, awful: a few barracuda in two days, nothing more. Captain Bob Smith turned out to be a treasure, though, a remarkably spry seventy-five-year-old who'd been fishing those waters for more than sixty-one years.

With few fish around we had a lot of time to chat and get to know each other. Bob had met his wife, Bonny, when she was working at her parents' hotel in Miami. The Saint John's Hotel thrived in the old pre-integration South by catering to black Americans who were not allowed to stay in "white-only" hotels. Some of the Saint John's famous clientele included baseball stars Jackie Robinson, Don Newcomb, and Roy Campanella and entertainment greats, including rocker Fats Domino and jazzman Louis Jordan.

Bob and Bonny had raised three daughters, all of whom are married and living and working in Florida. The elder Smiths had been married for thirty-eight years, during which time Bob had named two boats after his wife. Bob Smith's first fishing job, when he was fourteen, was catching bait for captains. He told me that he used to bring bait to Hemingway's captain on the *Pilar*, where his job was to keep Papa's fighting chair constantly turned toward a hooked fish. Hemingway later told Bob that he had been his inspiration for the young boy in his famous novel *Old Man and the Sea*.

Of course, I had to ask him what he remembered about the man. Bob said that Hemingway was well-liked in Bimini. In those early days, before he was widely published, Hemingway was remembered as a two-fisted drinker who loved to carouse and brawl and generally burn the candle at both ends. Bob said that he had a passion for arm wrestling with competitors like Bimini's own William Bryant—who, boxing under the name Yama Bahama, once beat the boxing champion from Cuba, Kid Gavilan, who was known for his patented "bolo punch."

Captain Smith said that these arm-wrestling matches would often erupt into drunken brawls with both men throwing roundhouse punches at each other. Then, as quickly as the fights began, the two combatants would be hugging each other, drinking, and singing with their arms around each other's shoulders like nothing had ever happened.

Captain Smith had caught a lot of fish in his life. Perhaps the highlight of his career came when he was inducted into the IGFA Hall of Fame, an honor brought to him in person by the Bahamian ambassador himself.

I asked him how long he planned to fish, and he said until he could no longer climb the six-step ladder to his seat on the bridge. Watching him scurry around the boat, I didn't think that would happen for a long time.

During the morning of the second and last day of my trip, I shared with Captain Smith that my passion was saltwater fly-fishing. He surprised me by calling ashore and lining up his brother-in-law, Ansil Saunders, to take me bonefishing that afternoon. In fact, when we got in, Ansil was waiting on the dock with the beautiful fourteen-foot wooden skiff that he had made himself. Happily, I had brought along my Loomis 8-weight fly rod and Islander reel, and we were in business.

As he cranked up his 40-horse engine, sixty-two-year-old Ansil told me that they had some big bonefish in Bimini. In fact, as the black-embroidered words on the pocket of his white captain's shirt proclaim, Ansil Saunders is a world record holder. In 1971, he guided an American named Jerry Lavenstein to a sixteen-pound, three-ounce bonefish, which he caught on twelve-pound spinning tackle for a world record that still stands.

I climbed down into Ansil's skiff, and we headed for the flats. About five minutes into the ride, we pulled up to a giant sixty-foot mud. As I finished rigging up, Ansil told me to throw into the head of the mud about fifty feet away. I really wasn't interested in catching one of the "schoolie bonefish" that I assumed were making this mud, but I knew what Ansil was trying to prove and decided to humor him. I made one false cast and threw my green Clouser Minnow fly fifty feet to the far front edge of the mud, stripped the line twice, got a hookup, and held the rod up high. As a three-pound schoolie pulled some line, I turned to Ansil and said, "OK, Captain Saunders, now that I know that you can find fish, and you know that I can catch fish, can we please go find a few grown-up bones?"

Ansil Saunders laughed and said, "OK, it's just that I see a lot of people with fly rods these days, and I like to know what I'm up against."

We both laughed. As we continued our journey, Ansil told me that he was waiting for the tide to rise and allow us to get onto his favorite big flat, appropriately named Big Flat. Ansil said that we had a few minutes and asked if I would mind catching him a few dinner fish. I smiled and said sure, guessing that if I hadn't known how to cast, those few minutes would have been used for a fly-casting lesson. I stowed my Loomis, and Ansil pulled out an old spinning rod rigged with a green tube lure. All of a sudden, I knew what he had in mind for dinner, as I'd played this game often in another Bahamian fishing spot—Deep Water Cay.

It didn't take long. My first cast produced ten pounds of angry and toothy barracuda. It took about ten throws to catch two smaller fish for the captain's neighbors. On the way to Big Flat, Ansil started calling me "Cuda Bob." I think he liked me.

A twisting waterway full of snappers took us half a mile to a huge lagoon where the water was about six inches deep and the tide was just beginning to rise. Everywhere you looked, were schools of bonefish on the move, with fish tailing in twos and threes.

I climbed out of the boat and started tracking a school of fish quartering at me from the west. "Cuda Bob," Ansil said in a loud whisper, "you walk like a large elephant!"

Now where in hell had this Bahamian seen a large walking elephant? Anyway, I changed to my dainty gait, caught the lead fish in the school, then six others in the five-pound range over the next hour before the fish followed the rising tide off the flat. Fishing doesn't always have to be a twelve-hour, sunrise-to-sunset proposition. The bite often goes off in fits and starts and a few hours can provide thrills and/or memories of a lifetime.

Ansil and I were giggling like schoolboys. It's fun to see the way even experienced older guides delight in watching their parties, or in this case new pals, catch fish.

As we packed it in, Ansil told me about some of the people he had taken out in his little boat, including Martin Luther King Jr. twice—the second time three weeks before the father of desegregation was murdered in Memphis.

Doctor King wrote the acceptance speech for his Nobel Peace Prize while sitting in a lawn chair on the bow of Ansil Saunders's skiff on the first day they went out together. He told Ansil that he was "totally consumed by the beauty and life of this place."

As we headed for home, I asked Ansil what he had talked about with the famous Doctor King. Ansil said, "I shared with him the 151st psalm."

"But, Ansil," I said, "there are only 150 psalms."

"I know that, Cuda Bob. The 151st psalm is the one I wrote."

"Boy, I'd really love to hear that, Ansil," I said.

"I'll do it for you right now," he replied, taking a right turn and idling his little homemade skiff out of the setting sun and into the shade of a nearby mangrove island.

He had me sit on the bow, holding the boat against the mangroves, as he stood up, cleared his throat, and started reciting his 151st psalm from memory. It was really quite moving, talking of creation and bearing witness to the unassailable evidence of the existence of the Lord from this outdoorsman's everyday experiences.

As the first verse drew to a close, some of the Lord's creations, the no-see-ums, discovered us and attacked from everywhere.

Captain Ansil Saunders shares his 151st Psalm. *Author's photo.*

"That's beautiful," I said, as the pesky gnats bit every exposed inch of my body. "Thank you, Ansil."

"There's more," Ansil said, seemingly oblivious to the insects, which now seemed to be growing in size as well as number.

As Ansil's psalm celebrated land and sea, sunrise and sunset, fish and fowl, I wondered if I would ever see the Big Game Club again or if I would be devoured by Bahamian no-see-ums half a mile from Bimini.

Ansil's articulate and heartfelt testimony finally ended. It was truly beautiful, and I told him so. I gave him a friendly congratulatory handshake and we headed for home. The 151st Psalm was the perfect way to end the day.

Flying back to the mainland, I felt that I had been strangely linked to Hemingway's Bimini. I'd been honored to meet and fish with two Bahamian legends. I thought a lot about Captain Bob Smith and Captain Ansil Saunders and wondered who would succeed them and keep the ancient spirit of Bimini alive.

MATANILLA REEF

Because I fish a lot and am often on the ocean, I am frequently asked the same four questions:

What's the biggest fish you've caught?

What's your longest fish fight?

What's your favorite fish to catch?

What's the most dangerous thing that's ever happened to you while fishing?

The first two questions call for quantitative answers and are, therefore, easily dealt with.

My largest fish was a 750-pound blue marlin off the coast of Africa.

My longest fight was five hours and fifteen minutes against a monstrously large Pacific sailfish (185+ pounds) near Crocodile Bay, Costa Rica, using 20-pound tippet on a fly rod.

The answer to the third question sounds facetious, although it's not meant to be.

My favorite fish to catch is the next one.

As far as question number four, that's a little more difficult. I've gone through some pretty hairy things. Sliding down the face of a twelve-foot wave in my forty-foot sportfishing boat in a sailfish tournament in Key West, filling the cockpit with green water over the transom, was right up there. Driving sixty miles an hour flat-out, at midnight with no moon, through the unmarked channels of Chokoloskee, Florida, with a slightly demented skiff captain was also pretty sobering. Being stranded overnight on a spit of an island in the Florida Keys called Carl Ross Key by a surprise lightning storm that would later be called the "Storm of the Century" was not my idea of fun, either. Stepping off the bow of a skiff while fighting a 125-pound tarpon being chased by bull sharks at a place called Ox Foot near Marathon, Florida, still brings nightmares. I guess I could go on and on, but suffice it to say that none of these finalists make the cut.

The most dangerous thing that ever happened to me while fishing was at Matanilla Reef.

> *There are things about the sea*
> *which man can never know and*
> *can never change. Those who describe*
> *the sea as "angry" or "gentle" or*
> *"ferocious" do not know the sea.*
> *The sea just doesn't know you're there—*
> *you take it as you find it, or it takes you.*[3]
> —R. M. Snyder, oceanographer

Let me tell you a story about Matanilla Reef.

I've been fortunate over my fishing career to form some wonderful friendships with fishermen I will never forget, men of the sea who are not only stoical seafarers but are interesting characters as well.

I had the opportunity to share an adventure with two of them as the twentieth century prepared for the onset of the year 2000, the dreaded Y2K.

Rusty Albury, a fishin' buddy of mine from the Florida Keys, and I decided to go marlin fishing in the Bahamas with another pal of mine, Pete Rose—not the Baseball Hall of Fame wannabe, but a white Bahamian commercial fisherman.

Rusty and I had known each other for over twenty years. Some fourteen years younger than me, Rusty is a sixth-generation resident of the Keys known as a Conch (pronounced konk). His ancestors were Loyalists who had moved from America's mainland to the Bahamas Cays and the Florida Keys to avoid fighting the British during the Revolutionary War. Like his forebears, Rusty is very insular and laconic, with little interest in what is going on outside his own world—the world of fishing.

Like many of his peers, Rusty was seduced in the late seventies by the chance to supplement his guiding income with a little smuggling, for which he later paid his dues. Now he has built his reputation as one of the finest backcountry and offshore fishing captains in the country.

Admittedly sparse on conversation, Rusty comes alive when the subject turns to anything about fish. In fact, I started laughing one day when we were fishing together on his skiff in Florida Bay at about two in the afternoon.

"What's so funny?" he asked.

"Rusty, you know, we've been fishing together for almost six hours and haven't spoken to each other yet," I said.

"Yeah, right," he said. "Good afternoon, Bubba."

"Good afternoon to you, Rusty," I said, and we went back to fishing together in silence. Believe it or not, peaceful contemplation is one of the things that draws me to fishing the most.

Marlin is a species I love to pursue. Unfortunately, they are not very plentiful anymore near Islamorada, Florida, where I live in the Keys, so I had set up a weekend marlin hunt with another friend in the Bahamas and had asked Rusty if he wanted to join me. We only had a few days to fish with Pete Rose, and I was sure it would be fun. Rusty said sure, so off we went on Saturday morning.

On the way over, I told Rusty a little bit about Pete. Like Rusty, his ancestors had come over from England to the "new world" and landed in the Bahamas. Actually, his dad, a horticulturalist, had moved his wife, six sons, and two daughters to the islands and taken up residency when Pete was only one year old. Growing up in Freeport, the ocean had been a big part of the boys' education, with fishing, diving, and conching as their daily pursuits.

Approximately the same age as me, Pete shared with Rusty the same outdoor fitness characteristic of men who had literally spent their lives toiling on the ocean. I don't think either of them carry an ounce of fat on their bodies. Their weathered, suntanned faces look like they've been cut out of the same piece of brown leather.

Pete fishes commercially for specific species that migrate through his home waters. He targets wahoo, allison tuna, and dorado and dives for conch when the fishing is slow. He sells all of his catch to local customers. Unlike Rusty, Pete doesn't take charters and always fishes on his boat by himself. He originally took me out wahoo fishing as a favor.

Pete Rose, center, the best wahoo fisherman Rusty and I know.
Author's photo.

Unlike Rusty, I found Pete Rose to be an interesting conversation-alist. Maybe it was our proximity in age that led to some in-depth con-versations on our lives, our dreams, and our plans. It even turned out that we had both grown up playing squash and shared a love of the game. We fish together a few times a year in fishing tournaments and always talk about our "ultimate squash challenge match of the century," a match that I think both of us know will never happen.

After a failed first marriage and rancorous divorce, Pete was remar-ried in 1974 to an attractive, dark-haired, London-born lady named Linda. She picked us up at the Freeport airport and drove us to meet up with Pete, who was waiting on his dock, his boat all gassed up so we wouldn't lose any time on our two-day fishing adventure.

We got to the dock at 9:00 a.m., I made the introductions, and we jumped on board, thanking Linda in advance for taking our overnight bags to the Port Lucaya Resort Hotel where we were staying. We said good-bye after agreeing to meet up later for dinner.

Pete told us that he fishes about 280 days a year on his Cummins diesel-powered, twenty-eight-foot Sea Vee. His boat, *Goombay Hooker,* is spartan to say the least, equipped with a compass, a GPS, and a depth finder. If he had a radio or phone on the boat, I had neither seen them nor heard him use them.

Rusty takes boating equipment, safety gear, and navigational aides very seriously, and I didn't really want to spook him before the trip. I'd also noticed that after a life spent on boats by himself, Pete respects the ocean and seems to commit himself to her every time he goes out. I won't go so far as to say that he has a death wish, but I would say that he seems very much at peace with the hard and dangerous life he has chosen.

As we left the dock, the wind seemed to be blowing a steady twenty out of the north, explaining our rather bumpy crosswind landing a half hour earlier. Pete said that these conditions meant that our best shot at marlin would be to the east.

The seas were calm in the lee of the island and we were comfortable all day, though we caught no fish. I really enjoyed being out there anyway, but to say that my two companions were short on patience would be a massive understatement. They were both proud fishing professionals, and I think they wanted to show each other what they could do.

That night, Rusty and I went out to dinner with Linda and Pete. Pete told us that he wanted to get an early start the next day. He was planning a two-and-a-half-hour run to the west that would put us in an area where he'd been seeing a lot of big blues. He said that we would pass Matanilla Reef, turn right, and troll toward Walker's Kay.

We said goodnight to the Roses, and Rusty suggested a nightcap. I, of course, went along only to keep him company. As the conch ordered his third brandy, I suggested we ought to hang it up and get some sleep since Pete would be picking us up at the marina dock at 6:00 a.m.

"Look at the wind blowing those palm trees," Rusty said. "No way in hell we'll be fishing offshore tomorrow!"

"I don't know, Rusty," I warned him. "I've fished a lot with Pete, and I've never seen him weathered out."

We walked back to the hotel and went to bed. At 5:30 a.m., the wind whistling in the halyards of the sailboats at the marina dock woke me from a deep sleep. I threw on my clothes, found some coffee at the office behind the checkout desk, and walked out to the dock just in time to see *Goomby Hooker* idling into the harbor. Rusty was nowhere to be seen. I called his room and, obviously, woke him up.

"What?" he answered, less than cheerful.

"Pete's here, and we're waiting for you," I said.

"You've got to be kidding," Rusty replied.

"I told you about Pete, pal," I laughed as the phone went dead.

"Where's Rusty?" Pete asked as he pulled up to the dock and threw me a line.

"He's on the way down," I said. "We went out last night, and I'm afraid he got over served."

We waited fifteen minutes for Rusty to finally show up. He was bundled in foul-weather gear and looked like he was still asleep.

"Morning, Rusty," I chirped in the most obnoxiously upbeat, cheerful voice I could muster.

Silence was the response as Rusty climbed aboard and looked for a spot to stand in the middle of the boat.

We motored out of the harbor under a full moon with the wind blowing out of the northeast at a steady twenty-five miles per hour. I noticed that we were the only boat up and about.

We were soon offshore and heading due west. We passed the famous Bahamian landmarks Sandy Cay, and, eventually, Memory Rock, the sun rising at our backs. The waves were well-defined and running about five feet. Pete's Sea Vee slid over them with ease, and, for the most part, we stayed dry. Pelicans flew by, mostly traveling east in formation. I wondered to myself where they were coming from and going to.

After running for two hours at about 3,300 rpm, I looked ahead to see what appeared to be a white wall against the horizon in front of us.

"What is that?" I asked Pete.

"That's Matanilla Reef," he replied. "Well, actually, it's waves breaking on the reef itself, which in some places is just a few feet below the surface. Those waves come the entire length of the Atlantic Ocean, and Matanilla Reef is literally the first thing to get in their way."

"Wow. That's quite a sight," I said.

"Yeah, but wait till you see it up close," Pete answered. Now Rusty seemed wide awake.

"How far do we have to go to get around the reef?" Rusty asked. *Good question*, I thought.

"Oh, we don't go around it, Rusty. We kind of pick our way through it," Pete said.

I looked over at Rusty. He looked as if he'd just seen a ghost.

The closer we got, the higher the wall looked. When we got within a hundred yards, Pete pulled the throttle back, turned ninety degrees to the left, and started studying the waves, apparently looking for the right angle of entry.

"Do you carry a life raft?" Rusty asked Pete.

"No, I've never needed one."

The waves seemed to break all at once over the reef. It was a frighteningly beautiful sight: a fifteen- to twenty-foot wall of white water accompanied by a constant roar, the likes of which I'd heard only at Niagara Falls.

"Rusty, isn't this the most beautiful thing you've ever seen?" I asked my pal.

Rusty said nothing.

Just then, Pete apparently saw what he had been looking for, turned right, brought the boat up on a slow plane, and headed right toward the wall of water.

"Is this safe?" I whispered to Rusty.

"I don't know, Bubba," he answered.

Have you ever done something that takes you out of your comfort zone and puts you a little bit on the edge of what you think is safe? Well, for me, this was it. At first it was exhilarating, a little intimidating, and then strangely relaxing. Maybe, I thought, this is how, and even why, we choose our hobbies. I was all of a sudden totally at ease as our captain chose his shot.

Pete stood quietly behind the wheel, then steered through a white-walled canyon of water. It was like shooting the curl in surfing; the crash of the waves may have been like thunder, but all I can remember is the sound of the engine throttling up and down as we crossed the reef and the wall of white water blocking the sun as we were all but swallowed up in the canyon.

Then, all of a sudden, we were out the other side, in the midst of the darkest blue water I'd ever seen. I glanced at the depth finder: seven hundred feet, eight hundred, nine hundred . . . then, all zeros. Just like that, we were in water a thousand feet deep, gently sliding over widely spaced waves rolling to about ten feet.

"Rusty, take the wheel, will ya, while I set up the lines," Pete said nonchalantly.

"Routine," I whispered to Rusty.

"Yeah, right," the Conch sneered.

We ended up fishing to within a few miles of Walker's Cay before skirting Matanilla Reef and heading for home.

We didn't catch any blue marlin that trip, and I couldn't have cared less. We'd not only seen one of the most breathtaking sights of nature but been a part of it and experienced a day on the water that I'll never, ever, forget.

> *There are moments of existence*
> *when time and space are more*
> *profound, and the awareness of*
> *existence is immensely heightened.*
> —Charles Baudelaire, French Poet

CATCH OF A LIFETIME

*Every fishing trip is a composite of all other trips; and it holds
irresistible promise for the future. The cup cannot be drained.
There are always greater fish than you have caught, always the
lure of greater task and achievement, always the inspiration to
seek, to endure, to find, always the beauty of the lonely
stream and open sea; always the glory and dream of nature.*
                                            —Zane Grey, introduction to
                               Tales of the Angler's Eldorado: New Zealand

T here are a lot of elements to a favorite catch, let alone the "Catch
of a Lifetime." It may not have been the biggest, the strongest, or
the fastest fish. It may not have been the longest fight—or the
shortest, for that matter. For me, location and company is every bit as
important as species.

All these things came together in perfect alignment to provide me
with my "Catch of a Lifetime," the one I'll never forget.

It happened late in the day in May of 2005. Mindy and I were making
our annual trip to the beautifully historic River Test in England, the
Mecca or birthplace of fly-fishing. Izaak Walton, William Shakespeare,
and Geoffrey Chaucer all fished the beautiful, gently flowing clear water
of this thirty-mile chalk stream in Hampshire in southwest England.

This trip would also be special, as we were sharing it with some good
friends, Jeanie and Johnny Morris, the founder of Bass Pro Shops, and
Bill Wrigley, the young chairman of the Wrigley Company. In addition,
we were introducing another close friend to our favorite river, George H.
W. Bush, the forty-first president of the United States.

We had first met when he was head of the CIA and a regular attendee
at Saint Columbas Episcopal in Bethesda, Maryland, where my brother
was the minister. I later visited him when he became vice president as
well. Our friendship really blossomed after he was out of the White
House and had time to pursue his passion, one which I share: fishing.

Our travel party's sense of excitement was heightened by the timing of our trip. It was the beginning of Mayfly Season, when the mayflies are hatching and struggling to the surface, where they are an easy target for hungry rainbow and brown trout, and large grayling as well. It was so easy to catch large trout fishing dry flies that the locals called it "Duffers' Fortnight." Not only was our timing perfect, but the manager of Lainston House, where we would be staying, said that the weather forecast was also ideal.

Lainston was a perfect headquarters for our Test adventure. It's a beautiful seven hundred-year-old country residence located between Stockbridge and Winchester. Their rooms are spacious and decorated with beautiful antiques and four-poster beds. Their common areas are also comfortable and look over acres of greenery and magnificent English gardens. Their oak-paneled bar is managed by an Italian mixologist named Franchesco, who is rightly proud of the fine, old, beautiful wines in his acclaimed cellar—as well as his mixed drinks, made up of secret ingredients.

As you might expect, the dinner menu of this country-situated refuge features a lot of local game like rabbit, pheasant, and venison, fish from the area like trout, and an array of locally grown organic vegetables.

While you can fish all day on the Test, the very best fishing is in the late afternoon and evening when the mayfly hatch goes off. Many avid anglers will fish until dark. Unlike most fishing, there is no premium on getting up and out early, so leisurely breakfasts, walking, and touring local towns are the pastimes of choice. It is, in two words, "very civilized."

The first two days of our three-day trip were idyllic, with some of the greatest dry fly-fishing I've ever enjoyed. The countryside intersected by the Test is incredibly scenic; the Test flows through many old estates that have been in some families for centuries. The British say that if there had been a Camelot, this is where it would have been.

Around every corner is a stone bridge or picturesque farmhouse or a barn or some other timeworn landmark. Periodically, a flock of large white swans would swim by foraging for food underwater. Owned and protected by the Queen, the swans' lazy motion seems to set the pace of life on the stream—until, that is, a hungry trout takes a dry fly on the surface and goes airborne and ballistic. Everyone was catching fish on almost every cast.

The third and last day of our fishing adventure seemed to come too soon. The shadows were growing long as we fished the middle beat of an old estate known as Compton. While we'd been somewhat spread out most of the afternoon, we seemed now to have all come together at a bend where the river makes a turn of almost ninety degrees. Mindy was on one side of me and Bill Wrigley was on the other. Across the stream, but very close, was Johnny Morris, fishing about thirty feet from President Bush.

The hatch was thick, and trout were rising all over the water. It was mystical. At one point, I sat down on one of the rough-hewn beaches that grace the well-manicured river banks, content to watch the others—particularly the President, who seemed to be catching three- to four-pound rainbows and browns on every cast.

Watching the sun setting on a beautiful cloudless day, I reflected on the good friends I'd made fishing, the beautiful places I'd seen, and the wonderful fish I'd fought. But reveries don't last long when big trout are slurping everything in sight. My wife and my three pals were fighting fish, and I think that I was the only one to see the huge bust on the far bank, followed in ten seconds by another huge bust in the center of the stream. After another pause, yet another bust by the near shore then back in the middle. While I couldn't really indentify the fish, it was apparent that he was large and very hungry, working his way back and forth across the river, stuffing himself on mayflies as if he'd been late to dinner.

I jumped up and stripped some line off my 3-weight Hardy reel and blew on the spent mayfly I'd attached a few minutes earlier, hoping the fish hadn't sunk down in the deep pool in front of me. There he was again, busting on the far shoreline. If he kept up this pattern, I knew exactly where he'd surface next. I threw one false cast and laid the fly in the middle of the stream and did a wishful countdown under my breath. Five, four, three, two, one . . . now. And *boom*, just like that, right on schedule and right on target, he crashed my fly, felt the hook, did a monster jump, and took off upstream, almost pulling my rod out of my hand. Everyone on the bank saw the fish jump, and we all knew he was huge.

He took me into the backing in only a few seconds before he stopped running and I could start taking back some line. With only 3-pound tippet, I really couldn't put any pressure on him.

We had two guides with us, and one of them ran for a net, although I knew this fight was far from over. Every time I got him corralled, the big fish would take off again. Three times he took me into the backing. The third time I brought him back, he dove into the pool in front of me that I judged to be about ten feet deep and hunkered down. He wouldn't budge, and I couldn't lift him. I began to worry that he had me snagged on a log or had become tail-wrapped.

A straight lift would surely break him off. It was time for some tactics. I walked up and down the bank to try him from different angles. I couldn't move him. I loosened the drag, reducing the pressure on the fish in hopes that he would start swimming again, or at least change position. He didn't. Almost as a last resort, I tightened the drag back up and started moving the rod in a horizontal figure eight over the fish, hoping that I could unloop the line if it was around his tail or a stick. Then there was a snap, almost like plinking the string on a guitar. The line hadn't broken, I'd freed him, and off he went again into the backing, obviously rested from his stay in the pool.

I brought him back again and could tell he was done. The guide climbed down the bank, opened the net, and managed to net the fish on the third try. He was a monster of a brown trout and hung out of the net on both sides. As often happens after such a long fight, the hook fell out of the side of the fish's mouth as the guide lifted him onto the bank.

"Let's weigh him, get a couple of pictures, and release him," I said, as everyone gathered around to get a better look.

Just then my friend Stan Conway, our senior guide, arrived on the scene and said, "No way." He reached into his pocket and pulled out a little wooden mallet-sized stick called a "priest" and whacked my fish three times on the top of his head.

"Stan, why'd you do that?" I asked, knowing that he was as much into "catch and release" as I was.

"Bubba, that's the biggest brown trout I've ever seen on the Test," he said, "and if you must know, I've got a good friend who does skin mounts

My catch of a lifetime, and a dear old friend. *Author's photo.*

in shadow boxes, and I wanted to have one done for you." Most mounts these days, by the way, are really fiberglass reproductions. Making skin mounts is something of a lost art, especially in the US. The process calls for a taxidermist to use the actual skin of the fish to provide a result that is far more authentic.

After handshakes and photos all around, we carried the fish back to the river hut where David, the seventy-year-old retired river keeper, produced a scale and weighed the brown in at thirteen pounds, two ounces. David agreed with Stan that it was the largest brown he'd ever seen caught on the Test.

It was indeed a thrill to catch this beautiful fish on light tackle on this historic river, with such good friends there to share the moment. I wasn't surprised to see that the most excited of everyone was President Bush. Perhaps, I thought, as a senior statesman and an older sportsman, events like this meant even more to him than the rest of us.

As often happens when one hits a goal or records some kind of landmark, feelings of joy are tempered with feelings of loss. What do you do next if you think you really have recorded your "Catch of a Lifetime"? On the way home, I thought of Zane Grey and his incredible fishing expeditions and hoped that he was right that "there are always greater fish than you have caught . . . always the glory and dream of nature."

ANGLERS OF THE OVAL OFFICE

Why do we fish?

Several years ago, I started a quest to answer this seminal question. More specifically, I set out to discover if there was any common interest that drove all of us anglers to the water in pursuit of fish.

My methodology was simple; I interviewed fourteen people from around the United States and Great Britain who fished for a variety of species with different tackle. I asked each one to tell me his or her favorite fishing story and then explored their history in the sport before asking each the ultimate question: "Why do you fish?"

One of the fourteen anglers who agreed to be interviewed was my friend and longtime fishin' buddy, George H. W. Bush, the forty-first president of the United States. His story was woven with events of his life in government service. Fishing became his release from the pressure-cooker geopolitical world in which the world's most important man must function. He also shared with us a love of the wonderful fishing available in Islamorada.

I compiled the interviews and shared my conclusion in a book called *The Fishing Club*. The answer to my research is best summarized by a popular Brit named John Buchan, the Earl of Tweedsmuir, who lived from 1875 to 1940. A renaissance man, who wrote spy thrillers in his spare time, he was a lawyer, war correspondent, intelligence officer, chairman of a news agency, a Tory member of Parliament, and governor-general of Canada. Buchan wrote: "The charm of fishing is that it is the pursuit of what is elusive but attainable, a perpetual series of occasions for hope."

That was the answer. It was all about hope. Hope was the motivator, the driver that pushed us on to the water to fish.

My book *The Fishing Club* was published in the spring of 2006 to some pretty nice reviews, and I set out on an ambitious series of appearances and book signings. Sales were good, and my publisher seemed pleased.

Out of the blue I got a call from a gentleman by the name of Roman Popadiuk, whom I knew as the executive director of the George H. W. Bush Presidential Library and Museum on the campus of Texas A&M University in College Station, Texas. Roman, obviously aware of the inordinately strong influence I wielded in my non-Cabinet role as "Presidential Fishin' Buddy," was calling to invite me to participate in the president's lecture series at the library, to be followed by a reception and book signing.

"Bubba: a lecturer at the presidential library!" I was thrilled, and of course I said yes to a date that was two months away. After thanking Roman and the president, I went to my laptop to find out what this series was all about.

Sponsored by Conoco-Phillips, the series had featured a very impressive list of guest lecturers. Colin Powell had made a presentation, as had Prime Ministers Brian Mulroney of Canada and Margaret Thatcher of Great Britain. Condoleezza Rice had been there, as had Brent Scowcroft and James Baker. I would be the second Bubba to appear, as even President Bill Clinton had been a guest lecturer. The audiences ranged from five hundred to seven hundred people, many of them former diplomats, business leaders, academicians, and of course, George and Barbara Bush.

All of a sudden my heart sank. What had I committed myself to, and what in the world would I speak about? Maybe I should call Roman back immediately with an excuse for why I couldn't appear, before they printed the invitations. This thing was taking me miles out of my comfort zone, even two months before my scheduled appearance. I wondered if there was a medical condition known as Advanced Premature Stage Fright.

I took a walk to think. President Bush was a friend, and we were scheduled to fish together in a few weeks in England. While intimidating, his invitation was also very thoughtful and flattering. I decided I would go, but just reviewing my book didn't seem to be appropriate for this forum. I needed a topic. Halfway through my walk, it came to me. While interviewing President Bush for my book, I had done some research and found that in its 230-year history as a nation, America had in fact elected several anglers to the office of chief executive.

Why, I wondered now, have so many American presidents been such avid anglers? Just what is it about fishing that stirs the souls of our leadership? And why have American voters repeatedly put anglers in the oval office?

I had a research challenge, and I had the title for my guest lecture: "Anglers of the Oval Office."

My challenge was to come up with an entertaining forty-minute presentation. I retained a journalist friend from Chicago, Mike Pehanich, to help me research and organize everything and to find supporting photographs, file footage, or news clips that my pals at Dog Eat Dog advertising agency in Buffalo could weave together to give me A/V backup.

While I liked my presentation, I still had a case of the jitters, and a week before the event I invited some family and friends to come along for moral support. Two of my sons who fish, Bob and Teddy came, and Teddy's wife, Nena, joined as well. Everyone met Mindy and me for the trip to Texas.

Also, Johnny and Jeanie Morris from Bass Pro Shop, who are also great fishing buddies of President Bush's, signed on. A last-minute add-on was our mutual friend, former Olympic downhill ski racer and tarpon-tamer, Andy Mill. Andy was reeling from his recent separation from tennis superstar Chris Evert. In retrospect, I don't think Andy really wanted to come along, but we knew the trip would do him good. While I told him I needed him there for moral support, I knew that it was really he who needed some friendship. Mike Pehanich, himself a fine bass fisherman, rounded out our contingent and ran my A/V for me.

The big day arrived, and the auditorium was packed. The President put me at ease with a nice introduction, and I delivered my lecture following the text below. I hope you enjoy it.

FROM SEA TO SHINING SEA

Long before Mark Twain created Huck Finn and Tom Sawyer, angling became entrenched in our concept of what American boyhood is all about. Many presidents fished in their youth and carried their love of the sport into their adult lives.

Why do we elect angler presidents? One pragmatic view has it that anglers have always comprised a large voting bloc. The American Sport-fishing Association counts 45 million fishermen in the United States today. That's a big number. In 1932, Herbert Hoover pointed out that 25 million fishing licenses had been issued that year.

"The whole allied world never had that number of men in armies at the same time," the thirty-first president said, with obvious angler pride.

The archetypal American character combines many of the virtues attributed to anglers—contemplative, wily, resourceful, patient, persistent, in touch with nature, linked to field and stream, and more. Whether sprung from those virtues or not, many a man aspiring to the presidency has donned fishing duds and flashed the angler image to the electorate.

Fishing also symbolizes freedom. Our right to fish elevates the height of American liberty, stretches it beyond that of even our "free" brethren across the Atlantic and in other parts of the world, where fishing is tied to privilege or wrapped in painful bureaucratic red tape. A *Gone Fishing* sign in a window has become almost a salute to that freedom. It means, "I'm leaving the world behind for awhile, folks!" It signifies clean air and pure water, a place where a man can cleanse his mind and spirit.

With the shadow of Hitler crossing the globe in 1936, *New York Herald Tribune* columnist Dorothy Thompson wrote: "As long as the President is fishing, dark omens of impending dictatorship will fade. Whoever heard of a dictator who was a fisherman? Mussolini plays the violin and rides horseback, but so did Nero. Hitler loves dogs, but so did Napoleon. . . . But none of these gentlemen would think of posing as fish-ermen. . . . For not only are fishermen inevitably believed to be patient philosophers, loftily elevated to Buddha-like wisdom above the strife of classes and parties, but they are known to choose as their counselors simple, honest souls whose prototype is the Maine guide."

From George W. to George W.

Our nation's *first* First Angler, George Washington, wrote about catching "Baricootas" in Barbados at the age of nineteen. Washington was an avid recreational fisherman who, in 1787, sneaked away during a ten-day adjournment of the Federal Convention in Philadelphia to fish for trout and, with sadness, relive the memory of one of the most brutal and historic winters in our history at a place called Valley Forge.

Washington fared only modestly as a sportsman. But he was richly successful as a commercial fisherman on the Potomac. In fact, he leveraged his fishing connections to feed his starving troops during the Revolutionary War on at least one occasion.

Not everyone likes fish, of course.

Historian Bill Mares writes: "The record shows that the troops responded to fish with as much enthusiasm as George Bush would greet broccoli."

Though we know relatively little about the angling prowess of John Quincy Adams, our sixth president, the American Museum of Fly-Fishing in Manchester, New Hampshire, displays his fly wallet. He is probably the first documented fly-fisherman president.

Biographer Ruth Painter Randall notes in a book called *Lincoln's Sons* that our sixteenth president Abraham Lincoln's solitary boyhood recollection of the War of 1812 was of catching a fish, and, like any proud angler, showing it off to a soldier that he met on the road. "Having been always told at home that we should be good to soldiers, I gave him my fish," recalled Lincoln.

While practicing law and serving as a member of the Illinois legislature in Springfield, Illinois, Lincoln took his children fishing on the nearby Sangamon River.

Our twenty-first president, Chester Arthur, prided himself on his fly-fishing expertise. Hoping to find evidence that Arthur was sponging off the American public with his fishing trips, the *New York Sun* ambushed the president on a trip to the Saint Lawrence River's Thousand Islands and demanded a photo. Arthur obliged amiably but asked that the photographer not ruin his image as a fly-fisher by showing his minnow bucket.

Arthur's enthusiasm for fishing helped to advance the popularity of the sport.

Conservation Heritage

Arthur's most significant outing may have been his 350-mile fishing and hunting trip to Yellowstone—during which he reportedly caught 105 pounds of trout in a single day. Coverage of that trip helped solidify support for our national park system.

Grover Cleveland, our twenty-fourth president, entered politics in 1881 when he was elected to be mayor of my hometown, Buffalo, New York. In his book *Fishing and Shooting Sketches*, President Cleveland established the First Angler's obligation to conservation when he wrote: "I believe . . . that those who thus by instinct and birthright belong to the sporting fraternity and are actuated by a genuine sporting spirit, are neither cruel nor greedy nor wasteful of the game and fish they pursue."

Cleveland was, as anglers go, "hard core." *Century* magazine editor Richard Gilder wrote: "Grover Cleveland will fish when it shines and fish when it rains; I have seen him pull bass up in a lively thunderstorm and refuse to be driven from a Cape Cod pond by the worst hailstorm I ever witnessed or suffered. He will fish through hunger and heat, lightning and tempest. . . . Thus, I have discovered, is the secret of Cleveland luck; it is hard work and no let up."

Rough Rider Establishes Conservation Ethic

Teddy Roosevelt, our twenty-sixth president, fished extensively as a youth and found some time to fish during his dashing career as president, hunter, adventurer, and rugged sportsman.

Roosevelt compelled America to step back and behold its beauty and bounty, to cherish that vibrant soul of nature from which the American spirit had sprung. Our woods and waters were both backdrop and players in his adventures. His waltz with them helped establish our conservation ethic and drew national attention to the value of our lands, waters, and wild creatures.

T. R.'s adventures also spanned the globe. According to great-grandson Tweed Roosevelt, T. R. "popularized the piranha and made it a widespread image of voraciousness" after encountering the toothy critters in South America.

Calvin Coolidge, president number thirty, was reluctant to allow the press to witness his fishing outings. Still, he was glad to have an audience on his fifty-sixth birthday, July 4, 1928, when he caught two trout on a single cast while fishing a pair of flies simultaneously on the Brule River in Wisconsin.

Herbert Hoover wrote the book—literally—of angling aphorisms. The thirty-first president's book *Fishing for Fun—and to Wash Your Soul* is a compilation of the president's reflections on anglers and the contemplative man's sport.

"Fishing is much more than fish," he said, capturing a realization that every soulful angler has come to at one time or another. "It is the vitalizing lure to outdoor life. It is the great occasion when we may return to the fine simplicity of our forefathers."

Hoover also loved how angling rekindled the spirit, made a man young. But he saw fishing as the great equalizer, too, the game that made presidents men of the people, like it or not. "[M]any a president of the United States has sought the Fountain of Youth by fishing. . . . Also, fishing reduces the ego in presidents and former presidents, for at fishing, most men are not equal to boys."

The 1932 Fish Off

The 1932 presidential election pitted Hoover against Franklin Delano Roosevelt—angler versus angler. The race prompted humorist Will Rogers to observe: "This campaign will be settled on fish. Do you want a deep-sea fisherman in the White House—flounders and cod—or a big trout-and-perch man?"

The electorate chose the deep-sea fisherman. FDR was elected our thirty-second president. He fished avidly as long as his polio-crippled body allowed. Frequently, he called upon the Secret Service to move him and his wheelchair to his many favorite fishing holes.

FDR even had a battleship outfitted for fishing—something I suggested the Navy consider doing for George H. W. Bush on the aircraft carrier named in his honor.

Truman to Carter

Harry Truman, our thirty-third president, enjoyed the angler image. America frequently saw Give 'em Hell Harry beaming with his catch in magazines and newsreels. But the truth was that his wife, Bess, was the more avid and accomplished angler.

Truman ceded the presidency, however, to one of our most accomplished fly-fishermen, Dwight D. Eisenhower, number thirty-four. Ike liked dry fly-fishing for trout on cold Colorado rivers. He enjoyed the challenge of sizing up streams, weather, and insect hatches.

Ike must have wondered what he was getting himself—and perhaps the nation—into when he took his vice presidential running mate, Richard Nixon, fishing. By Nixon's own account, their first outing was a disaster. Nixon hooked tree limbs on his first three casts and snagged Eisenhower's shirt on the fourth.

Ike and Dick never became fishing buddies. But there *is* a happy postscript to the misadventures of this angling "odd couple."

Eisenhower's grandson David—after whom, by the way, Ike named the presidential retreat known as "Camp David"—met Julie Nixon, daughter of our thirty-seventh president. Julie and David fished together, got married, and, well, lived happily ever after.

Oddly enough, Nixon and trout fishing helped preserve a historic presidential retreat, too.

In his book *In the Arena*, Nixon claimed that he convinced the newly elected thirty-ninth president, Jimmy Carter, to spare Camp David from the chopping block in 1976 during Carter's purge of presidential perks.

"If getting away from the Oval Office helps a president make better decisions, he should get away," Nixon advised.

Democrat Carter took the former Republican president's advice and kept Camp David, which became the site of the peace agreement between Egypt and Israel, today called "The Camp David Accords." The event was one of the highlights of the Carter presidency.

By the way, Vice President Gerald R. Ford, who ascended to be the thirty-eighth president, by appointment after Nixon's resignation, grew up fishing in the lakes of Michigan as a boy and also loved deep-sea fishing later in life in locations like the Bahamas and the Caribbean.

Size Matters

President John F. Kennedy was not a dyed-in-the-wool fisherman by any means. Nevertheless, our thirty-fifth president could not conceal his envy of Canadian Prime Minister John Diefenbaker's mount of an eight and a half-foot marlin. After challenging the catch, Kennedy finally admitted: "I spent $50,000 trying to catch one of those."

Kennedy's vice president from Texas, Lyndon Baines Johnson, our thirty-sixth president, fished a bit himself, but not as much as the Democratic Party's next president. Jimmy Carter, number thirty-nine, is an accomplished angler who has fished all his life. He chronicled many of his memorable outings with his wife, Rosalyn, in his book *An Outdoor Journal*.

Carter and his wife, Rosalyn, enjoyed fly-fishing for trout at Camp David and at Spruce Creek in Pennsylvania. According to historian Bill Mares, Carter regarded his conversion to fly-fishing as "one of the most gratifying developments of my life!"

America's last two angler presidents both carry the name "George Bush." The forty-third president, George W. Bush, is an avid bass angler who often retreats to his ranch in Crawford, Texas, to fish.

As I mentioned earlier, I have had the good fortune to fish with his father, George Herbert Walker Bush, number forty-one. Our trips have ranged from my winter home waters in Islamorada, Florida, to the Tree River in Alaska.

I described his fishing character in *The Fishing Club*:

> He combines optimism and patience with an almost childlike enthusiasm for the pursuit of fish. He's a great tactician and loves the preplanning that goes into an outing as much as the actual trip itself. . . . He has boundless energy and is usually the first on the water and the last to leave it. "Around the campfire," he is engaged and engaging and mixes wonderful stories of the fishing day—or fishing days gone by—with tales of events from his life, punctuated once in awhile with some of the world's oldest, corniest jokes.

Reservoir of Hope

It is hope that drives anglers to the water, and hope may also explain why so many fishermen have ascended to the presidency.

As for me, I like to think of them going to their favorite waters to rejuvenate their spirits and to rekindle the light that must always shine for them . . . a light that has drawn millions from across our oceans, away from civil strife and oppression and into the arms of freedom and opportunity.

Besides, what quality is more important to our leaders than hope—hope for a strong and healthy nation, hope for us, and hope for our children in a world in which freedom overcomes terrorism and tyranny?

What is America anyway, if not a deep reservoir of *hope*, filled with ideals, dreams and aspirations . . . perhaps only one last cast away?

I finished my lecture to a great round of applause, my third of the day (but who's counting), and a standing ovation. *Nailed it*, I thought, as I invited Mindy, Andy, Johnny, and Jeanie to join me on the stage with President Bush, to serve as an impromptu panel to field fishing questions from the audience. Pretty soon, we had to shut it off. It was apparent that the audience was either the world's politest or really into fishing.

Before I closed, we executed our prearranged little surprise for the president. While fishing together on the River Test in England the month before, the president had landed a large brown trout of over ten pounds, a magnificent and beautifully marked specimen.

Unbeknownst to my fishin' buddy, I'd had our guide spirit the fish off to a famous British taxidermist, who created a mount in a large glass shadow box that I'd had shipped to College Station.

As I thanked the president and the receptive audience, the curator wheeled the trophy onto the stage for me to present to him on behalf of all his fellow anglers who loved and respected him as our leader and as a fine sportsman.

President Bush was generous in his praise and promised to add his fish to the new fishing exhibit the library was planning. He brought the program to an end with another standing ovation—or maybe everyone was just standing up to walk to the bar.

The folks in my book signing line were also very complimentary, but the best compliment of all came from Barbara Bush, known by her family and friends as the Silver Fox, who signed on to our next summer's trip to the River Test.

SEARCH FOR A GRANDER

Day One
Los dos Gordos
Alegre

It was day one of our big adventure; Captain Greg Eklund from Islamorada and I were trolling four miles off the coast of Sao Vicente, Cape Verde, on a beautiful blue ocean with light swells and gentle seas created by one- to two-foot waves.

I was sitting in the cockpit of a brand-new forty-foot Cabo sportfishing boat, watching our teasers and four lures faithfully following the boat. Sharing my vigil were Xie (CHEE) and Mario, our two young mates. We were all hoping to see our lures attacked by the flailing bill of a "grander"—a thousand-pound blue marlin. Some say it's the most spectacular sight an angler can see, which causes some anglers to spend a lifetime in their pursuit. Don Tyson, the famous "chicken king," literally mounted a relentless, ongoing worldwide quest for these enormous fish; he caught six. Other anglers, like the famous Jerry Dunaway, have found fame and enjoyment fishing around the world but have never caught an elusive thousand-pound blue marlin.

Greg was sharing our vigil on the bridge of our boat, appropriately named *Beast*, with its captain, Zak Conde, a native of Cape Verde who has also fished the globe in search of these beauties. His own quest has taken him to many stops along the marlin highway from the Ascension Islands to Ghana, from the Azores and Madeira to the Canary Islands, Australia, and Hawaii.

Over the low growl of the boat's two 800-horsepower Man diesel engines, I could hear the two young captains discussing fishing exploits past, present, and future. I could tell over cocktails at our first meeting at the hotel the previous evening that these two guys would get along famously, and I was right. It's interesting to me how fishermen are so

231

often drawn together and how they are bound, not only by a shared passion for their sport, but by a common bond of optimism. If you want to surround yourself with optimistic people, go fishing.

Anglers universally believe that the next cast, the next drop, the next troll, the next drift can produce the memory of a lifetime—no matter how slow the day may be. This morning we seem to be testing that resolve.

It was only yesterday morning that we dropped off my wife, Mindy, and three of her girlfriends in the town of Maun, Botswana, where they will connect with a small twin-prop plane to begin a weeklong African safari.

Mindy actually gets credit for the trip we're all on. Last fall she started arranging a fishing trip for me where I could realize a lifetime adventure of catching a grander. Her first wise decision in the process was to enlist the aid of our friend Greg Eklund, who runs a charter boat named *The Cloud Nine*, a popular sportfisher located on the dock at Bud and Mary's Marina in Islamorada, where we live in the Florida Keys. Greg was a perfect choice as he had worked for two years running a worldwide sportfishing expedition for a young entrepreneur who had sold his investment company for several billion dollars and still retained some $4.5 billion in stock. (Yes, that's billion with a *B*!)

Anyway, Greg did his planning and scouted locations for a perfect time, place, boat, and captain. Then Mindy wrapped it in a package complete with a bow and surprised me with it for my birthday in January. What a wonderful gift—far better than a new necktie. To add to the fun, Greg agreed to come along on the trip, help me find my fish, and keep me company.

Mindy is an accomplished shallow-water angler, known in the Keys as a monster tarpon tamer. She is also honing her skills up north as a fine stream fisher.

To say that she is not an offshore fisher is an understatement. She gets violently seasick and refuses to join me on the high seas. In fact, a few of my friends, knowing her condition, suggested that I name my first offshore boat *Home Alone Two*. But staying at home is the last thing on Mindy's agenda. When I hit the waves, she often books one of the fine backcountry guides in Islamorada, like Craig Brewer, and goes on her own fishing quests for the many species that inhabit the beautiful and haunting shallow waters of Florida Bay.

Similarly, on this trip she arranged a safari in two locations in the wilds of Botswana. Sharing tents with her will be three longtime friends, Sue Moret, Barbara Gisel, and Patti Gilbert. They are an adventuresome group, indeed. Last year, they all enrolled in a weeklong cooking school together with five other pals at the Culinary Institute of America in Hyde Park, New York. The program was called CIA Boot camp, and they had a ball. Their safari will also be a great adventure for the friends, and I'm sure they'll have a lot of stories for Greg and me when we see them next Saturday.

They are all true gamers. Sue Moret and her husband, Sandy, run a fly shop and fly-fishing school in the Keys. She has a flair for design, which is well-represented by the clothing she chooses for sale from the shelves of the Florida Keys outfitters. She's the eldest of the friends and the most conservative. She often tries to act stern and take charge like a true adult, but she fails miserably. She has a high-pitched giggle that signifies surrender to the humorous escapades of the others.

Born in my hometown of Buffalo, the sister of my protégé and CEO of our company, Barbara Gisel moved to Main Line Philadelphia several years ago and started a very successful interior design business. After a failed marriage, she married an old college chum of mine, Albert Oehrle, and together they are one of our favorite couples. Barbara is tall and willowy, inquisitive, and incorrigibly upbeat and happy. Her throaty, earthy laugh is like music to our ears. It's no wonder that she is such a favorite of men and women alike.

Patti Gilbert, a true free bird and blithe spirit, is the hardest to describe. She and Mindy were best pals growing up in Cincinnati, and she moved to Aspen after college. She later moved to Los Angeles and joined a commercial real estate broker with one of the largest firms in the business. At about five foot two, Patti is on the go 24-7 with a huge appetite for adventure and an insatiable curiosity. A good athlete, she has developed many friends in southern California who have watched her grow into one of the most successful brokers in her business. While her wit and devilish demeanor have attracted men to her like a magnet, her private life remains a shambles of failed relationships. She goes on, though, undaunted, ever in search of a new sport like fly-fishing or photographing critters on safari.

Mindy rounds out the troop. The original "Brown Eyed Girl," she took my life by storm. When we first met, I was a forty-three-year-old recycled bachelor with four children, and she was the most creative (and attractive) account executive at the largest ad agency in town—a dynamic shooting star at age 27. Tall with long, dark-brown hair and penetrating eyes and disarmingly beautiful, she was a true out of the box thinker—before the term was invented—with the most positive attitude of anyone I know.

Raised in an era before Title IX scholarships heralded the coming of equal opportunity for women in sports, Mindy proved to be a gifted athlete, a good skier, and a better fly-fisher.

A lifetime baseball fan by her birthright of being born in Cincinnati, Mindy took over leadership of our company's three professional baseball teams and served in a variety of capacities at Rich Products before becoming vice chair of our board of directors. She also serves on four other corporate boards. Anyone who knows her knows she has earned her success and did not merely "sleep her way to the top" of our company.

I dedicated my first book, *Fish Fights* to her and said that she was my first female friend. Today, twenty-six years later, she has become much more than that. I think of her as a true partner and best friend and relish her unique point of view and positive advice and counsel.

I know that these are qualities and talents that her three tentmates have come to admire in her as well, but this week they will be able to be just best friends, exploring together the wilds and wildlife of our world's most fascinating continent. The childlike looks of joy and anticipation on their faces as they boarded the small plane for their adventure said it all, looks that I'll never forget. I can't wait to see the pictures and hear the stories.

The trip to Africa and Cape Verde really worked out well, as we were already scheduled to be in South Africa for some business meetings in Johannesburg.

Back on the *Beast*, two hours passed quickly as the rising sun burned off the last of the morning haze. Greg had now left the bridge and joined me in my watch, sitting together on the large fishing cabinet that so often doubles on fishing boats as a waiting station and observation platform.

Conversation always comes easily for us. Greg is a bright and handsome thirty-seven-year-old mechanical engineering graduate from Purdue University who chose a career in the charter boat industry. Raised in Kentucky, he is from "good stock." His father was a very well-acclaimed professor in solid-state physics at Penn State University with a never-ending list of academic awards and innovative accomplishments; his mother is also a professor at Penn State, specializing in gifted education.

Greg is a big man, six feet tall and strongly built, with Nordic blond hair and blue eyes. His high school tennis team pals nicknamed him Shamoo for the "whalelike way he glided around the court." He never ceases to amaze me with the range of subjects about which he can talk, from quantum physics to rigging marlin bait, from business to equestrian sports, from mechanics to government policy. Greg is a true renaissance man. When he jumped into charter boat fishing in Islamorada, he hit like a big blond hurricane. A real lone wolf, he outworked and outfished a fleet of crusty old captains and built a good business of loyal customers. Not only did he tweak their noses on the water, but he really piqued their ire when he fell in love with and married a beautiful, tall blonde girl who was recently divorced from one of the most well-liked charter boat captains in the fleet. Together, Greg and his wife, Lynn, are raising a seventeen-year-old daughter by her first marriage and a precocious seven-year-old daughter of their own. Both the girls are promising equestrians with the older, Alexa, almost ready to burst onto the international riding circuit. Look for her in a future Olympics.

I think our fishing trip has special meaning for Greg. His dad passed away at age sixty-four on August 12 after a twelve-month bout with bladder cancer. They were close, and I can see in his eyes the sadness of someone grieving over the loss of a special friend. We've talked a lot about his father, and perhaps it has been of some consolation to Greg. It has certainly enlightened me about the career of a world famous physicist who left his family and colleagues way too early. This I know for sure: this father must have been very proud of the son he and his wife of forty-two years reared.

By then it was 10:45 a.m., and we'd been trolling four lures and two teasers[4] for two and a half hours. So far, the highlight of our sightings had

been a small pod of killer whales swimming in a tight formation to protect three new-born calves. We did get a bit of a start when a large spotted
leopard ray jumped twice behind our lures, a tactic they use to rid themselves of sea lice, remora, and other ocean-dwelling parasites.

The sun was really beating down on us, and even the gentle breeze
was feeling oppressively hot. As often happens on a fishing boat during
the first morning of a trip when no fish have been sighted, conversations
seemed to slow as anglers, captains, and crew began to settle into their
routine and their private thoughts, dreading that their quarry have left the
area or are simply just not home.

Captain Greg, obviously better at fishing than posing. *Author's photo.*

Greg passed me a plastic quart of ice water, which was well-received. All of a sudden there she was, a large, hungry blue marlin attracted from the depths by our bright yellow starboard teaser, setup close enough to the boat that we all got a good look at her.

Xie was the first to react and yelled something in his native Portuguese that I'm sure translates to "there she is," the classic words that anglers throughout the ages live to hear. The fish swatted the teaser three times with her bill and then she "dropped out," disappearing leisurely into the sea. You will notice that I refer to these large marlin as females. That's because males only range in size up to around three hundred pounds. It is the females that we were in search of.

Zak kept the boat moving in the same speed and direction and yelled down from the bridge, "Be ready, she'll be back." After two minutes that seemed like thirty, there she was again, this time grabbing the nearby port lure in her mouth only to drop it as quickly as she had grabbed it. Our next interval of waiting was far shorter, as the big fish made a beeline for the portside long lure, gulped it down in a flash, and kept on trucking directly away from the boat. As Zak had instructed earlier, I left the rod in the rod holder (or "Rodney," as Greg calls them), watching in awe as line literally flew off the reel as the marlin turned on her full power.

"Now!" Zak yelled from the bridge, and I wrenched the rod from its holder and struggled to take it with me and place it in the metal holder called the gimbal which was situated between my legs in the fighting chair. The crew quickly reeled in the other three lines and Zak brought in the teasers from the bridge to clear the way for the fight that was about to happen.

The minute I lifted the rod, the big fish must have felt the pressure. She turned to her left and started a series of incredibly acrobatic jumps. Leaping, greyhounding, tailwalking, twelve leaps in all to rid herself of the annoying object that had stuck her in the side of her mouth. Greg was quick on his feet and captured it all on tape for what I'm sure will become a wonderful DVD to show our friends and save the memory.

After the jumps, the fish turned right back toward the boat, swimming fast as Greg buckled the clips of two chains connecting the reel to the bucket harness. I was sitting in the fighting chair. What a feeling to be "joined at the hip," so to speak, to this huge, beautiful creature, hooked, angry, and no doubt shocked and scared as well.

I started reeling frantically to return as much line to the reel as I could; taking the belly or slack out of the line is important in all fishing. Slack lines allow fish to shake out hooks, no matter how sharp.

All of a sudden, I couldn't feel the fish. From the bridge came the words we all hate to hear, "I think she's off." I didn't agree and tried to gather line faster. All of a sudden, the line came tight again and the fight was back on. The big fish swam at medium depth just out of our vision, first to the right, then to the left, then away from the boat while I lifted up and reeled down quickly to stack the yellow 130-pound monofilament line on the Shimano Tiagra reel.

I think of catching a fish as a prize fight. The fish pulls out some line and wins a round, then the angler pulls back some line and wins the round, and so it goes until one of the fighters tires first and the other wins. For me, there is no ultimate loser as on any boat I'm on we free every caught billfish so it can fight another day. I'm a strong proponent of "catch and release" fishing and am thrilled to see it becoming a way of life for so many captains and anglers at home and around the world. In fact, I was thrilled to find out that our captain on this adventure, Zak Conde, had won a citation from the International Game Fish Association (IGFA) the previous year for the most billfish releases of any captain in the Atlantic Ocean!

As the snap swivel on the end of the leader rose from the ocean, I thought about my favorite blue marlin quote by angler Herb Schaffner: "Perhaps nothing compares in angling to seeing a thousand-pound fish leap fifteen feet in the air, shaking its head violently to dislodge the hook as its ten-foot body cartwheels in the air to crack against the water. Nothing in angling is as physically challenging as bringing such a fish to the gaff. And nothing in angling takes as much moral courage as releasing that extraordinary predator to live and fight again."

But this fight wasn't over yet. As the leader came out of the water, Xie put on his heavy gloves and started taking wraps around the heavy monofilament that connected the hook to our quarry. No doubt feeling the extra pressure, the fish surged and shot away from our boat, pulling the leader out of Xie's hands. After the first surge, the fight changed and the fish felt like dead weight, sinking straight down directly under my rod tip.

"I think she's tail wrapped," I shouted to Captain Zak. Sometimes when a fish jumps or surges, she might create a loop in the line that will wrap around her tail and restrict or remove her ability to swim. Zak made the same guess I did and eased the boat ahead slowly so we might change the angle of the line and thus float the momentarily incapacitated fish to the surface.

Our tactic worked; within five minutes, we had the spent fish on the surface. Now lying on her back, Xie reached over and removed the loop of leader from around her tail. When he did, our big hook fell out of her mouth and she floated away, ten feet from the transom. "Four hundred pounds," guessed Zak, backing the boat to the exhausted fish so that the mates could grab her and turn her over. We would revive and tag her and let her swim away. Over the next five minutes, you could see her coming to and gaining her strength until she slowly swam away to continue her day—but probably with a temporary loss of appetite.

Just like that, at 10:45 a.m., after a half-hour fight, we'd released the largest blue marlin I'd ever caught. She wasn't a grander but was a wonderful adversary whose picture will grace my wall and whose memory will last a lifetime.

The rest of the day went slowly as we failed to raise another marlin. We returned to the dock at 6:30 p.m.

The waters at the pool of our hotel, Foya Branca, were soothing and the rum and cokes were refreshing. At dinner, Captain Greg and I went to the outdoor restaurant at the hotel and both selected from the menu. It is literally a feast of grilled steak, lamb, chicken, and sausage, brought to the table on skewers with knife-wielding waiters. We washed down numerous helpings with native drinks called *capariñas*—which tasted suspiciously like Cuban *mojitos*: cool, refreshing, and deadly. We laughed a lot, especially when Greg toasted the caught-and-released marlin as my "starter fish."

We went to bed early, both no doubt dreaming about the day to come.

Day Two
Greg in the Chair

We had strong coffee in town at our new favorite café before climbing aboard *Beast* for our day-two adventures. A handful of locals looked at us with what appeared to be mildly interested bemusement as we sipped our *cafés con leche* and talked fishing.

The people in Cape Verde all seemed very attractive and friendly to us. Over 80 percent of them are Creole, a mix of the white European men who settled the islands and the black slave women who were brought here from Africa. They all seemed well-weathered, many from working outdoors, many on the sea. The women seemed to be equally industrious and occupied. There doesn't seem to be much standing around, at least during the workday. Today it was Greg's turn in the chair, and I could tell that he was pumped. "When did you catch your last big blue marlin?" I asked him.

"Fifteen years ago off the island of Peleliu, Micronesia," he replied. "Eight hundred and fifteen pounds." His specificity on the weight tells me that they killed that big fish and weighed it on the dock. "Good fish," he added. "Fought her for four hours and twenty minutes. My equipment wasn't the best."

"Peleliu has quite a history. In World War II, it was held by the Japanese. When the Marines went in, they found the enemy well-entrenched. Five thousand Americans lost their lives and ten thousand Japanese were killed before the Battle of Peleliu ended one month after it started."

"Let's go get you another big one, Greg."

"Lead the way, Bubba."

As we steamed out of the harbor, it looked like the day's weather and seas would be a carbon copy of the day before: cloudless, with a light chop driven by variable winds of around eight knots out of the northeast.

Greg was especially excited as he helped the crew drop back some of the lures he had brought for the trip. The spread set, Greg began doing something curious. He strapped himself into a stand-up harness, like the

Zak helping Greg adjust his stand up gear. *Author's photo.*

ones we use on fifty-pound sailfish in the Keys, instead of sitting in the chair. He adjusted the straps and tested the gimbal.

"What are you doing?" I asked.

"It's a standup harness," he said.

"I know what it is bud, but why are you in it? You're not thinking of fighting one of those beasts in that, are you?"

He just smiled and said, "We'll see."

He kept on smiling as we settled in on our tackle cupboard seats and began the watch. The day before, we had waited until 10:15 a.m. for our first bite. This time, the left long went off at 9:15 a.m. A nice fish had inhaled Greg's black-and-purple Mold Craft Wide Range lure. My pal gave the fish about a minute with rod and Rodney, then picked it up easily and opted to slip himself into the fighting chair instead of using the standup harness; as his fleeing fish picked up speed, I snapped him into the bucket and the battle was on.

Good choice, Greg, I smiled to myself.

This big fish was obviously a beast, but it was clear from the first minute that she'd met her match. In a phrase that I hate, but which seems appropriate here, Greg "opened a can of whoop-ass" on her. He got after the fish from the get-go, never giving her a minute to rest. Our light-hearted banter was gone; this angler was in full concentration, speaking only to the captain to let him know exactly what the fish was doing so that he could keep the boat positioned safely.

I noticed that he had quickly shaken off any rust and had settled into a smooth rhythm to subdue the beast. He would sit back slowly then reel himself up to a standing position, taking line in as many handle turns as he could get. I'm sure in the back of his mind he was thinking, *This fight's not gonna last four hours and twenty minutes.*

Unlike my marlin, which had stayed near the surface, Greg's preferred the depth and fought to stay deep, tough on the photographer and tougher on the angler.

Finally, after half an hour, as if to see what was going on, the big fish came to the surface not thirty yards from the transom and did two beautiful jumps in quick succession. We liked what we saw. She was a monster—way bigger than mine. She apparently didn't like what she saw and sounded like a whale, dumping several yards of line off the reel in an instant. This turn of events would have discouraged less experienced anglers, but the sight of this beautiful fish only steeled Greg's resolve and seemed to refresh him.

It took Greg only ten minutes to recover the line he'd lost and enough more to bring the fish to the leader. Bending low over the transom, a gloved Xie began taking his wraps while Greg stayed in the chair in case the fish surged away from him . . . and that's exactly what happened and happened again, leaving this strong angler to regather line.

The third time was the charm, and Xie hauled the marlin straight up to the surface on the port side of the boat so that Mario could get a release tag into her and we could get a good look at her. She was indeed a monstrous creature. "Over seven hundred," Zak shouted from the bridge. Just as I snapped a picture, the camera-shy fish surged under the boat and almost immediately chafed off the 800-pound leader on the corner of the transom and was gone, back to the depth of the Atlantic where she had come from forty-five minutes earlier. It was almost as if the fish was saying to her adversary, "OK, you won this time. You caught me, but I'll release myself!" In another time, on another boat, with another angler, that fish would never have had that choice or chance. A stout kill gaff would have broken her spine and she would have been hauled through the transom tuna door by a braided rope tied to her tail.

As the war whoops erupted from me and the crew, I saw a look come on Greg's face that I'd never seen before. He was beaming, full of adrenaline, and obviously proud of what he had just done—a more-than seven hundred pound marlin subdued in only forty-five minutes, a great accomplishment and rush that very few anglers will ever get to enjoy. Then, after generously thanking the crew, the captain, and even me, the photographer, the smile disappeared. It was replaced by a look that I would call appreciative contemplation as he sat down on a gunwale and let his head sink and then rise. He seemed to be staring at the far off mountains of Mindelo and I, the chatterbox, went inside to let him enjoy his moment of peace.

The rest of the afternoon, like the day before, was uneventful, and we hauled in the lines and headed for the dock.

On the way home, Captain Zak asked us if we'd like to run south to another island the next day, overnight there, and spend a few days fishing some new water. It sounded like a wonderful adventure, and we signed on immediately, both making mental notes to pack some extra clothes for the journey.

Over a cold local beer on the way in, I congratulated Greg again on a good job and remarkable feat.

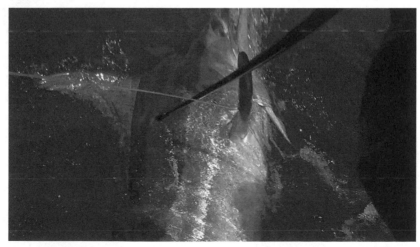

Greg's 700-pound blue marlin; caught, tagged, and released. *Author's photo.*

"You tired?" I asked.

"No, just satisfied," he replied.

"What were you thinking of, fighting that fish?"

"I wanted to assert myself and get after her right away. I've seen too many bad things happen when anglers relax and let a fish control the fight. I'd felt her power, then I wanted to tame the beast."

"What were you thinking about after you caught her?" I asked the seminal question I'd been wanting to ask all day.

A thoughtful smile came to his face and he said, "Well, first I was thinking how thankful I was to be in this place and to have the opportunity to catch that beautiful creature."

"And second?" I drilled down.

"Second," he said, as if knowing my next question, "I had a little conversation with my dad, dedicated the fish to him, and I told him I missed him but not to worry, that we were all right. Also, I thought about how lucky I was that I could have those kind of talks with him and still feel that he is very close to me," he added.

After a swim in the hotel pool, a long, hot shower, and a few rums, and several unsuccessful attempts to reach the girls on our satellite phone to see how they were doing, we headed for the inside dining room, both famished. We ordered a bottle of local white wine that turned out to be a great accompaniment to our broiled lobster dinners. First, though, Greg insisted that we each try an appetizer of whelk. I know what you're thinking. I had no idea what it was either, but what's a friend to do? Greg said it was small chunks of meat from some crustacean that attaches itself to shoreline rocks. Tasty, eh? Well, was it ever! It was served hot in a rich brown sauce with diced onions and tomatoes. The meat was succulent and melted in your mouth.

Both of us returned to our rooms, stuffed and ready for bed. I resolved that it would be whelk for dinner every night for the rest of our trip.

Day Three
The Ride

Day three started early, at 6:00 a.m., when I was awakened by a strong wind rattling the windows of my beachfront room. I walked out on the porch and guessed it to be blowing a steady twenty knots out of the southeast. In spite of the wind, the temperature was already reading seventy degrees. It was apparent that we were in for a long, bouncy ride in a hot cockpit.

Greg and I had each packed an overnight bag with a change of clothing, and, skipping our favorite café, we made our way straight for the boat and a strong cup of Zak's black coffee, microwaved in the salon of *Beast*. Having gotten to know us a little better, he opened up and told us a little more about himself and some of his big-fish catching exploits around the world. Greg had done some extensive research on this experienced captain, and Zak's stories added the spice to his impressive resume and explained categorically how he had built such a strong reputation with blue marlin chasers all along the mystical "marlin highway."

Sun and sea had weathered this thirty-seven-year-old veteran to the look of an older man. The occupational stress of his job had also aided the aging process and it had left him with a chronic ulcer. Born in Cape Verde, his native language was Portuguese but his schooling, combined with global exposure to fishermen, has helped him practice his English, which he uses flawlessly to communicate. I think that I eased his stomach pain by sharing the results I had read in a *USA Today* poll listing the job of fishing guide as the number one most stressful occupation in the world. Go figure. I guess the stress of having to meet and put strangers on fish everyday takes its toll.

As Zak climbed the ladder to the bridge, Greg whispered to me, "You made that up, didn't you?"

"No, no I didn't," I promised, inwardly pleased that I had imparted a true fact to these young professionals about the careers they'd chosen of which they were both unaware.

Xie and Mario cast off the dock lines, and we headed out through the harbor, which was surprisingly calm considering the wind that was blowing.

The calm seas changed dramatically as we sailed past the now-familiar volcanically formed cliffs that provided shelter to the small but busy port of Mindelo. Two miles out, the boys put out the lures as we headed south for the island of Saõ Nicolau, forty-eight miles away, which Zak told us translates to Santa Claus Island in English. Great, I thought, I've fished off Christmas Island and now maybe Santa Claus Island would gift me my grander in September. Feeling the Cabo buck in the waves, I knew I'd have to hold that thought for later, as there'd be no writing in my journal in this chop. I've been out in a lot worse, but it was one of those days where you couldn't stand up without holding on to something.

I won't drag out the account of this day, a day by the way, spent in foul weather gear—lots of conversation, but no marlin, although we had one major take down by a large mystery fish at 11:00 a.m.

Our fishing highlight was Xie's tuna fish sandwiches followed by catching a small yellowfin tuna that weighed in around twenty pounds. I knew when I saw the fish that it was a "gazinta" (as in, it "gazinta" the cooler . . . for that night's dinner).

At 7:00 p.m., the seas had mercifully begun to lay down as we pulled the lines and steamed into the harbor of our destination island, Saõ Nicolau.

On first sight, you could see that this port was all about commercial fishing. Fishing vessels of all shapes and conditions filled up the dock space or gently rocked on anchor in the clear harbor waters of the small, hilly, green island. Brightly painted houses and buildings spread from the shoreline up the foothills as if laid out specifically to watch boats and small ships coming and going. On the docks, Cape Verdean seamen scurried about, concurrently securing their boats for the night while preparing them for the next day's fishing trips.

At the space we selected to dock there were several young boys, standing shoulder to shoulder, greeting us as if we were rock stars and fighting to catch our mooring lines and fasten them to weathered old dock cleats that looked like they were designed to tie up much larger craft than our forty-footer.

It was apparent from the greetings and salutations that Zak, Xie, and Mario had been there many times before. The hero worship for these fishermen by the youngsters on the dock was pleasant and engaging.

Zak walked Greg and me to our lodgings, a three-story guest house/hotel, or *pensión*, on a central square. He introduced us to our hostess, the middle-aged lady who ran the house, cooked the meals, and oversaw the operations. Our rooms were on the second floor, small but immaculately clean and cared for, both overlooking the town square. Dinner would be served in two hours in the small dining room on the third floor, giving us time to shower and pay a quick visit to the small café/bar that we'd noticed across the street.

The hot shower felt great, and I dressed quickly in shorts and T-shirt to join my fishing buddy at the café. It had no signage, so I will call it the "No Name." Greg arrived there before I did, and I found him sitting at an outside four-top surrounded by Zak's young groupies and giggling over his recent discovery and acquisition: a bottle of his favorite Cuban dark rum. He had bought the fifth for $8.50 (US), and the bartender had thrown in two cokes and the use of two glasses for free. Ice, by the way, was not an option—as it is a not-to-be-trusted, potentially unfiltered third-world tourist trap for unsuspecting gringos like us, Montezuma's revenge or the green apple two-step waiting to happen.

By the way, the little groupies weren't the only ones surrounding Greg at the table. Hovering over his shoulder were two comely young waitresses, obviously smitten by Greg's Nordic looks. Blond hair and blue eyes were definitely not a common appearance in downtown Saõ Nicolau. I could also see that the activity at Greg's table was getting its share of critical attention from the gents scowling at us from the surrounding tables.

I joined my pal and his entourage, filled and emptied my glass a few times, and delighted the natives with the function of my digital camera. Pictures all around as Zak, Xie, and Mario joined us for a drink before dinner.

Time, and our bottle, went quickly before we headed back to of the third floor of our pensión for a delicious dinner. I guess Cape Verdeans love soup, and our señora started our meal with a heaping bowl of steaming vegetable soup followed by fresh salads, homemade bread and butter, our yellowfin tuna broiled to perfection, rice, and fresh asparagus with a side of whelk—my new favorite—all washed down with a bottle of a fruity Portuguese white wine. Strong, dark coffee followed, accompanying vanilla ice cream and peaches.

I was stuffed. Xie and Mario excused themselves with that look in their eyes common to young twenty-year-old guys, which made it apparent what they were planning to look for that evening. As Greg and Zak's conversation turned to things mechanical, I started to yawn. Zak suggested we fish these waters the next day and stay over another night, and we agreed. The two captains then started talking about buying another fifth of Cuban grog at our café, and I jumped at my exit cue. Age teaches discretion over valor, and I wished the cappies well and headed for my berth, reeling a tad—no doubt from the day's big seas, I tried to convince myself.

Day Four
Wahoo

Day four had a quiet 8:00 a.m. start. Greg and Zak weren't talking much, and both looked a little green around the gills. My inquiries about the night before drew only grunts and one-word answers. I suggested that they might have been over served the night before (by themselves).

In Cape Verde, all the guys wear football (soccer) shirts everywhere, so Greg and I got a pretty good laugh when we showed up for the ride back to Mindelo in new, colorful soccer shirts we'd acquired.

Thankfully, the winds and big seas of the day before had subsided dramatically. I don't care how often you go to sea or how much you drink on a regular basis, hangovers are much easier to manage on a calm day on the water. We stopped at a beautiful and efficient ice-building facility for ice and fuel. Zak explained that this facility was built for the island by the

Japanese longliners, the scourge of the seas for sportfishers. Their commercial boats troll thousands of yards of baited hooks; along with bottom draggers, they "lead the league" in the indiscriminate killing of any and every species large enough to take a baited hook. The Japanese call it aquaculture or harvesting of unspecified protein. I believe that it is one of the main reasons for butchering and decimation of some of the world's greatest sporting fish like bluefin tuna, swordfish, and, yes, blue marlin.

And as for the Japanese, they dismiss our concerns and say that they are feeding their people, and that, unlike us Americans, they do not "play with their food." I wondered how many granders those guys killed every week.

Interesting debate, I thought as we left the harbor, but one that I wouldn't resolve that day.

Zak searched the horizon and headed straight for a group of twelve or so small native fishing boats—eighteen-foot wooden craft powered by small outboards, each boat with two, three, or four fishermen trying to handline yellowfin tuna. Knowing that big marlin feed on these tuna, Zak's strategy was to circle the fleet, hoping to tease up some hungry blue marlin.

The strategy almost worked, except for the wahoo. Another predator of tuna, wahoo follow their schools and feed on the slow or injured. Wahoo are the speedsters of the ocean. Billfish without bills, they are incredibly fast killing machines. Voracious eaters, tinged in blue with horizontal tiger stripes, they are a wonderful target species and one of the most tasty and delicious fish found in the ocean. No sooner had we put our lines out than we had two takedowns—a wahoo double-header. Greg brought in one and I brought in the other, a forty- and a fifty-pounder. Then bang, another takedown. A huge run, then, in typical wahoo strategy, a buttonhook and a run right toward the boat. No surprises there except for its size—sixty-five pounds, a monster, my largest wahoo ever. A prize on light tackle, but no fight on 130-pound marlin tackle.

One hour out and we had landed three huge wahoo. This was going to be our day! Not. That was it. Greg jumped out of a midday nap screaming that he saw a huge monster stalking our starboard long line. I think he was hallucinating. We headed for Santa Claus at 6:30 p.m. with no marlin flags but a great wahoo dinner, once again with all the trimmings. This time, no one was interested in another after party. We all went to bed early.

Day Five
Homeward Bound

Day five dawned clear and hot with fifteen-knot winds out of the north. We left the dock and all the kids were there to say good-bye. It was kind of special, these beautiful youngsters waving good-bye to strangers-turned-friends after two days. I wondered what would happen to them. I doubted that we'd ever see them again and suspected that we would never know their fate, nor they ours. The night before, one by one, their moms had come to the café, ostensibly to fetch their children home but moreso, I believe, to see these fair-haired visitors whose cameras showed pictures instantly and who bought their kids soft drinks and bags of chips.

It was rough on the water, but the small fishing boats were still out there, handlining tuna as they and their ancestors had done for years.

We didn't waste much time around them that day but instead headed north toward Mindelo, our home port. On the way we trolled past two Japanese longliners, and I wondered what role they had played in our "shutouts" and how many granders they'd hauled in over the past month.

Two days without a marlin—not the way I'd envisioned it, but it didn't seem to matter. We'd had a great experience! We'd been part of a community and made new friends even though we didn't even speak the same language. Marlin? Oh yeah. . . . During the last couple of days marlin hadn't really seemed to matter. But that was then. Now, day five, with only three days left to find the big girl, we refocused.

Nothing seemed to work all morning. By noon we were the only ones biting . . . Xie's ham and cheese on fresh-baked rolls. I began to think that Saõ Nicolau was Portuguese for "no marlin."

Two big marlin in four and a half days. This was defintely not the way I'd envisioned this trip. I'd told Greg up front that I wanted to alternate catching. I'd caught the first on day one, he'd caught the second on day two. That left me up on watch for the last two and a half days, watching for a bill or a dorsal fin.

It was sweltering, but I left the shade of the cooler perch, pulled up my Lycra face shield, and sat in the fighting chair, braving the direct rays of the early afternoon sun in hopes of a strike.

In ten minutes it happened: the port long line went off, and I was hooked up. This fish jumped way away and looked huge. Having honed my technique, I had new confidence and used it to lean on her. In ten minutes, I had her to the boat. She had shrunk from a thousand to about four hundred pounds—still, a wonderful fish and a great adversary, and we were back in business.

Now Greg was up. "Good luck, Pal," I said, "you can watch for the next two days."

Greg didn't have to wait that long. Captain Zak retraced his path, and an hour later, bam, another hookup. Greg jumped all over this blue marlin, which had struck our starboard flat line. Clearly in the groove, Greg bested the fish in twelve minutes, so fast that we barely got a look at her. We guessed her weight at 450 pounds, but we didn't get a long look because she broke off after Xie got the leader but before we could bring her up for a tag and a photograph.

As we motored back to Mindelo, Greg seemed reinvigorated. He'd caught our fourth fish, and I was back on deck.

We sailed into the harbor past a beautiful three-masted sailing ship flying under the flag of the Brazilian navy and manned by about a hundred young sailors, all, I'm sure, looking forward to a little shore leave in Mindelo.

Xie went below and brought up two marlin flags, which he attached and raised on the starboard halyard, upside down, signifying that we had caught and released two marlin that day. I'm sure that was salt in the wound for the other sportfishers on our dock who were flagless, but it was inconsequential to, and unnoticed by, the one hundred or so Brazilian sailors who's hunt to catch and release quarry was just beginning.

Our return to Foya Branca was unextraordinary, like no one knew we had been gone. After a welcome swim, Greg and I walked to the restaurant for an early dinner. Lady, our favorite pretty waitress surprised us each with a double-order of whelk. Dinner was fun. We were both tired, but we'd started the day with two big marlin in four days and finished with four in five days. In these waters it's never boring; you know you are in the land of the giants. There are only big fish, and you know that the next takedown could be your fish of a lifetime.

I was back on deck for day six.

Day Six
Home Waters

It was day six; was I mistaken, or were the guys in the café happy to see us? The waiter brought us our coffees, one black and one with cream, without our even asking. The old guy at the table by the door who I'd complimented on his blue cowboy hat covered with commemorative pins from God knows where looked over, pointed to his hat, and smiled a toothless grin that warmed my heart and made me feel at home.

Just like our third day, the wind was really whipping up the seas, creating close-packed waves that don't allow you to get into any rhythm moving around on the boat.

Around 11:00 in the morning, while we were trolling past some tuna fishermen, I got a great takedown.

"Big tuna," Zak said as the line played off my Shimano reel.

Down and dirty, the big fish kept on going and going, taking about half of my line. Two hundred yards of line, I figured. Still going, I said, "Hey Zak, do you think we better get after this one?"

"Take the drag up to thirty pounds," he said as the boys collected the other lines and we started to back down on the fish.

Reel, reel, reel! I was thinking my right arm was going to fall off after fifteen minutes when our big tuna jumped about thirty yards from the transom disguised as a 450-pound blue marlin. She had exhausted herself after her long run and came in pretty easily after a few great, flailing head smashes. Photos, a good tag, and nice release preceded some high fives all around and some kidding for our captain on his false fish identification, a mistake that anyone could have made.

Greg was on deck again. In the fighting chair after a one hour wait, just like the day before, we got a huge strike and takedown on the long port rigger. By now, Captain Greg was dialed in, smokin' this fish like it was something he did everyday. As I manned the camcorder, I watched his technique as he brought the marlin to the leader after three nice jumps. Xie got the wraps, and number six was tagged and released just like that, in eighteen minutes.

"Five hundred pounds," Greg half-intoned and half-begged, looking up at Zak, our impartial referee on the bridge.

"Maybe 425," Zak opined as Greg first hung his head and then looked up, flashing a huge smile. Six huge fish in five and a half days. Who could complain about that? And that is how the day ended.

We cracked two beers as we headed for the dock with two inverted marlin flags flying from the halyard for the second straight day. We were heading to port with one day left to find our grander and we were scheduled to meet the girls for dinner the next night. Catch her or not, the trip had been great, full of moments we'd never forget.

The pool swim, with rum and cokes in plastic cups before an early dinner, felt great.

Day Seven
Last Chance?

On day seven, we got a nice "*bom dia*" from the guys at the café.

On board *Beast*, we trolled lures over a calm sea. The air was oppressively humid, and we were all sweating profusely. After four hours of nothing, I stood behind the fighting chair and reflected on our trip, fighting a sinking feeling that in spite of the great adventure we'd enjoyed, my prize was going to allude me.

"What're ya thinkin', Bubba?" Greg asked.

"I'm not, Greg" I answered. "I'm in a trance, trying to conjure up a grander."

We both laughed and returned to our vigil. Our hopes seemed to be dwindling under the merciless noonday sun.

Then, all of a sudden, as if in a dream, a monstrously enormous mass of color lunged at our port side teaser, then disappeared.

"Get ready, get ready," Zak shouted from the bridge, "that's her and she's coming back, hot!"

I couldn't believe it. I thought maybe I should consider a career as a conjurer.

With all of our eyes glued on the spread, a monstrous explosion went off on the port rigger lure, almost too large, violent, and fast for the mind to comprehend. It looked like someone had dropped a Volkswagen out of an airplane. The rod in the gunnel bent over double as the black Dacron loop affixed to the 130-pound line snapped out of the outrigger clip and came tight immediately. The yellow monofilament screamed off the reel, creating a sound I'd never before heard.

"Pick it up, Bubba," Greg almost whispered in my ear. "This is what we came for."

I wrenched the rod out of the rod holder, climbed back into the chair as Xie and Mario snapped me into the fighting harness. I thought, *This must be like being strapped into the seat of a jet fighter plane.*

All I could do was hold on and watch the line fly. I knew that we had three hundred feet of monofilament connected to seven hundred feet of Dacron for a total of one thousand feet of line; but still, I prayed that I wouldn't get spooled. Obviously sharing my concern, Zak tried to be patient as he watched his crew clear the other lines then started backing down toward the fleeing fish.

I kept hoping for some jumps that never came. A fish expends more energy jumping than sounding, and it's easier to take back line from a fish on the surface. For now, there would be no retrieval. We had set the reels up with thirty pounds of pressure, and all we could do was keep a good bend in the rod, watch, and wait.

Then, after several minutes and down to a quarter of the spool, the fish stopped pulling. Just like that, the reel stopped spinning. I responded by reeling as fast as I could, trying to lay the slack line back evenly on the spool, hoping against hope that my quarry hadn't pulled the hook or broken me off, but rather that she was swimming back toward us. Reeling as fast as I could, I couldn't catch up or come tight. Zak eased *Beast* forward, trying to help me collect line if the other beast was still hooked up.

After what seemed like about ten minutes, to our collective relief, the line came tight again. Feeling the pressure, the big fish took off again in the same direction as before, with the same stamina. While I'd been reeling, she's been resting.

I've caught some big fish before, but never had I felt the power of such a fish on a rod. She had a heaviness that defies description.

An hour went by with Zak moving the boat around then backing down toward the fish to give me some advantage in this tug of war. Following Greg's instructions, I reeled myself up and sat back down, over and over, in a kind of a rhythmic repetition.

Greg handed me a quart-sized plastic bottle of ice water. I drank a quarter of it and poured the rest of it over my head.

This was another real prize fight. She'd win a round, then I'd win a round. In between, we'd just kind of pull on each other in a bit of a Mexican standoff.

An hour and a half into the battle, Greg tried to bolster my spirits. "She's really getting tired now, Bubba!" *She's not the only one,* I thought. Jamming the controls on the bridge, Zak was backing down hard on the fish, sending water and spray over the transom. The entire cockpit and everyone in it was soaked.

Then all of a sudden, the black Dacron rigger clip appeared on the surface.

"She's a rigger length away now," Greg yelled, "Only 150 feet!" *Only,* I thought, every inch of my body on fire.

Another fifteen minutes passed. I knew that I had her now. For every foot of line she took, I took back two. Then we "had color," that mystical time in a fish fight when you can see the silhouette of your adversary swimming twenty or thirty feet underwater. She was indeed huge. Just as she came into view, she seemed to see the boat and marshal up her last ounces of strength to rocket toward the surface, launching herself in a giant, breathtaking leap, her sword-like bill flaying and her entire body stretching skyward out of the sea not ten feet from the transom. She crashed back into the water with a splash that soaked all of us.

We knew the end was in sight. Xie and Mario put on their heavy gloves, stepped back to the transom, and got ready to take some wraps on the leader and bill the fish. Greg walked over to Mario and said, "Mind if I do the honors?"

Mario handed him his gloves with a smile and went to get the tag stick. Greg slipped the gloves on and ducked under my rod, ready to grab the leader. The first time he got it, the big girl surged and pulled the line out of his hands. On the second try, he got a few good wraps and was able to get a firm hold on the bill, which he handed off to Xie while Mario stuck a tag in the fish's back, near its dorsal fin. Xie worked the lure out of the corner of the fish's mouth then, with Greg's help, and moved the fish to the side of the boat while Zak motored ahead slowly.

After five minutes, the saltwater flowing through her gills revived the fish, and, with a slap of her large tail, she pulled away and swam off, looking perhaps a little dazed but none the worse for wear.

I released myself from the fighting harness, stood up, and gave Greg a big hug.

"Well done, Bubba," he said.

"My grander?" I asked, fully knowing she wasn't a thousand pounds, but more like seven hundred and fifty.

Greg smiled and said "Bubba, she is certainly the grandest fish we've caught this week."

Just then, Zak said, "Good timing, here come the girls." We looked up to see the plane descending through the puffy mid-afternoon clouds and starting its final approach onto the long runway at Mindelo's airport.

With handshakes all around, we headed for port and Greg got that sad look on his face.

"What's the matter?" I asked him, knowing what was on his mind.

"I'm disappointed," he said.

"Chill, pal," I told him, "we did great. We hit our goal."

"But you didn't get your grander."

"You don't understand," I said, "a grander is a concept, no more, no less. We gave it a shot, caught some big marlin, and had a great time. That's what we came here for."

"What about the grander?" Greg persisted, "Aren't you upset you never caught her?"

Not a grander, but still a wonderful fish. *Author's photo.*

"Not at all, Greg. As I said, she's a concept—the concept of a hunt for a big prize. So she's still out there, bigger than ever, a reason to come back or a reason to do something else. She's still out there, stronger and more magnificent than we can ever imagine, swimming in our dreams amidst memories of a wonderful adventure."

"No regrets?" Greg asked sheepishly.

"Not a one, pal. And I've even discovered whelk!"

Postscript

The girls arrived safe and sound after their safari, brimming with great stories. Zak joined us for a farewell dinner at the hotel and was able to serve as a bridge between quest and safari and enjoy the stories as well.

While proud of my big fish, I thought the best tale of all came from Mindy, who talked about a large wild elephant who seemed to adopt their group and eat and sleep about ten feet from their tent, snoring heavily and breaking wind incessantly, making her feel, no doubt, that she was back at home trying to sleep next to yours truly.

BOOK 4
SCENES FROM THE WAYSIDE

THE FIGHTING MANATEES

"Dive in, Aqua Man, and do ten laps as a warm-up before we start today's practice."

Standing on the starting block at the end of the pool, looking over the vast expanse of fifty meters of water (164.5 feet), I whined, "You don't understand, coach. What is a warm-up for you is a career for me."

Shivering as I hit the water at 6:30 a.m., I started to think about how I got into this masters swimming program in Florida.

For years I'd been plagued by sinus infections. I blamed everything. Work, stress, grandkids, pets, air travel, cold, heat, air conditioning—everything. No matter what remedies I tried, nothing worked. Antihistamines, antibiotics, heating pads, cold compresses, sinus rinses, acupuncture, booze—nothing. Specialists said I wasn't a candidate for surgery and that I should just live with it.

Finally, after about ten years of severe on-and-off pain, during one extreme episode where I thought my head was going to explode, my wife, Mindy The Wise, suggested that I try swimming. "It may be about pressure, and the water might also open your nasal passages" she said, probably for the hundredth time before I'd considered listening. By then frantic, I agreed. I went over to the Buffalo Club, which had a fifty-foot indoor pool, ready to try anything. My guess was that my wife was just trying to get me out of the house.

I'd swam a lot as a kid, but not competitively—except for once as a fifth grader at Buffalo's Public School 22 against our arch rival PS 63. Being the youngest on the team, they made me swim backstroke. I think I lost by about five lengths and cracked my head open when I slammed into the metal ladder at the end of the pool. The gash required five stitches to close and provided an inglorious end to my short aquatic career.

Remembering that day, I decided to swim freestyle, or the Australian crawl, or whatever they called it. The Buffalo Club was one of those dinosaur old-man-only hangouts where you could paddle around with nothing on but a smile and a borrowed pair of swim goggles, which I did. (This always made it easy to swim with your head down and not check out adjacent lanes underwater.)

I climbed in, kicked off, and swam. After about five laps, the pain went away, I kid you not! I was pain-free and lovin' it. Mindy should have been a doctor. Anyway, I stayed in for about an hour, not wanting to risk the sinus pain coming back. On the way home, I stopped at a sporting goods store and bought myself a pair of swim goggles. I decided that I was going to swim as often as I could, home or away.

Traveling a lot for business, I even began choosing hotels by the length of their pools. As far as swimwear, I decided to stay with my baggy Vineyard Vines swimsuits. While I knew that they were less than hydrodynamic, they did cover up more figure flaws on a full-size guy, if you get my drift.

Finding available pools in the winter up north is not that easy, so I was glad that, after Thanksgiving and with the snows beginning to fly, we were heading south to our home in the Florida Keys. In Islamorada, the place to swim is easy: either the ocean or the pool at Founders Park. A few years before, we voted to incorporate our village. One of the first and best decisions our new town council made was to buy up and develop a large tract of land that they humbly named after themselves. The pool at Founders Park is a beautiful L-shaped, Olympic-sized pool with all the trimmings, with an adjoining diving pool complete with two one-meter and two three-meter boards.

We arrived in town around midnight on a Thursday, and I was checking in at the door at Founders by 8:00 a.m. Friday morning. After paying a nominal fee and taking a warm shower, I was in the pool, baggy trunks and all, by 8:15 a.m. I swam a mile in about an hour and five minutes and was really comfortable. Happy with myself, I began wondering if even Mark Spitz could keep up with me.

Only being able to turn my head one way, to my right, while swimming, I looked over and saw that another swimmer had entered the pool. It was a young guy, very thin, in a Speedo suit, and he was passing me. That wasn't so unusual. What was unusual was that he was swimming the length of the pool underwater with his chin almost on the bottom and his arms by his sides, doing the dolphin kick. I touched the far end and headed back. Halfway to the near side I looked to my right side again just in time to see another guy passing me doing the same stroke, the dolphin kick, underwater, with his arms at his side—only this time he was upside down with the back of his swim cap almost running along the bottom of the pool.

That's it, I thought, reaching the end of the pool. I ducked under four lane dividers, found the ladder, and pulled myself out of the pool. Taking my goggles off and finding my towel, I asked the lifeguard, "Who the hell are those guys?"

"Oh, those are the Olympians," he smiled back nonchalantly.

"You mean guys who want to make the Olympics?" I asked, knowing the 2008 Olympics were coming up in Beijing, China, the next summer.

"No, they are Olympians," he said. "Look, while you were swimming, there were four other guys that got in the pool with you. Between them, they've already won sixteen Olympic medals."

That really put it in perspective for me. All of a sudden feeling like a tow barge on the Erie Canal, I sat down at the base of the lifeguard stand to watch them.

What a sight; each one more ripped than the next. Each one doing warm-up strokes that I'd never even seen before nor thought possible. It looked like a fashion shoot for Speedo as I watched about twelve more of these mermen dive into the water, filling up the lanes along with about four female swimmers as buff as the guys and absolutely beautiful.

Just then, an attractive blond walked up to me, said hello, and asked me if I wanted to join the masters program.

"No thanks," I said. "I'm about to announce my retirement from swimming."

She looked puzzled at first, then looked around, threw her head back, and started laughing as I tied my Snoopy beach towel around my waist to cover up my baggy shorts.

"Don't be intimidated by them," she said. "That's the Race Club; they swim for two hours every morning after the masters are done."

"Who are these people?" I asked.

"Well, first of all," she said, extending her hand, "I'm Christina Boland. A few years ago, my uncle, Gary Hall Sr., moved here from Phoenix and started a program for training Olympians using some rather unconventional approaches to conditioning—like periodic spear fishing outings—and I help him with the program."

"Wait a minute," I said. "I recognize that name; wasn't your uncle a two-time Olympian and medalist for the US in the seventies?"

"Three-time," she corrected. "He swam in Mexico in '68, Munich in '72, and Montreal in '76."

"Is your uncle here today?" I asked.

"Yeah, he's the guy in the big straw hat standing next to the coach."

"And who's the coach?"

"He's Mike Bottom," she said. "He coached at University of Southern California and then Cal Berkeley for ten years before coming here to coach the Olympians, who've come from all around the world to train."

"And your cousin, Gary Jr., I remember him as an Olympic medalist, too."

"Yeah," Christina said. "He was in the last three Games: Atlanta '96, Sydney '00, and Athens '04. He's trying to make it four by qualifying for Beijing this summer. That's him in lane 3."

Wow, I thought. I remembered him as the big, blond, cocky kid who paraded into the aquatic center in Athens dressed up in a red, white, and blue Everlast robe and shorts like Rocky Balboa. He then disrobed and smoked everybody to win gold in the fifty-meter freestyle.

Pretty good company for a small-town pool in the Keys.

"So how 'bout it?" Christina persisted. "You wanna join our masters program?"

"Tell me a little more about it."

"Sure," she said. "We're part of the national US Masters Swimming program. We have a coach here three mornings a week, Monday, Wednesday, and Friday, from 6:30 to 9:30 a.m., and we swim before the Race Club starts their daily practices."

"You pay a minimal amount for dues and are also eligible for regional and national competitions. We know a lot of our swimmers travel a lot, so there's no mandatory attendance. Swim when you can."

"Do I need to bring anything?" I asked.

"Well," she said, "you'll need goggles and eventually your own fins and a kick board for some of the drills. And . . . that Snoopy towel will work nicely, but you might want to ditch those baggies for a Speedo suit or the like."

"Now that could be problematic," I said.

Laughing, she said, "Don't worry, you'll look fine. We all wear them here and you'll be amazed at how much faster you'll swim."

"OK, Christina, I'm in," I said, thinking to myself, *How hard can this be anyway?*

Six-thirty in the morning of the appointed first day of masters class came very early. It wasn't the early hour; all of us fishermen in the Keys are used to getting up early. Rather, it was because of a fitful sleep the night before. I kept dreaming of a sea cow that we call a manatee, trying to shoehorn itself into a tropical-flowered Speedo.

Oh, well, what's the difference? I've been embarrassing myself for years. Why should this be any different? I put on my new swimsuit and a pair of sweats and headed for Founders Park.

When I arrived there was only one guy, obviously the coach, standing at the end by the pool. Looking a little closer, I realized that there were seven swimmers in their lanes, swimming laps. I introduced myself to the coach, Mark Hill, who looked to be about thirty with a swimmers build. He wore shorts and a whistle around his neck.

"Lane 2 is open, and here's a copy of today's program," he said, handing me a photocopy of something that looked like hieroglyphics to me—and that was before I took off my glasses:

WARM UP

300 FREE
200 I.M. (KICK / DRILL BY 25)
100 CHOICE
4 × 50 VARIABLE ON 1:10

25 EZ / 25 FAST
25 FAST / 25 EZ
ALL FAST
ALL EZ

PULL

4 × 200 BREATHE 3/5/7/3 BY 50 R:45

MAIN

6 X (100 FREE BUILD R:20, 50 FAST CHOICE)
R 1:00
BETW EA

KICK

2 X 300 (MIDDLE 100 STROKE)
W ↓: 200 CHOICE
I 3300M

"Thanks; what should I do with it?" I asked, knowing I was looking stupid already.

"Wet it and stick it on the wall at the end of the pool so you'll know what drills to swim."

"And what do all these numbers mean?" I asked sheepishly.

"For the most part, it tells you how many laps to do of each stroke," Mark said, "for now, why don't you just jump in and do ten laps to get warm? I'll keep an eye out for you and give you instructions after your warm-up."

While swimming laps I noticed that, not for the first time in my sports career, I was the only guy. Well, that's OK, I thought, I'll be the fastest one in the pool. Within three laps, I realized that I was, in fact, the slowest. This was not a good thing.

We all swam for a couple hours until practice ended. I climbed out and put in a very good time in my new event, "the twenty-five foot sprint to the Snoopy beach towel." As the other swimmers emerged and took off their bathing caps and goggles, I realized that I knew three of them: Caroline Wightman, the wife of a legendary Key's fishing guide Captain Eddie Wightman; Eliza Colmes, who'd worked for years for the veterinarians in Islamorada and was also married to one of my charter boat captain friends, Jeff Colmes; and Beth Kamenstein Levy, the wife of our former village mayor Ron Levy.

They were all attractive and fit middle-aged women who I'd known for several years. I was flattered that, perhaps feeling my awkwardness, they seemed to be going out of their way to put me at ease.

All except for Beth, that is. "Nice Snoopy towel, Bubba," she said, laughing.

It wasn't too surprising that Beth would take a shot at me. You see, I'm a nicknamer, and I gave her my very best. Beth is a potter of some renown from New York City who learned her trade as a coed at the rather artsy-craftsy all women's college Bennington, in Vermont. Having been a proud member of a *National Lampoon*'s *Animal House*–like fraternity at nearby Williams College, I always had a soft spot in my heart for Bennington as a prime road trip destination.

That's why Otter's road trip to a women's college in *Animal House* struck a chord with me. If you remember, Otter (Tim Matheson), traveling with three of his frat brothers, did his homework and researched a young woman who had been killed in a kiln explosion. Asking for the deceased girl at her dorm, he introduced himself to her attractive roommate as the girl's fiancée, causing the roommate to have to disclose the news of her sad demise. Bursting into tears, Otter said he didn't want to be alone and asked her if she would come out to keep him company—and as a footnote, asked if she had three friends to match up with his friends in the car, Pinto, Boone, and Flounder.

And the name of the recently departed potter? Fawn Leibowitz, the nickname I gave Beth! All right, sophomoric, I admit, but as any nicknamer will agree, the real success of a nickname is that it sticks. That's why I was so proud when Beth a.k.a. Fawn had called me a few months earlier feigning rage because her mother in New York had started calling her Fawn. OK, maybe she wasn't feigning.

My new masters pals didn't seem to be in a rush to leave as the Olympians of the Race Club arrived, disrobed, and started their stretching.

"Oh, I get it," I said. "You've all turned into cougars and are lusting after these young guys."

Their spontaneous laughter gave them away. Their halfhearted denials fell on deaf ears.

I may not be able to keep up with those young Olympians in the pool or match up with these women for that matter, but on dry land I figured I could hold my own. My swimming career was relaunched.

The winter percolated right along. The more I tried my best to understand the sport, the more Mark the swimming coach seemed to ignore me. Then one day, as I was finishing a workout, he came up to me and said, "You know, I really admire you for coming out here."

"Thanks, Mark," I said, somewhat shocked, and added facetiously, "Why's that—because I'm so old?"

"No . . . well, that too," he said, adding, "because you don't know how to swim."

"Thanks, coach, thanks a lot," I said. "I've been out here for six weeks. Why are you telling me this now?"

"'Cause I didn't know how serious you were," he said.

"Well, I'm still here, aren't I?" I said. "Why don't we start again right now?"

"OK," he said. "Start rotating your hips and take fewer breaths and work on your dolphin kick and stop doing that frog kick with your butterfly stroke. That went out in the sixties."

All right, I thought, *I've co-opted my last critic.* Now I'm ready to chop off some seconds. The digital poolside clock was running constantly, so you could always tell how you were doing.

There was a lot of activity at Founders, and it was fun sharing the pool with the cougars and the Olympians. It was even more fun when some of the older guys started showing up, like my friend, offshore captain Rob Dixon. He had been married to my pal Rusty Albury's cousin and was thus known as an in-law. Then they got divorced, so I thought it was a natural to nickname him "The Outlaw," and it stuck.

Fifty-six-year-old Gary Hall Sr. started working out with us, too, and demonstrated the kind of things that you needed to bring to be successful in the water. His fitness and work ethic were without parallel. Inadvertently I started calling him "The Legend," which I thought he was, and that nickname stuck, too.

Apparently he didn't mind because I started to get messages on my voicemail saying "Aqua Man, it's me, Legend. How about a workout tomorrow? Call me."

That was kind of cool, I thought, even though I knew I swam more like a manatee than Aqua Man.

That, in fact, led to the formation of our swim club. We were supposed to go to a meet, and all the other teams had names like the Dolphins, Sharks, Marlins, Barracudas, and so forth. I asked one of our fellow swimmers, John Timura, who was in the T-shirt business, if he would make up some shirts with a fanciful logo on the front and the words *The Fighting Manatees*. I also asked him to personalize them with names on the back like "Fawn Leibowitz" for Beth, "The Legend" for Gary, "The Outlaw" for Rob, "Mrs. Robinson" (from *The Graduate*) for Caroline, "Aqua Chic" for Eliza, and "Aqua Manatee" for me.

Thus our swim club had a name, and Fighting Manatee Wear was launched.

It took off, and all of a sudden, shirt sales, with revenues benefitting swimming at Founders, were booming and people were clamoring for manatee nicknames. I even started seeing some of the Olympians wearing Manatee shirts or hats.

Around about Easter, Christina approached me and said, "We're putting a team together for 'The Swim Around Key West' and wondered if you wanted to join us."

"You can't be serious," I said. "I swim slower than a manatee, and that's a long way through shark-infested waters. It's gotta be ten miles."

The team poolside at Founders Park in Islamorada. *Author's photo.*

"Actually, its twelve and a half miles," she said. "They've been doing the race each summer for a few years, and no one's been eaten yet. You'll do fine. We'll have a six-person team and split it up so everyone swims about two miles each. You do more than that every practice. You'll do just fine."

"Sounds doable, Christina," I said, "but open water's a different thing than pool swimming with all those waves out there and creepy, crawly things. You know, I fish a lot and I've seen a lot of strange things happen—like the time a bull shark ate a 140-pound tarpon in two bites."

"We're planning some open water training sessions," she said, "and don't worry, you don't look much like a tarpon."

"Well, why me, Christina?"

"Because you're a gamer, Aqua Manatee."

She had me. To say "no" would be saying that I wasn't a gamer. "OK, when's our first open water swim?"

"I'll set it up. We've already got four swimmers, counting you. There's me, Mike Bottom's wife, Laura Lynn, and a guy named Bharat Sachdeva from India, who swims with the Olympians. Maybe you could choose two more to fill out our team."

"Great," I said, already thinking of who my first choices would be. My son Ted and his wife, Nena, were swimmers and were always trying to get me to do an open water swim. I knew that they'd be up for Key West, and they were. Game on!

Race day arrived in June, just as the American Olympians were packing up for the time trials in Omaha. It would be a farewell swim for Laura Lynn, who was leaving for Ann Arbor, Michigan, with her children and husband, Mike. Mike had just accepted the head swim coach job at the University of Michigan, which had produced some great swimmers like Michael Phelps.

My fishin' buddy Rusty Albury had secured a boat and had agreed to come down to Key West to drive it as our "chase boat" and to watch out for sharks. My wife, Mindy, came along as our coach and timer. We loaded the boat with water, fruit, sunblock, and five swimmers and left Bharat on the shore at Smathers Beach to swim the first leg for us. We figured that, being a sprinter, he would be able to take us out fast. The rules called for each swimmer to swim for at least half an hour before the team could go to ten minute rotations, but always in the same order.

Bharat had us near the front of the pack of a hundred or so swimmers when he gave way to Nena for the second leg. A strong swimmer in high school, Nena used a long, steady stroke with high elbows to take us around the corner and past the marker at the southernmost point in the United States. Christina was up next and she really burned up the water. She had been a college swimmer, and, before jumping into the water at Key West, told us a bizarre story of what had influenced her decision to quit competitive swimming. She had been swimming in a meet at Erie Community College in Buffalo when someone called in a crank bomb threat, forcing all the teams to immediately evacuate the building. Being in the pool at the time, she had to run out of the building barefoot, still in her suit, soaking wet, into the dead of winter. It took the fire department about twenty minutes to reach the stranded swimmers with blankets. In the meantime, she said her wet hair froze and she felt like she was turning blue. "Lycra swimsuits aren't very good winter wear for Buffalo," she joked, shivering compulsively to punctuate her story.

Now, Christina was swimming a great leg and almost leaving a wake as she passed several other swimmers. She turned it over to my son Ted as we approached two of the large cruise ships tied to the dock in Key West Harbor. Ted is a triathlete, and while he's slight of build, he has the heart of a warrior. You could tell that he was out to pass people and not be passed. In fact, the only thing that did pass him was a large, hooked tarpon fleeing the angler in a boat right next to us. This provided a rather tense moment for the Fighting Manatee Race Club as well as our shark spotter/captain.

Ted finished his leg and Laura Lynn dove in for her turn. A fine ex-college swimmer, she took us past the Coast Guard station and around the corner into the channel and under the bridge that connects Key West to Fleming Key.

I was up next, ready to put real meaning back into the phrase "Anchor Leg." The swim along the backside of Key West is really quite beautiful, in gin-clear shallow water over coral heads, sand, and rocks. It was like swimming in an aquarium, which made it quite hard to avoid getting caught up in looking at all the colorful tropical fish as you swam over them. I tried to concentrate and speed up my strokes, but I am sure that I got passed by some of the teams that we'd passed earlier.

All of a sudden, my time was up and we started our ten minute rotations. Everyone looked strong, and we started passing swimmers again. My next time in the water was a swim I'll never forget. My turn came up as we hit Cow Key Channel, appropriately named after me, I think. It's a channel, seventy-five feet wide by one mile long, that separates Key West from Stock Island to the north. We got to the channel just at the middle

The original Fighting Manatee swimming like one. *Author's photo.*

of the falling tide. Riding the fast moving water flowing to the ocean, I felt like I was surfing more than swimming or that I had an outboard motor tied to my backside. I was flyin' and I knew nobody was going to pass me.

Back to the ocean, we pulled up behind a team of young girls who were calling themselves the Topless Torpedoes for obvious reasons. I think the women on our team took this personally and went into overdrive. Boy, I thought to myself, this is a lot more fun than swimming with those old naked guys at the Buffalo Club. We basically reeled them in and left them far back in our wakes as we passed the finish line and all jumped in to swim to shore together.

At the reception after the race, we found out that our time of five hours and twenty-six minutes was good for third place and trophy conch shells that I think we all still treasure.

After the race, Gary Hall Sr. called and said that he'd like to be on our Key West team next year. Ted, Nena, and I stayed on the team and added Ted's cousin Kiley, a college swimmer, Gary, and our friend Dr. Marc Harrison, head of the pediatric ICU at the Cleveland Clinic and an eight-time Iron Man. Showing the growing popularity of masters swimming in Islamorada, we were now just one of three teams that entered the race representing the Fighting Manatees. Our time was slower because of a rising tide at Cow Key Channel and we finished fourth, fifty yards behind one of our other boats that had also "Olympic-upped" with a US sprinter from the '92 and '96 games, Jon Olsen, who'd won four gold medals and a silver.

The highlight of the race came when The Legend, in a blue full-body suit, caught up with Jon and swam stroke for stroke with him before passing him by twenty-five yards at the end of his half-hour swim. Of course, Jon was somewhat disadvantaged when his drawstring broke, causing him to literally swim out of his red bathing suit. As an unexpected consequence, he mooned the folks all along the length of the deck of the cruise ship, getting a huge ovation from the passengers and gaining him the new nickname Moon Manatee.

One week after Key West, in the 2008 US Trials in Omaha, Gary Hall

Jr. failed to qualify for a trip to Beijing in spite of swimming the 50 meter free in a time that was faster than his gold medal time in Athens four years earlier. He ended in fourth place in Omaha, and only the top two made the team. The swimsuit technology that the winners used has now been banned.

The Race Club from Islamorada was well-represented in Beijing that summer by seventeen of their swimmers from fifteen different countries. They were led in medals by Nathan Adrian swimming to a gold medal for the USA in the 400 meter free relay. And who will ever forget Serbia's Milorad "Michael" Cavic's loss to Michael Phelps by less than a fingernail (one one-hundredth of a second) in the 100 meter fly, which enabled Phelps to win eight golds while Race Clubber Cavic had to settle for silver.

As an interesting footnote to that race, it fell upon Cavic's coach, Mike Bottom, to file that protest against a living legend who trained at Michigan University—where Bottom was on his way to coach.

Back in the US a month after the Olympics, Gary Hall Sr. competed in the US Master Championship with a "reunion" team from his alma mater, Indiana University. Swimming on a team they called the Hoosier Daddies in honor of their legendary coach, Doc Counsilman, Gary won seven gold medals, four in team relays and three individuals in the 100 meter back, the 50 meter back, and the 50 meter fly.

As for the rest of the Fighting Manatees, our cougars have survived the departure of the Olympians and now, not distracted, are training harder than ever. Our ranks have swelled, and through a variety of local fundraising events and clothing sales, we have been able to make some nice contributions to youth swimming in the Keys.

As for Aqua Manatee, I'm still waking along and enjoying looking at our beautiful new coach, Katy LeVasseur, Mama Manatee, much more than I enjoyed looking at Mark Hill, who has gone to Michigan to join Mike Bottom's coaching staff. And, oh yes, I'm still headache-free.

STRAIGHT ARROW

I've never hunted—never shot at or killed any of God's creatures. The only time I fired a gun was in army basic training at Fort Dix. The prize for qualifying as "Expert," besides the army medal, was a weekend pass. Man, I looked like Chuck Connors in *The Rifleman* on TV. Shot a flawless round with my M1, won the Expert medal, which I still have somewhere, and used my pass to weekend in New York City with a local college girl . . . ah, but that's for another story.

The way I see it, there are two kinds of men (and women) in the world: those who hunt and those who don't. My theory is that if your father hunted, you hunt; if he didn't, you don't. Simple as that. Dads who love guns pass that love along. Dads who don't like guns shield their children from them. I grew up in the latter camp. My Dad was big into team sports, and guns were never allowed, let alone spoken of, in our house. The only exception was when my father would read random newspaper articles to us about children who accidentally shot themselves.

My dad had an accomplice in my mother who was constantly reading *Bambi* to us. It wasn't until I grew up that I questioned why someone would read a story to their kids about a bunch of dumb deer, especially one with such a sad ending. Now that I think about it, I guess you'd have to list Walt Disney as an accomplice as well.

Some would call it healthy respect, but it was really a fear of guns. For me, that fear turned into genuine dislike one fall day when I was ten years old. My best friend and I were playing cowboys and Indians in our yard. As the cowboy, he got to carry the rifle and I got the damn bow and arrow. He sneaked around a large elm tree one way while I was sneaking around the other way, and I ran right into his rifle barrel and knocked out my front tooth. I've never been very comfortable around guns.

I fish a lot, so I'm always asked if I hunt as well. I guess because fishers and hunters share the same stage, the outdoors, it's a natural assumption that hunters are fishers and vice versa. For some reason, maybe not to stop the conversation and/or sound like a wimp, I always answer, "Just a little wing shooting and some sporting clays." Truthfully, I don't even really know what that means—unless its birds and those clay things that somebody throws in the air when you yell "pull."

I've got a lot of great pals who are passionate hunters. I have no problem with that. I don't fully understand the allure of the pastime, but I do admire their resolve and the travails they go through to shoot their prizes. At the same time, I am repulsed by those Saturday morning outdoor shows on hunting that push fishing off the air, especially with the approach of the fall, when most shooting seems to take place. I believe the programs are disgustingly predictable. Wayne walks over hill and dale with his trusty, laconic guide, Steve, in search of big things to kill. As they approach their quarry, they start whispering. They set up and *bang*. Cut to the next scene, and there's some big critter lying on the ground with its eyes rolled back and tongue hanging out. Wayne and Steve kneel behind it, stroking its skin. "Isn't she beautiful?" Wayne asks Steve, rhetorically I'm sure.

"No, Wayne," I answer, sometimes almost shouting at the TV screen, "she was beautiful ten minutes ago, before you blasted the life out of her!" Then I change the channel and look for an early football game.

Enough of "Bubba on Hunting" before my good pal Johnny Morris rescinds my Favored Shopper's Card at Bass Pro Shop. (John's son, John Paul, like his dad, is a great guy and one of the country's best bow hunters. I asked him once how he sleeps at night with all of those animal mounts in his bedroom, staring at him, and he just laughed.)

So how come I went hunting? I've obviously been invited before and had turned down all previous invites. Well, we were visiting the Greenbrier Hotel in White Sulphur Springs, West Virginia, where we had become members of the local sporting club. While the state is beautiful, a real gem of mountains and forests and twisty roads, it is also a dichotomous tale of two cities. West Virginia leads the country in illiteracy and unemployment but also is one of the best hunting and fishing destinations. It's safe to assume that almost every West Virginia male you meet is a hunter. Ask a stranger if he got his deer on opening day and prepare for a smile and a hunting story that usually begins with, "Yeah ah did, and here's how. . . ."

The head of The Sporting Club is a young man named Larry Klein.

Larry Klein—hospitality professional. So-so with a fly rod.
"Straight Arrow" with a bow. *Author's photo.*

Larry is a handsome chap with an identical twin who is also in the hospitality industry in Jackson Hole, Wyoming. A Michigan State graduate in his thirties, Larry stands straight and tall with the thin build of a triathlete—which he is. His black hair is starting to show a little salt and pepper now, probably from having to deal with sporting club members like me. He's initially very serious and a little retiring, but a twinkle in his eye belies a good, albeit reserved, sense of humor. Above all, he seems to be a standup guy and a straight shooter.

I like Larry, and when he called one day to invite me to join him on his day off to go trout fishing on some "new water," a farm called Stoney Brook that I'd always wanted to fish, I was quick to accept. The fact that he'd also invited another friend, Jacob Ott, to join us made it that much more special.

Jacob is a homey; he was also born and raised in Buffalo. One of his claims to fame is that his dad was named Mel after big league pitcher Mel Ott, who was admired by the senior Ott, who himself pitched for the Buffalo Bisons. Thirty-something like Larry, Jacob discovered hunting and fishing at twelve years old and his future was determined. After school he moved to West Virginia and became a guide and eventually the river keeper for The Sporting Club. Shortly after Jacob became river keeper, I complained to him about a family of otters that were ravaging the stream where I love to fish. Otter love trout and have ravenous appetites, two facts that led Izaak Walton to brand them the worst enemy of the angler in the book *The Compleat Angler*, first published in 1653. Jacob promptly dealt with the menace by calling the West Virginia Department of National Resources and securing a permit to trap and relocate the critters. In the process, he earned himself the nickname "Otter."

He's the consummate outdoorsman: knowledgeable, stoic, and passionate about conservation. On this day, however, he would be joining Larry and me in no other capacity than fellow angler.

Back to my phone call with Larry Klein: my cell phone started to ring as Larry told me how glad he was I could make it. After the second ring, indicating another incoming call, Larry said, "I'll let you go," and added, "And maybe we'll shoot a deer in the afternoon on the way home."

"Yeah right, great," I said, hanging up. "See ya."

Do what? I thought to myself, picking up my incoming call. *Oh well,* I thought, *I'll call him back later.* But I didn't.

The next morning Larry called to confirm a time to pick me up. I was flattered by the excitement in his voice. "You're still in, aren't ya Bubba?" Larry said.

"Yeah, of course I'm in, but about that hunting part?" I managed.

"Man, I love hunting," he said, "Picked it up when I moved here. Had never once hunted before then, can you believe it?"

"Yes I can believe it, Larry and. . . ."

Before I could finish any sentence, he continued, "Tuesday will be the fourth day of bow season, and I've got my equipment ready. Is your bow ready to go?"

"Well no, Larry, actually it's not," I said, not actually lying, since I've never held, shot, or owned a bow, not counting that toy one I had when I was ten and got my front tooth knocked out.

"No problem, we'll bring an extra," Larry volunteered. "See you Tuesday at 11. We'll bring lunch. See ya then," he said and hung up.

Oh great, I thought. Why was I such a coward? Why didn't I say something? Oh well, why not? When in Rome. At least it's a reasonable hour for a departure. He did say bows. I remembered a lot of my friends in Buffalo going out for opening day of bow season and seldom seeing a deer, let alone shooting at or killing one. Maybe I'd get lucky and we'd get skunked. I wonder if skunked is a term you use in hunting like fishing, or do hunters say they got catfished, or something else? Maybe we'll have such great fishing, they'll forget about the hunt. Maybe it'll rain. Maybe it'll snow. Maybe someone'll get sick. (By the way, did I tell you that while not a hunter, I'm a world-class rationalizer.)

By Monday night, I actually had myself not only resigned to, but built up for, the trip. How could so many of my hunting friends be wrong? I remembered, for example, how Buffalo Bills Hall of Fame quarterback Jim Kelly had all hunting opening days committed to memory and religiously scheduled around them. Having grown up in East Brady, Pennsylvania, in a family with three brothers, Jim had dual religions, Catholicism and hunting, and took them both very seriously. "Jim, what if opening day was scheduled for the same day as a Super Bowl you were supposed to play in?" I once asked him jokingly.

Without smiling, he pondered the question for a couple of beats and finally said, "Bubba, that would be a tough call."

Who knew, maybe I'd like it. It was supposed to be a beautiful day, and I could always shoot and miss. Now I was really getting into it. I decided to call a few of my hunter pals, kind of make small talk, ask them what they were doing tomorrow, wait for them to reciprocate and ask me what I was doing, then drop the bomb. None of them did. When I told them I was going hunting, they all laughed and said good-bye, thinking I was just pulling their legs.

So be it, I thought as I got into bed and turned out the light. *I'm committed and I'm excited*, I thought to myself. What's the worst thing that could happen? Famous last words!

Tuesday dawned crystal clear and crisp with a few billowy cumulous clouds drifting by, a gentle breeze, and temperatures that were supposed to climb into the mid-seventies. There was no rain in the forecast.

I got my kit together and was dressed in my fishing waders and ready to go by the appointed hour. Larry and Otter were right on time, and off we went on a forty-minute drive toward our destination. My pals told some good hunting stories that made me laugh in spite of myself. Larry told my favorite: He was involved in planning for a very lavish wedding for the daughter of a Sporting Club member at the Greenbrier. The father of the bride had ordered white doves be released as the bride and groom kissed. The next day he led a Sporting Club dove hunt, and the hunters were surprised to see that white doves mixed in with the usual migratory target species. OK, I guess hunting humor may be a tad twisted.

Stoney Brook, in one word, is breathtaking. Fifteen thousand acres of farm and woodland, it's set in a beautiful valley but spreads into upland forests with streams that run to a series of lakes that help water the fields where they grow and harvest corn. Owned by Jim Justice, the new owner of the Greenbrier and himself an avid hunter and fisher, Stoney Brook is home to game animals of all kinds. Deer, black bear, and wild turkey seem to mingle with pheasants, doves, grouse, and a lot of other birds that I cannot identify. Driving in the front gate, we were greeted by a majestic bald eagle who performed a flyby not fifty feet from our SUV.

As we would discover after a great early lunch of West Virginia fried chicken, the streams were literally stacked with large, hungry rainbow trout. The owner claims that these big fish have been there for generations. Based on many of their banged-up noses and bitten-up tails, I suspect that most of them were recent immigrants from the local hatchery. Stocked or not, the fish were as beautiful and plentiful as the beasts of the field and the fowl of the sky, making Stoney Brook a true sportsman's paradise.

Scooting around the property on a four-wheeled vehicle called "The Bad Boy Buggy," we caught trout measuring up to twenty-four inches in every spot we fished. They were a nice matchup for my eight foot six inch House of Hardy 3-weight rod. I fished dry flies exclusively then, and did not feel disadvantaged by the nymphs and streamers that Larry had brought.

I glanced at my watch, and it was already 3:30 p.m. and there had been no mention of hunting. Maybe they'd forgotten. But no, as if reading my mind, Larry piped up, "Well, we better get going if we want to get our deer by dark."

Damn, I thought, *I'm trapped.* "Where do we look first?" I kind of whimpered.

"Oh, not here," Larry said. "We're going to drive over to Richard's farm. He's expecting us."

"Great," I lied.

Richard's farm was about a half-hour away and my soon-to-be "huntin' buddies" explained that Richard Aides is the retired owner of a local department store who loves to spend time in his beautifully restored hunting cabin on a very pretty farm drinking beer and watching the deer and bears who seem to have befriended or adopted him. (The beer part I was to confirm a few days later when I ran into him checking out at the "Less than 20 Items" counter at the local Walmart. I couldn't help noticing that the contents of his cart qualified him for the line: two 24-bottle cases of Bud and a giant frozen pizza.)

Richard, in his sixties, matches his white hair with a bushy white mustache. The racks that fill his walls attest to his legendary hunting skills. As we chatted on the porch, Larry excused himself and walked upstairs to the john. I found Richard to be a man of few words. *Maybe he used them all up selling hunting supplies*, I thought. As we watched what looked like four dozen deer grazing in his fields, he told me that he now runs hot and cold on hunting. "I really haven't done much shooting in the last two years," he said. "I'm really more into fishin' now." *Bless you, lad, bless you*, I thought to myself. Someone walked down the stairs to join us dressed from head to toe in green and brown camo clothes.

"Oh my God, is that you Larry? If I hadn't heard you on the stairs, I'd never have known you were here," I said, feigning surprise.

"Very funny," Larry smiled. "Where's your camo?"

"Oh darn it," I said. "It's, it's, it's at the cleaners. Yeah, that's right, it's at the cleaners."

"No matter," he shot back. "You've got a lot of brown on, and we can hunt from a ground blind."

"Oh, swell," I said.

"Got your hunting license?" Otter asked.

"Oh shoot," I answered, wondering if I should say that it was in my "imaginary" camo pants pocket at the cleaners. "I forgot it."

"No problem," my new ex-friend Jacob said. "I'll run you over to the local C-store and we can get you one. It'll only take a few minutes."

"Gee, Otter, that would be great, but I even forgot to bring my driver's license so I have no ID," I said, afraid to look at Richard let alone think about what was going through his mind about this city slicker who was invading his private refuge.

"You know, fellas," I tried. "You know what? The sun's already getting low in the sky. Why don't we just get started? You know I've done a lot of this, and I've actually brought along my camera and want to get some good footage of this while it's still light."

"Really?" Richard asked skeptically. "What kind of camera you bring? Canon, Minolta?"

"No, it's called a FLIP, Richard. Fits right in my shirt pocket. Well, we better get started."

The silence that ensued was palpable. I swear, I could almost hear deer chomping on the corn that Richard had obviously been spreading on his lawn for the last month. *I think these guys are wise to me, messin' with me*, I thought. I think Larry, the perpetrator, knew full well that I wasn't a hunter—probably looked me up on Google under "Sissies."

"OK, let's go," Otter said. "I'll drive you . . . hunters to a ground blind."

Jacob dropped us at our destination and headed back to the cabin in a four wheeler.

"Aren't you staying, Jacob?" I asked.

"Might be a little crowded," he said, pointing over at this thing that looked like the shipping crate for a refrigerator lying on its side.

"That's it?" I said.

"That's it," Larry answered, biting his lip. "C'mon over. I'll give you a tour."

A tour—yeah, right, it was a wooden box with one large peephole and two folding lawn chairs. This blind, I'm sure, made the prisoners' accommodations at Guantanamo Bay seem palatial.

Anyway, we ducked our heads, stepped in, and sat down on our lawn chairs, Larry with his camo and bow and arrow and me in my Patagonia fishing clothes and FLIP camera. What a pair!

"Hey Larry," I had to ask, "what is that strong smell around here? I know its urine. Is it human or animal?"

"Maybe a little bit of both," he said, now whispering like the guys on TV. "Here are the rules," he continued, "talk and move as little as possible. Whisper and move very slowly. And now, we wait."

And we didn't have to wait long. As I prayed to the Deer Gods to communicate our location, there came a scratching noise from behind us. As we had no rear window, I assumed it had to be a deer. For some reason, I had assumed they would all come straight at us from the wooded ridge that surrounded the beautiful green pasture we gazed upon from our peephole, which was about twelve inches wide and six inches high.

Within fifteen minutes, we were surrounded by deer, large and small, young and old, bucks and does, grazing and cavorting. It was mesmerizing; they were everywhere. There were at least twenty-four in our peephole view. Of those, six were bucks—three spikes (young bucks with two pointy antlers), two eight-point, and one nine-point. As we watched, the bucks circled, ate, and occasionally enjoined each other in little mock battles. First they stood on their hind legs and swiped at each other with their front legs, almost looking like they were boxing, then they backed up, lowered their heads and banged into each other, their antlers rattling. Then they backed up, looked around, and started feeding again like nothing had happened.

"None of those bucks are much over three years old. They're only sparring now," Larry whispered, jolting me out of my reverie. "In a month or so, when the rut starts, the fights will get more serious." I nodded my understanding, not exactly sure what he meant but pretty much able to figure it out.

Before we'd left, Richard had asked us not to kill any of the young bucks. I was pretty sure that was why Larry hadn't drawn a bead on any of those bucks, especially that young nine-pointer, and was concentrating instead on the older and larger does.

We watched for about fifteen minutes more. I was enthralled. It was like being a voyeur or becoming a part of the deer family. I started to notice individual characteristics of the animals and how they related to each other. A couple of the older does clearly did not get along and menaced each other while moving around and eating, as the males did their mock fighting. One smallish spike messed with everybody, encroaching on their space and even bumping them occasionally. *Maybe if he spent more time eating and less time fooling around, he'd grow bigger, faster*, I thought. I opened my mouth to share this with Larry but thought better of it. I even noticed that one of the does seemed to sneeze a lot and another had a bad wheeze, making me wonder if deer caught colds. One little doe came closer and closer and all but put her face into our peep-hole, only to lose interest in our blind and go back to her grazing.

Larry broke the silence. "Maybe it's time to get things going. Which one do you want me to kill?"

Inwardly horrified, I stammered, "Your call, pal," thinking to myself, *No way I'm going to play that role, I'm already enough of an accomplice.*

Larry sat forward a little and changed the grip on his bow. It was quiet. The only thing I could hear was the growling of my stomach. It sounded like an earthquake. I shouldn't have eaten that third piece of fried chicken.

Larry started to raise his bow. What should I do? Should I fake a cough or a sneeze? All of a sudden, the silence was broken by the unmistakable refrain from Queen's "Bohemian Rhapsody."

"I see a little silhouetto of a man, Scaramouche, Scaramouche, will you do the fandango." Damn, the ringtone I'd selected for my cell phone. I had forgotten to turn it off! Maybe it was the deer Gods calling. Twenty-four heads lifted as one, forty-eight white ears perked up like radar, scanning the air for a point of focus. I shut the phone off through my pants pocket and sneaked a peek at my huntin' partner, whose glance was more of amusement than anger. Amazingly, the herd dropped their heads and went back to grazing, maybe inwardly knowing that a 70s rock band like Queen would never hurt them—even though I think Queen had another song called "Another One Bites the Dust."

The hunt went on; fifteen minutes later, Larry lifted his bow, drew back, and let fly an arrow at a target that was out of my sight, some forty feet to our right.

"Get her?" I asked as the remainder of the herd bolted away.

"Yes," he said, as the herd surprisingly stopped about fifty yards away and started eating again as if nothing had happened.

"Well should we go get her?" I said.

"No," Larry said, settling back in his lawn chair. "That would be a rookie mistake. Let's just sit back, relax, and watch the herd for awhile. She won't go far."

Sitting in silence, watching the herd return, and thinking about what had just happened, I couldn't help but be impressed with Larry's cool confidence and expertise. He had told me what he was going to do and he did it, calmly and unemotionally, before and after the shot. There were no high fives or war whoops. Something else was going on that might hold the key to why people do this. Larry was already starting to think about finding his deer before dark and getting her to his butcher. In the pasture, life went on as normal.

Twenty minutes later, Larry said it was time to get started, so we exited our wooden "Frigidaire" box.

"Now what?" I asked, trying to stretch out the stiffness from my attempt to sit motionless for an hour and a half.

Author's note: What follows may be a little harsh for young readers, but *Harry Potter* is no "day at the beach," either.

"First we find the arrow," Larry said.

"Isn't she wearing it?" I asked naively, dropping any pretense that I'd done this before.

"No; with sixty-five pounds of bow tension, the arrow went right through her. Finding it will help show us where she is."

"How?" I asked.

"You'll see."

The arrow was stuck in the ground of the pasture about fifty feet from the blind. Larry knelt down, pulled it out of the ground, and gave me a hunting lesson.

Fingering the feathers on the end of the arrow, he said, "Look: good, rich red blood, some bubbles. Indicates a good lung shot." Working his way toward the point of the arrow, he lowered his head and smelled the arrow. "If it had been a gut shot, you'd expect to smell it on the shaft of the arrow."

Fascinating, I thought, *this guy knows his stuff.*

"Shall we fan out and find her?"

"No," the teacher told the student. "We've got to find the blood trail that will lead us to her. Fan out and you may never find her."

Larry bent over and all but got on his hands and knees like someone looking for a lost contact lens. It paid off: in five minutes he called me over to look at a few drops of blood on a blade of grass. "Here it is," he said, while looking for more blood.

Our search went to the right of our blind, through an unmowed field and the top of a ravine. The obvious choice would have been for the injured deer to go downhill, but Larry remained disciplined and insisted that we continue to search for the blood trail.

It was getting late and night was falling; it was getting too dark to follow any trail. Larry kept his cool and suggested we descend the hill, me to the left, him to the right.

We split up, and five minutes later he said, "Over here, Bubba."

"Blood trail?" I asked.

"No, dead deer," he answered.

I walked over to find him standing over his doe, who had fallen against a downhill tree and had clearly expired. Her wound showed that his assessment had been correct and his aim had been true. While she was about 150 yards from where she'd been shot, it had been an almost per- fect hit. Larry told me that this was about the average distance for a deer to run and/or fall after it's been hit.

Hoping that he wasn't about to kneel down beside her and ask me, "Isn't she beautiful?" I asked, "Now what?" inwardly fearing that I knew the answer.

"We field dress her," he said.

"Can't we call someone to do it?" I asked facetiously, knowing my rookie cover was blown and wanting to give my friend some ammo for *his* story.

"No Bubba, it's up to you and me. Do you want to make the first cut?"

"Ah, no thanks, Larry. Go ahead."

Field dressing is the act of eviscerating the kill, removing the entrails including colon, intestines, stomach, liver, lungs, kidney, and heart to make the deer ready for the butcher.

Reality sunk in, and my heart sunk too. *We killed Bambi's mom*, I thought as Larry began his butchering in silence as darkness closed in on us.

Later, as we dragged the gutted deer to a spot we could reach her by vehicle, I thought a lot about what had just happened. On one hand, I felt my beliefs about hunting had been confirmed. On the other, there had been no hedonistic disrespect of the quarry celebrated ritualistically as a show of weekend machismo.

Deer are plentiful. We'd killed one and were rushing her to be butchered, packed, and chilled while the meat was still fresh.

Yeah, the hunter could afford some steaks from cows or breasts from chicken, but he had chosen venison from a deer that he himself killed. I had no doubt in my mind that this deer's meat would be 100 percent consumed. I'd also learned that day about a group called Hunters Against Hunger that donated unwanted deer meat to needy families. That surprised me.

We loaded the deer in our truck for the drive back to another Larry, Larry the butcher in White Sulphur Springs, and said thanks and goodbye to Richard. Several things had become patently clear to me—some thoughts old, some new. Yes, deer hunting is a blood sport and is not for everyone, that I knew. But the hunters I'd spent the day with were special, all wise and thoughtful conservationists with a profound understanding of their environment and its creatures, not beer-guzzling Neanderthals drinking before, during, and after their trip to get away from the missus and hang out together.

Larry, Otter, Richard, I'll put them and their knowledge up against any animal rights advocate I've ever heard of, read about, or met. Overpopulation of deer is a well-reported problem throughout the US, and the solutions range from the sublime to the ridiculous.

Poison 'em. That's real bright. Poison the environment and kill anything that comes along, including wandering house pets.

Neuter 'em. Dart them with drugs and then neuter them so they can't reproduce. Yeah, right.

Ignore the problem. Not a solution.

So what? My friends dropped me at home. I poured myself a scotch and sat at my desk and continued to think about the day I'd had. I'd gone huntin'. That was new. I'd seen some serious guys do their thing. I'd spent some time, albeit a brief time, living amongst some animals. I'd been there for a kill and a field dressing and a visit to a butcher to bring him something and not to pick up something.

Hunting versus fishing—I'll still take the latter. In fishing you cast a rod and the fight begins. In hunting, when you shoot a gun, the game is over. When you hunt, one of the combatants must die, when you fish, both the angler and fish can live to fight another day.

What about my old hunting friends? I have a new understanding and appreciation of them and their motivation. They are not perverted, blood-thirsty cretins. (Well, at least most of them aren't.)

Now I've made some new hunting friends. Otter and Larry were great fun to be with. I was especially surprised at Larry's expertise in the field. A friend like that deserves a nickname. Let's see, earlier I described him as being a straight shooter. Hmm, that's it, from now on, Larry Klein shall be known as: Straight Arrow.

So will I go hunting again? Categorically *no*!

Postscript

I skipped dinner that night, unable to choose between red meat or fish.

I tossed and turned for a few hours before falling into a fitful sleep.

My dreams turned Elizabethan. I dreamed of Shakespeare and his Scottish masterpiece, *Macbeth*, and of Lady Macbeth's madness after talking her hubby into whacking their houseguest, the King, Duncan the Meek. Her malady increased, manifesting itself in her obsession with imaginary blood on her hands, stains that she could not remove no matter how she washed and rubbed her hands.

I woke up at 4:00 a.m. drenched in sweat and headed to the bath-room—not for the usual nocturnal purpose, but rather to wash my hands. In my dreams, I had become the tortured accomplice, and my name was Lady MacBubba. There and then, I swore an oath that I had gone hunting for the last time.

BABE

"I've always wanted a puppy."

"What?" she asked, putting down her current book as I continued staring at the late winter fire burning in our fireplace.

"Mindy, I've always wanted a puppy."

"You mean another dog?" she asked, luckily still smiling.

"No, a puppy that I can raise, housebreak, train, feed, walk, bathe, groom. You know, all that good stuff."

"And you'd be the primary care giver?" she asked quizzically, peering at me over the top rim of the reading glasses she'd started wearing a year earlier.

"Well of course I would be," I replied, perhaps a little too emphatically, trying hard to demonstrate a small amount of righteous indignation. "I've had plenty of dogs before, you know."

"Yes, but you've always ignored them." *Good point*, I thought to myself as I continued to stare at the now-dying embers. "And what would our Mattie think?" she asked me. "She's been the only dog in the house for quite awhile and may be a little spoiled."

Mattie is our ten-year-old "Gucci" crossbred labradoodle, one of those hypoallergenic mixes. In this case, Labrador retriever and standard poodle. They were only recently legitimatized and considered a registered breed by the International Kennel Club (IKC), after several years of rather contentious debate.

She's an OK dog, I guess. She's loving and loyal but not into the things that labs love to do, like swim and fetch, unlike her "half-sister" Lilly, our chocolate lab, who died peacefully at eighteen years old two winters previous. Lilly had a particular game that she loved. You could throw a small stone into the water and she would dive to the bottom and retrieve it on the first try, in fresh- or saltwater, up to about twelve feet. I'm not kidding. It was remarkable, and she'd do it over and over until you stopped throwing.

Mattie loves to pose. I've tried to get her to fetch but I think she figures that if you're throwing something away then you must not want it anymore. *Author's photo.*

I've always loved labs. For me, they set the bar, and maybe to be truthful, just maybe, I've always been just a tad embarrassed telling "the guys" that I owned a dog called a labradoodle and answering the always-asked follow-up question, "A what?" All right, I'll admit it, I have started telling people, when asked, that she is a curly haired lab.

Mattie often exhibits very un-lab-like behavior, like positioning herself under a window and jumping straight up and down with the vertical leap that would be the envy of any NBA basketball player. On the top of every jump, she looks in the window, hoping that someone will see her, take pity, and let her in. Cute, you say, but it always makes me mutter that "her poodle is showing."

She's also the best and most stealthy food thief I've ever seen. She can take food off a four-foot kitchen counter. Her best snatch-and-grab so far has been an entire homemade pie last Thanksgiving. It was hard to get mad at her when she sheepishly tried to rejoin the dinner party in progress with her light tan face covered in purple blueberry juice.

"I'm sure Mattie would be thrilled to have a puppy in the house to, ahh, keep her company," I answered, kind of lamely.

"Well I'm not so sure," she said, adding, "maybe you should go to bed."

"I'm serious, Mindy."

"I know you are, dear. We can talk more about it in the morning."

Well, I know when I'm being patronized, but at least she didn't say no. In our family, my wife, Mindy, is the practical one, the voice of reason, and still-undefeated champion of household debates. *Darn it*, I thought to myself, wending my way upstairs, *she's just too smart for me*.

Mindy had clearly been right about one thing: my "absentee ownership" of more than a few pets. Traveling a lot to run a multinational company, raising four kids, getting two divorces, and spoiling eight grandchildren had been time-consuming and had probably offered me perfect excuses to ignore old Bowser or whatever the current dog's name was. And yes, two divorces. Until I met Mindy, I think the book on me was "a good date and a bad husband." OK, "so-so date." In fact, I thought it laughable that my classmates in both high school and college in our senior polls had voted me as "First to Marry" and "Last to Marry"—and I was.

Lying in bed, I couldn't help but question myself about the idea of really taking care of a young dog. Was this one of those mid-life or later-life crisis deals? Was I reverting to my childhood, or was it one of those "I'll show you I can really do it" kind of things? Did I really want, or could I really handle, the responsibility? *Well*, I thought falling asleep, *there's only one way to find out*.

Blame Eliza

Mindy and I didn't discuss the subject the next day nor the following week, for that matter. Then, something very peculiar happened.

"Hi, I've got a puppy who needs a home, and I thought of you," blurted out the familiar and perky voice on the other end of the phone. It was Eliza Colmes, a member of our not-so-fearsome swim club, The Fighting Manatees.

Eliza, manatee name "Aqua Chic," is a well-known and very popular resident of Islamorada in the Florida Keys, where we live. Forty-five-ish and full of energy and enthusiasm, she worked for the local veterinarian for fifteen years. I think of her as a "Young Mother Earth in Training." Taking in strays or caring for her fishing guide husband and two very nice teenage children, she always seems to have time for a new cause. She is often asked and never says no. I like Eliza, consider her a friend, and every time I see her I think of that old Carpenters song, "Bless the Beasts and the Children." Everyone loves and respects Eliza. I'm sure if she wanted to she could run for, and be elected, mayor.

"Well, do you want her?" her voice persisted.

"Whoa, Eliza," I said, wondering how she'd thought of me when we'd never discussed my "puppy dream." "We already have a dog," I stammered, thinking this was too coincidental and wondering how I'd ever convince Mindy it wasn't a setup.

"I know, Silly," she answered. "I've taken care of Mattie for ten years at the vet's, remember?"

Ignoring the fact that aging guys hate having their memory challenged, I said, "Well, I'm not sure; how do you think Mattie would react?" I was really thinking, but not saying, *How do you think Mindy would react?*

"I'm sure Mattie would be thrilled to have a puppy in the house to, ahh, keep her company. Might even make her feel younger and live longer," she said.

Oh, my God, I thought, *those are the exact same words I used with my wife, with the added argument on longevity.* Actually, that was probably her best point. Ironically, we had brought Mattie home to keep Lilly company, and I think it added years to the older dog's life.

"Boy, Eliza, I don't think. . . ."

"How 'bout I bring her over for a play date with Mattie tomorrow morning and pick her up around noon?" she interrupted me.

Now I've never understood this modern-day nuance called pre-arranged "play dates" for children, let alone animals. Seems jaded and contrived to me. *When I was a kid, we just went out and found someone or something to play with*, I thought, wondering if I was turning into CBS's Andy Rooney without those bushy eyebrows.

"How about 9:00?" Eliza persisted.

"Oh, oh, oh yeah, fine," I managed to blurt out. "By the way, what kind of dog is she?"

"She's an adorable four-month-old yellow lab puppy. You'll just fall in love with her!"

"That's what I'm afraid of," I said, thinking to myself that this was getting weirder and weirder. The "play date" on, we said good-bye, and I went downstairs to tell the missus. I found Mindy in the kitchen serving up a hefty pancake breakfast to three of our grandchildren, Mae, Amelia, and Nate, ages three to nine, who were winding down a two-week spring break visit with us.

Maybe I better wait a little while and not tell her in front of the kids, I thought to myself, knowing I was taking the coward's way out. Well, "a little while" turned into a longer while, and all of a sudden it was tomorrow.

Waking up, Mindy asked me, "What are you going to do today?"

The time had arrived; I had to come clean. "I'm having a play date," I almost whispered.

"A what?"

"A play date?" I answered with a question mark.

"That's what I thought you said," Mindy said with that cute quizzical look she gets on her face.

"Well, it's not actually for me," I tried to explain.

"Who's it for then, the grandkids?"

"Well, no," I said, knowing the moment of truth was fast approaching. "It's for Mattie."

"Oh, really? Who's coming over?"

I took a deep breath. "A yellow lab puppy," I managed, knowing I probably had some 'splainin' to do.

Mindy shook her head and feigned annoyance, but I could see a little smile beginning to curl her lip . . . well at least one side. By sharing this story that was so bizarre, I thought that she'd have to believe me, and she did. That's what I love about this woman. Pragmatic on the outside, she's really a softy on the inside who, by the way, grew up with and loves dogs. Who knows—come to think of it, maybe she even cooked up this plan with Eliza to give me a morning to either get over my obsession, or if not, to really insure that I was going to take care of this pooch. She was always dreaming up fun surprises and cool stuff for everyone in our family. One way or the other, I knew I'd better not let our play date visitor poop on the living room rug. Did I mention that Mindy's just too smart for me?

The Big Moment

The appointed hour arrived. At five of nine, Mindy asked, "With the kids here and to avoid a little confusion, do you think we should put Mattie in her crate for awhile 'til the kids go out for an early lunch?"

"Sure," I said and walked Mattie toward the door. Just as I was going back in the house, up pulled Eliza's four-by-four. She bounced out of her seat, waved hello, and walked around to open the back hatch where I could see she kept a large crate. Reaching into the crate, she pulled out the cutest little dog you've ever seen (unless you're only a fan of another breed, like maybe poodles). She gave the pup a snuggle and put her on the ground, safely tethered to a small collar and leash, both pink. From the get-go, I could see that she wasn't shy. She made a beeline to me, her little tail seeming to wag her whole body like only labs can do. Typical of the breed, she had that doleful expression on her face that makes you want to hug them.

"Do you want to bring her in?" I asked Eliza. "Can you stay for a few minutes?"

"No," she replied. "I'll say 'hey' to Mindy, then I've got some errands

Meet Babe—
love at first sight.
Author's photo.

to do," she said, handing me the end of the leash. "Here, you do the honors."

Wow, I thought, *if I'm being hustled on this one, Eliza's really good.*

Inside, the ladies greeted each other and the grands went crazy.

"What's her name, what's her name?" asked nine-year-old Nate.

"It's Haley," Eliza responded.

"Can we keep her?" Amelia, the seven-year–old, asked.

"No, honey, I'm afraid not, you all have to fly home the day after tomorrow and Haley has to stay in the Keys," Mindy answered.

Three-year-old Mae was understandably more reserved, given the fact that she and Haley were roughly the same size and I think it must be a little intimidating at first to meet an animal that looks you in the eye from the same level.

Speaking of Mindy, I knew she liked this new little one although she seemed to be trying not to show those feelings. As the kids played with Haley, Mindy asked Eliza a series of questions, all of which I hadn't thought about.

"Has she had shots, and has she been spayed?"

"Yes and no. She's still a little young for that."

"What about her parents?"

"Two black labs from not too far away. She was the smallest of a litter of eight, all black except for her."

Hmm, I thought to myself, unable to conjure up memories from high school sophomore biology, my deepest academic dive into the pool of science. I nodded my head as if understanding how this strangely mixed dog family could be, vowing to sneak away and call the vet after Aqua Chic headed out for her errands.

"She's as gentle as she is beautiful and friendly," Smiling Eliza, the Friendly Used Dog Salesperson, chimed in.

"If she's all of that, Eliza, why aren't you keeping her?" Mindy drilled down.

"Well, I was going to, but I've got a fourteen-year-old lab, and the more I thought about it, the more I couldn't do it to her."

"Should we be concerned, then, about Mattie?" Mindy continued.

"No," Eliza said, "I don't think so. Dear Mattie is much more relaxed than our Chessie. Well, gotta run. I'll call before I come back for Haley at noon. Hope the play date goes well. See 'ya."

I said good-bye to her back as she headed for the door, and just like that we were alone, with the puppy in limbo.

"If we can't keep her, can you, Bubba?" asked Nate, the precocious one. "Then we could play with her when we come to visit. She's such a babe!"

I think that one got to the missus, who bent down to pet the pup who responded with another round of full-body tail wags and wet kisses.

"Gee, I don't know, pal," I jumped in, feeling things going pretty well. "Don't you all think we'd have to give her our own name first?"

"Oh, yeah," they all said almost in unison. "Let's give her a new name."

"Well, who's got an idea for a name?"

Not surprisingly, Nate jumped in. "She's such a babe, why don't we just call her Babe?" And just like that, almost before it started, the naming contest was over. Mindy and the two girls jumped up to give Nate high fives, and the puppy started wagging again and, in her excitement, let us hear her first bark, which caused laughter all around.

"OK, then, Babe it is," I said as everybody cheered and gave her a new round of snuggles.

Just then our son Ted and his wife, Nena, walked in. Hearing the cheering, they asked, "What's up, gang?" At that point Nena saw Babe and said, "Oh, no, Bubba, you didn't."

Nate jumped to my defense. "No, Mom, she's not for us. She may be Bubba's new puppy."

Relieved, no doubt, they joined in the love fest for awhile before Ted chimed in, "OK, guys let's leave Bubba with *his* new puppy and grab some lunch."

Off they went, leaving Mindy and me looking at each other, knowing that it was time for the play date to begin. Mindy said, "I'll go get Mattie. Why don't you give Babe a chance to pee first?"

Babe finished fast; we came back in, and I took her off her leash. Just as she was lying on her back so I would scratch her tummy, in bounded Mattie with Mindy in tow. The curly haired lab seemed to have a little extra spring in her step, as if she knew something was going on but she wasn't sure what. She ran into the middle of the living room and came to a screeching halt four feet from Babe. Her eyes opened wide and then closed as she literally fell over on her side and didn't move.

"Oh, great," I said, "do you think she just fainted?"

Before Mindy could even answer, Mattie's teeth clenched, her closed eyes opened and rolled back in her head, her body went into convulsions, and she started frothing at the mouth.

"I think she's having a seizure. I'll see what I can do," Mindy said, "Go call the vet. Her numbers are in the directory on the desk."

Being Saturday, I was relieved when the vet's office answered on the second ring, and I told them what was going on. The vet said to stay close, watch over her, try to keep her comfortable and bring her in as soon as we could.

Thinking how fortunate we were that the grandkids hadn't seen this, I walked in to see Mattie sitting up as if nothing had happened, intently eyeing Babe as the puppy tail-wagged her way all around her.

"We're supposed to take her in to the vet's," I said. "I'll crate Babe while you walk Mattie to the car."

When I got to the car, I found Mindy and Mattie in the back seat with Mattie lying down, her head in her mistress's lap, getting a gentle ear scratching. The dog looked a little drowsy but didn't appear to be in pain.

Now, rightfully wracked with parental guilt, I got behind the wheel and started the car. Mindy was being very uncharacteristically quiet. I felt glad not to be a mind reader.

As we pulled out of the driveway, my wife said to me facetiously, "Well, that went well, I think."

A few nervous chuckles about what she said and how she said it broke the tension, and we were off to the doggy hospital.

Mindy and I delivered Mattie to the vet then sat together holding hands, not talking much, and worrying about our labradoodle.

The vet came out after about forty minutes, and we stood to greet her.

"Miss Mattie's doing just fine. I gave her a thorough examination and did some blood work and couldn't find anything. Sometimes these seizures just happen. She may have another one sometime, or she may not. I gave her some phenobarbital and would like to keep her overnight as a precaution so we can keep her under observation, but don't worry, she's going to be just fine."

"Thank you, doctor," Mindy and I said almost in unison, feeling relieved.

Then Mindy asked, "Do you have any idea of what caused it?"

"Not really, but seizures with older poodles are somewhat common," she said, adding "Did she have any emotional strain recently?"

I jumped in, "You said she's going to be all right, right?" The vet nodded her head, still looking at me. "Good then, ahh, no, I can't think of any emotional strain she's experienced," I lied, afraid to look at Mindy and not wanting to take on anymore guilt. Wait a minute, I thought, was that a little smile I saw on the vet's face? Maybe she's a part of this right- or left-paw conspiracy, too.

"OK, fine," the vet said. "Stop by and pick her up in the morning. We'll take good care of Miss Mattie. We love her visits."

By the time we got home and I walked the puppy and brought her back to the house it was 11:45 a.m., fifteen minutes before Eliza would call. My wife and I watched the grands playing together on the beach and then walked into the kitchen. Mindy asked me, "Do you want me to fix you some lunch?"

"No, thanks, I've kind of lost my appetite," I smiled, adding, "I guess we should tell Eliza that this isn't going to work and have her come and get Haley."

"Nonsense," Mindy fired back. "Babe is a sweetheart, she'll be great for us and great for Mattie. They'll have fun keeping each other company. Mattie's a wonderful loving dog and a diva. She'll adjust and love that puppy like we do. I think you should go out and get Lilly's old crate out of the storage room; Babe's going to need somewhere to stay," she added.

I gave my wife a big hug.

Just then the phone rang. It was Eliza, right on time. "Well, how'd the play date go? Are you ready for me to come over and pick up Haley?"

"Well, Eliza, we'd love to see you, but there's no Haley here, just Babe, and she's staying!"

POSTSCRIPT

Mindy was right again. Babe's a love and is totally housebroken, and I'm the designated caregiver. She loves to fetch, and, unlike me, loves to hunt, so we often go along on hunts with friends—they do the shooting.

As for Mattie, fully recovered, she's all but adopted Babe, and they play together like puppies. She's working on teaching the younger dog how to jump up and look in windows. Oh, and last week, she performed her greatest trick ever—she jumped up and took a steak right off the barby without burning herself. She even shared her prize with Babe. Ya gotta love those labradoodles!

LORD BUBBA

*G*enealogy *(from Greek: γενιά, genia, "generation"; and γνῶσις η, the gnosis, "knowledge") is the study of families and the tracing of their lineages and history. Historically in Western societies, the genealogical focus was the kinship and descent of rulers and nobles, often arguing or demonstrating the legitimacy of claims to wealth and power.*[5]

I believe that most people are interested in their genealogy at least twice in their lifetimes. The first time is when they are very young, in their wonder years, when they're inquisitive, wanting to know as much as they can about who they are and where they came from. The second is when they become older, aware of their own mortality, and more reflective on their lives—what they have done and where they fit in.

In between the curiosity of youth and introspection of age, most people seem to live in the moment, making their livings, raising families, building reputations, and seeking security.

Now, lest I become accused of over-generalizing, let me add that I have met several people obsessed with their family histories (maybe with too much time on their hands) and even people who make a living by helping others "climb their family trees," even selling titles for "coin of the realm." I will tell you about a few of the more interesting ones in this short thesis.

As for me as a child, if it wasn't about sports, it held little interest. My mother and father had told me that we were Scottish/English, and that was fine with me. My father had also told me that I came from a long line of English royalty, and that was OK with me too, though it was rather superfluous information, since it had no value if I couldn't trade it for a baseball card. I also figured that royalty stuff might be somewhat suspect, as it was, after all, information coming from an adult. I thought it might just be one of those fairy tales made up by all parents.

As a background for the Waspy life I was raised in, being of British descent was comfortable and made sense. I left public school in sixth grade for First Form, not seventh grade, in an English-style, all-boys private country day school. Little did I know then that I would complete my formal education through a master's degree in classes with no women. At the time, it didn't seem right or wrong. It was just the way it was. If anything, maybe I was relieved 'cause everyone knows that girls are smarter than boys.

Anyway, I grew up, kind of, and got on with my life. Lineage was something I never really thought about until the mid-nineties when I ran into one of my favorite cousins, Judy, while attending a family funeral. From the time she was a child, Judy was a beauty. With dark hair and beautiful skin, she had a tiny little voice that demanded close attention, which was rewarded with great, albeit naïve, tales and a priceless lilting

Growing up, happiness was getting to sit in the front row for a family picture between my beautiful girl cousins, Judy and Marty. *Author's photo.*

laugh. I was ten months older than Judy, and she was so becoming it made you wish she wasn't your cousin, if you get my drift.

Anyway, there was Judy, whom I hadn't seen in at least two marriages, telling me about her latest passion for researching family history. It was kind of boring, but I loved her voice and was hoping for a laugh.

Her starting points, ironically, had come from extensive research done by a sister of our grandmother on one side and a sister of our grandfather on the other. She also told me about a second cousin of ours, on my grandmother's side, with the unforgettable name of Dorothy "Dottie" Popham who, with her hubby, had done three years of research to support Dottie's acceptance into membership in something called the Order of the Crown of Charlemagne.

"You mean we're related to Charlemagne?" I asked.

"Yes, we are, and I'll send you the backup study," she said.

"Great," I answered, not really caring and added, "Wasn't he from Europe?"

"Of course, Bobby," she said with that great smile and laugh, as if to say, "you're still my semi-lovable, stupidest cousin." "He lived from 742 to 814 and was King of the Francs, which included France and Germany. He defined all of Western Europe and was called the Emperor of the West. He also conquered Italy and established the Holy Roman Empire."

Now feeling totally stupid, I was searching for something to say to claw my way back. I considered, "Oh, *that* Charlemagne," but settled for, "Oh, I thought we were Presbyterians."

Pretty dumb, I know, but at least she laughed.

Having been a Protestant all my life and nervous about my discovery of having Catholic roots, I decided to change the subject ASAP. "I'm really most interested in Grandpa Rich's side of the family."

"Oh, me too," she said. "In fact, right now I'm researching Riches who fought in the Civil War."

"Were we Yankees or Rebels?" I asked.

"A few fought for the Confederacy," she answered, "but most of our ancestors fought for the Union."

"And what about Great Britain, Judy?" I asked her. "Don't we come from some royalty?"

Van Dyck's portrait of Sir Robert Rich, the Second Earl of Warwick, hangs in the Maritime Museum in London. *Author's photo.*

"Well," she said, "like all family history, ours is a mixed bag. We had some knights but some scoundrels as well. I'll send you a report done by our great Aunt Georgia. You'll no doubt love the reference to your name-sake, Sir Robert Rich, the Second Earl of Warwick," she added.

"That's my guy!" I said.

Judy laughed again and said, "That may be, but when you start up the tree, you've got to be prepared to take the bad with the good."

We said good-bye, and somehow I knew that Judy would send that information as promised. It's interesting about families that are separated by geography: at first you only see each other at family weddings, then oh-so-quickly only at funerals. It's sad, I guess, but inevitable as well.

Judy was good to her word, and a few weeks later I received Dottie Popham's thorough evidentiary research on our connection to Charle-magne on my grandmother's side and Aunt Georgia's equally well-researched study on my grandfather's side showing our ancestry from Sir Robert Rich. I gave the former a cursory look but was more intrigued with the latter, maybe because it felt more comfortable, and I related more to a knighted ancestor from the sixteenth century.

Aunt Georgia's research was voluminous, tracing our family back to the battle of Hastings in 1066. Echoing my cousin Judy, she started out with this wonderfully candid disclaimer, which probably speaks to anyone embarking on a historical review of their family roots.

"In this short space we have traced our family name from its earliest origins and connection with English history. We have found saints and sinners, lawyers and statesmen, authors, soldiers, and travelers; Riches who were knighted and Riches who were beheaded."

I was fascinated with perhaps the most noble, a guy named Edmund Rich (1190–1240), who was consecrated Archbishop of Canterbury in 1234. During his lifetime, he challenged the pope on the church's dealing with other religions, for which he was excommunicated and fled to a monastery in France where he lived out his life in exile. After his death, his body was returned to England for burial at Westminster Abbey. Later on, he was beatified and became Saint Edmund.

So there was the saint Aunt Georgia referenced, but where was the sinner? It was easy to find the worst, present company excluded. Sir Richard Rich (1498–1564) was categorically the worst. His life was high-lighted, make that low-lighted, in the film *A Man for All Seasons*. A lawyer by trade, he served no less than three kings and a queen. His two specialties were perjury and religious persecution, with a little torture thrown in for good measure. He became Lord Chancellor under Henry VIII and spent a great deal of time suppressing monasteries and pun-ishing bishops.

Given his proven skill set, he became a natural for Henry VIII to turn to when he needed a special favor. The King had petitioned the pope to annul his marriage with Queen Catherine so that he could marry his long-time sweetie, Anne Boleyn. His then-chancellor, Sir Thomas More, refused to recognize the King's power over the Catholic Church and snubbed Anne by refusing to attend their marriage ceremony.

King Henry retaliated and had More removed from power and thrown in jail in the Tower of London. Next, the King looked around his court for someone who would bear false testimony against More. His choice was obvious: Sir Richard Rich.

Sir Thomas More, known for his candor, did not go gently into that good night. In her best selling novel *Wolf Hall*, author Hilary Mantel says that, at his trial, after Rich had perjured himself by lying about alleged confidences from More, Sir Thomas went on the attack. He literally turned from being the accused to the accuser when he assaulted Rich with these words: "I know you of old, Riche, why would I open my mind to you? I have known you since your youth, a gamer and a dicer, of no com-mendable fame even in your own house. . . ."

More's defense fell on deaf ears and Rich's perjury prevailed. More was convicted under the Treason Act in 1534 and beheaded as a traitor, and his head was fixed upon a pike over London Bridge for a month. For his service, Sir Richard was awarded the title Earl of Warwick and later became Chancellor. Before he was done, he also brought to death two other famous Thomases—Cromwell and Seymour. (By the way, King Henry later ended his marriage to Anne Boleyn by having her beheaded as well. Her crime: failure to bear him a male heir.)

To show you how bad Richard Rich was, in 2006 he was selected by the British Broadcasting Corporation's *History Magazine* as the sixteenth century's "worst Briton."

The second-worst Rich was probably the notorious Henry Rich, who was called "the handsomest villain in Europe" and beheaded in 1649.

Rich women weren't exempt from villainy either. I was fascinated by the story of Lady Penelope Rich, who "won the admiration of Sir Philip Sidney at age fourteen" and continued an affair with him even after her forced marriage to one of Richard's sons. After Sidney's death in 1601, she took up with and "lived in open adultery" with Lord Mountjoy until her hubby dumped her in 1605.

So anyway, I decided to overlook Richard, Henry, and Penelope—kind of psychologically "prune them from the family tree" and concentrate on focusing on Richard's grandson, and Penelope's son, Robert.

Sir Robert Rich, the second Earl of Warwick (1587–1658), proved that you can overcome some evil ancestry to become a superstar. A seafaring adventurer, he occupied himself primarily with the colonization of America (and a little privateering on the side).

He was referred to as the patron of Bermuda and also played a major role in the British presence in Barbados in the Caribbean. In 1643 he was appointed Lord High Admiral of the British Fleet and Governor of all English Islands before his independence caused him to be "estranged by the court." Lord Rich exerted his authority in support of religious freedom and was granted the Rich coat of arms, *"Garde la Foy"* (Keep the Faith).

I was fascinated with Sir Robert the Earl of Warwick and wanted to learn more about him. Every year, my wife and I schedule a trip together on the date of our wedding anniversary. After reading the family history, I asked Mindy if she wanted to visit Warwick Castle. She jumped all over it, and we put it on the schedule.

My former neighbor and mentor in Buffalo, a Cambridge-educated lawyer, Howard Meyer, used to wax euphoric at the mere mention of Great Britain. At the end of our conversations he would sigh and say, "I can die now that I've seen London." My passion for the place does not equal his, but I do look forward to our trips to "Jolly Old." From the southern coast of Portsmorth to the northern moors of Northumberland, I feel a kinship with the people and the place. I always wonder if that's part of one's heritage: to feel a bond with your ancestral home and her people in spite of growing up somewhere else. Can it really be in the blood?

While fond of the country life of the Cotswalds and Hampshire, for me, the ultimate destination is London. I love its mass and majesty, its river and buildings, its shops and food—though often maligned—its green spaces and statues, its pomp and ceremony. Most of all, I love its tradition. Singer–comedienne Bette Midler said that "When it's three o'clock in New York, it's still 1938 in London."

Critics often complain about the sometimes-incessant rain. I like Groucho Marx's quote, "I'm leaving because the weather is too good. I hate London when it's not raining." For me, London and rain just go together, and the rain makes the sunny days there that much more special.

English poet Samuel Johnson summed it up for me when he said, "By seeing London, I have seen as much as the world can show," and "When a man is tired of London, he's tired of life."

Having offices and manufacturing facilities in England, I've had many opportunities to travel there. I always get a kick out of the location of our offices in a town called Stratford-Upon-Avon. It makes me think of myself "the crown prince of cream puffs," kind of mingling with William Shakespeare, the bard.

Besides visiting Warwick Castle, we decided to go the full tourist route and throw in the Tower of London, Stonehenge, and Edinburgh Castle for good measure. I like driving on the wrong side of the road, so we usually rent a car. Research had told us that Warwick is an hour and a half train ride from London. I decided that would never do for our first visit to *my* castle, so we reserved a car and driver. Also, our friendly travel agent from the Travel Team in Buffalo, Jeanne Covelli, knew of a British woman, Hermione, who did genealogical studies and worked as a tour guide. We decided to go first class and sign her on as well, first sending her all we had on my heritage so she could work it into our tour.

We could not have made a better choice; Hermione did her homework well. As we drove from London, she downloaded some interesting facts. There had not been one Earl of Warwick in our family, but eight between the years of 1618 and 1759, four named Robert. The unbroken line continued until 1759, when the direct male line ceased.

The title should then have gone to descendents of the heirs of the second son of Earl Robert, who had gone to Cape Cod. In fact, Richard Rich, my ancestor who had led our family to America, refused the title saying that "American citizenship was worth more than a dukedom." Our sea-faring family used to jest that they "wouldn't exchange a fishnet for Warwick's dukedom."

After the Riches moved to the colonies, some family named Greville moved into the castle. Boy, I was really getting into this. While I was feeling proud of my ancestors who settled in the United States, I was also feeling a growing sense of proprietorship about this castle that I had never even seen. Mindy felt my mood and as we approached the castle gates she warned me to behave and not embarrass myself.

My first sight of Warwick Castle was unforgettable. Built on a bend overlooking the River Avon with its massive walls and towers, it dominates the rolling landscapes and is the true definition of a medieval castle.

Hermione had prepaid our admission, so we sailed past the ticket takers. Now a little miffed that no one recognized me or that there was no one at the door to announce us, I looked for someone who could give us a tour.

Standing by the registration desk was an older, white-haired gentleman dressed in a grey wool suit with a red poppy in his lapel. Red poppies are worn to commemorate the British soldiers' lives lost in the First World War. The octogenarian pensioner was serving as a docent, giving castle tours and, now looking at his pocket watch, probably counting the last sixty minutes of his shift before the castle closed and he could go home to his supper.

Man, I thought to myself, *I'm the last thing he needs today*. I walked up to him, but I couldn't help myself. I felt Mindy cringing by my side.

"Good afternoon," I said. "I'm Robert Rich, the true heir to Sir Robert Rich, the Second Earl of Warwick, and I've come to claim my castle and lands."

He did not look amused. In fact, he seemed to be looking around for a guard to give me the old heave-ho if necessary, but he did straighten up a little, I noticed.

Before he could respond, I ended the mini-charade and said, "I'm joking. I'm not really here to claim anything, but I am who I say I am and just wanted to look around."

He broke into a broad smile, and as we shook hands, he said, "That's good, because your ancestors never really lived here. They enjoyed the rights and title, but they actually lived in a large estate in Sussex that recently burned down. But, how about a good tour, then?"

This is going to be fun, I thought, looking around to see that Mindy and Hermione were getting into it as well.

The tour was great. We started covering every square foot, including the towers and dungeon and places where many tourists are never allowed. William, our guide, was a font of information and told us historical facts and stories about every room.

An hour went by quickly, and it was closing time. "Never mind that," William said. "We've got a lot more to see." His gait was spritely, and I could tell that he, too, was enjoying our visit. Soon I looked at my watch, and it was 6:30 p.m. We'd been touring for two and a half hours. I thanked William for his hospitality and begged our leave. He was very gracious and invited us to come back.

"To stay?" I asked.

He laughed and said, "As you wish; you'd make a fine Earl."

Years went by. The Tussauds museum folks that had bought the castle added many features and turned it into one of the great tourist attractions in England, now complete with medieval battle reenactments and fanciful ghost stories for fans of the paranormal. It's promoted now as "Britain's Ultimate Castle." Check it out on their super-slick website, Warwick-Castle.com.

As for me, I bought a copy of the Van Dyke painting of Lord Robert that hangs in the Maritime Museum but have decided not to pursue my claim to the title, although I know in my heart that Warwick Castle really belongs to me.

Some years later, reminiscing with Mindy about our Warwick adventure and with me no doubt bemoaning my lost title, she said, "You know you can buy titles?"

"No," I said. "Where did you hear that?"

"Well," she said, "I was talking to our friend Julian Tomlin, the manager at Lainston House, and he said that titles do come up for sale, often when older, titled Brits fall on hard times and need some money. If you really want one, I'll buy it for you as a Christmas present."

"That'd be cool," I said "but I'd like to find one that was in our family."

"That could be tough," she said. "What else do you want for Christmas?" and that was the end of the conversation.

Last year, my son Ted accepted a promotion to run our European operations, which required him to move with his family to England. Mindy and I volunteered to help them get settled. One of the real estate agents we worked with was Lord Michael, and something about his title rekindled an old ancestral fire. I decided that it was time to revisit the subject of titles.

When we got home, I searched the Internet and found out that not only were there vacant titles for sale, but that there were also individuals and companies that actually sold titles along with all the appropriate certifications of authenticity. You can even buy titles on eBay!

Amid the e-mail addresses of these title sales agents were numerous warnings about the sales of titles being fraudulent and vilifying the sellers as being scammers. I placed a call to our attorneys in England and was told that many of the agents had, in fact, purchased the titles and were able to legally sell them. While opportunistic and distasteful to some Brits, the agents couldn't be indicted on a practice that some considered tasteless and gauche. It was, I determined, a case of "buyer beware." It also seemed to me that a lot of the complaints were coming from disgruntled British gentry who felt that interlopers were invading their turf.

History also instructed that many titles changed hands under far more scurrilous circumstances. Kings and queens were constantly giving and taking away titles, which became inducements for favors. Also, titles were constantly being contested, traded for, bought and sold, and even killed for. I decided to continue.

I culled the agents and found one that seemed to be knowledgeable, with some staying power, Noble Titles Company. Established in 1996, they represent themselves as "Heritage Researchers and Purveyors of titles, with over twenty years of experience in Genealogical Research," buying and selling "genuine titles."

I e-mailed my interest to NoblesTitles.com and received a prompt and courteous response from a gentleman named Lord Graham. He told me that the title of Earl of Warwick was not available, as I suspected, but that as per my inquiry he thought that there were other titles available that had been in the Rich family. "Give me a week, Lord Robert, I'll research what's available and get back to you."

Lord Robert, nice ring to that, I thought as Lord Graham and I said good-bye. A few days later, he called to tell me that his research was going well and that he was zeroing in on a few of our previously held family titles and would send me an e-mail in a few days. "By the way," he added, "I've discovered how your family came to England. Would you like to know?"

"No thanks, Lord Graham," I stammered. "Why don't you just tell me in your e-mail?"

I was still taken aback by finding out that my grandmother's side wasn't originally from England and now felt that the second shoe was going to drop. My self-image as being British was being threatened. I resigned myself to this pending disclosure. Maybe my relatives were Saxons or Angles, the fierce Germanic tribes who settled England after the Romans left in 410 and gave the country its name. That would be OK.

Two days later, Lord Graham's e-mail arrived, starting with the usual cordial greeting and then his findings.

"The Rich Family came over (to England) with William the Conqueror (Duke of Normandy) in 1066, and they were Knights Templar, namely 'Edmund Rich' (Riche in France from Loraine). The Rich family crest has French Templar crosses on it."

That's it, I thought. I should have put two and two together. Saint

Edmund's grandfather had been Riche. I'm not English at all; I'm French! What about all those rude French jokes I'd told? Like when, for example, the French refused to join us in the war effort in Iraq, causing General Schwarzkopf to make the dismissive comment, "Going to battle without the French is like going hunting without an accordion."

This discovery was going to take some time to get used to. Meanwhile, Lord Graham had found three available titles that had been in our family. My favorite was the Lordship of Bedlington, a small town in Northumberland.

I e-mailed Lord Graham that I'd get back to him in a few days and wondered if I should rethink my lifetime aversion to French toast.

The next day, I shared the story with my longtime pal Doctor Toby Cosgrove, head of the world-famous Cleveland Clinic. He got a kick out of the story and asked me if I was going to go for it. I said I thought I would and he laughed and said, "Why don't you get me one, too," and then, I'm sure, he forgot about it.

I called Lord Graham the next day and started my negotiations. "My Lord," I asked, "do you offer discounts for quantity purchases?"

"Well, My Lord," he responded, "it is Christmastime, and we are throwing in real gold royalty rings for free."

This was getting good now, I thought, just like ordering a membership in the Sky King Fan Club, sending in two Ovaltine labels, and getting a genuine decoder ring for free.

"Well, your lordship," I said, "the rings will be nice, but I was thinking about a discount as well."

"How much of a discount?" he asked.

"Oh, let's say 20 percent," I haggled.

"I can do 10," he countered.

"Deal," I said. "Merry Christmas, My Lord."

The wire transfer took place and the documentation and "real gold rings" arrived in time for Mindy and me to surprise Toby after a Cleveland Clinic Board of Directors meeting. He started laughing so hard about his Christmas gift that he nearly slid off his chair at dinner.

So from now on, if you run into the good doctor, tell him that Lord

Certificate Of Title

TO ALL AND SINGULAR

Know Ye from this day forth the 10th day of December 2009 in the reign of our sovereign Lady Elizabeth (II) keeper of the faith of the United Kingdom of Great Britain.

Robert E. Rich, Jr. of Buffalo, New York

Hereafter known as, at all times and in all records, deeds, writings, and transactions, private as well as public shall adopt and be known as

Lord of the Manor of Bedlington

In accordance with the laws of England notice having been declared to the entire Kingdom due claim to the said title, the above named person shall now and forever more swear by their sword of honour and title, obedience to the monarchy and respect for the Crown.

A family title reclaimed.

and Lady Rich of Bedlington send their regards, and please use his proper title, Lord Toby of Wangey. I think he's amused with his new honorific; Lady Wangey—not so much.

My son Ted was also amused. He came home for Christmas and brought me a red scarf from the Bedlington Terriers professional football (soccer) team. "You can wear it at one of their games, Dad," he said.

"Brilliant, lad, brilliant," I replied, "because I just contacted them and made arrangements for us to sponsor their team next season."

Lords must act lordly. Perhaps we'll be able to schedule a test match next year against Wangey.

POSTSCRIPT

To date I haven't gotten up the nerve to use my title, but I do wear the ring and smile every time I look at it or someone asks me about it. Upon reflection, I believe that nobility comes from actions, not by titles. I am proud to be known as Bob Rich from Buffalo.

Au revoir,
Lord Bubba

THE FINAL WORD

"Far better it is to dare mighty things, to win glorious triumphs, even though checkered by failure, than to take rank with those poor spirits who neither enjoy much nor suffer much, because they live in the gray twilight that knows not victory nor defeat."

—Theodore Roosevelt,
twenty-sixth President of the United States

So what's the bottom line? Charlie Chaplin said, "In the end, everything is a gag." For me, there is some humor in it, but life is still about games—some more serious than others.

I consider myself blessed to have had some wonderful mentors along the way, not just to teach me the rules but to help me learn to play:

A father who woke me up at six every morning for a push-up/sit-up competition, who made all sports available, and showed me that business is a game as well;

A teacher who taught me that you cannot work too hard for what you want;

A coach who gave me permission to be myself and play the game my own way;

A sportsman/entrepreneur/civic benefactor who told me, "A day without working up a sweat is a day wasted," and "Always pay your club dues first";

An ex-president friend who jumps out of planes at eighty-two and still loves the adrenaline rush of competition;

And a wife who walks at my side, no matter, at times, how bizarre the trip may be.

NOTES

1. To "spell" the starter is to take over and give the starter a break.

2. Ernest Laurence Thayer, "'Casey at the Bat': A Ballad of the Republic Sung in the Year 1888," *San Francisco Examiner*, June 3, 1888.

3. Patrick Dillon, *Lost at Sea,* New York: Dial Press, 1998.

4. Teasers are brightly colored plastic lures with no hooks, designed specifically to attract or raise fish.

5. *American Heritage Dictionary*, 1st ed., s.v. "genealogy."

BIBLIOGRAPHY

American Heritage Dictionary, 1st ed.

Berners, Dame Juliana. *The Book of Saint Albans*. New York: Charles Scribner's Sons, 1903.

Bolt, Robert. *A Man for All Seasons*. London: Vintage Books, 1962.

Dillon, Patrick. *Lost at Sea*. New York: Dial Press, 1998.

Mantel, Hilary. *Wolf Hall*. London: Picador Publishing, 2010.

Mares, Bill. *Fishing with the Presidents*. Mechanicsburg, PA: Stackpole Books, 1999.

Overfield, Joseph M. *The 100 Seasons of Buffalo Baseball*. Kenmore, NY: Partners' Press, 1985.

Rich, Bob. *Fish Fights, A Hall of Fame Quest*. Guildford, CT: Lyons Press, 2001.

———. *The Fishing Club, Brothers and Sisters of the Angle*. Guildford, CT: Lyons Press, 2006.

Swados, Robert O. *Counsel in the Crease, A Big League Player in the Hockey Wars*. Amherst, NY: Prometheus Books, 2006.

Thayer, Ernest Laurence. "'Casey at the Bat': A Ballad of the Republic Sung in the Year 1888." *San Francisco Examiner*, June 3, 1888.

Violanti, Anthony. *Miracle in Buffalo: How the Dream of Baseball Revived a City*. New York: St. Martin's Press, 1991.

Walton, Izaak. *The Compleat Angler*. New York: Modern Library, 1998.

INDEX

Page numbers in **bold** indicate photos and captions.